ASIA BOND MONITOR
JUNE 2020

ASIAN DEVELOPMENT BANK

ADB

Contents

Emerging East Asian Local Currency Bond Markets: A Regional Update

Highlights

Key Trends

- Investor sentiment soured as the global economic outlook weakened due to the outbreak of the coronavirus disease (COVID-19).
- Governments and central banks globally took decisive fiscal and monetary policy actions to mitigate the negative economic impact of the pandemic.
- Between 28 February and 29 May, the 2-year local currency (LCY) bond yield fell in nearly all emerging East Asian markets in line with the shift to more accommodative monetary stances.[1] On the other hand, 10-year bond yield movements diverged owing to market-specific factors.
- Equity markets in the region fell, domestic currencies weakened, and risk premiums increased for most markets in the region, reflecting worsening economic conditions and weakening investor sentiment.
- Rising risk aversion and declining investor sentiment also led to capital outflows from most markets, resulting in a decline in the foreign holdings' share of government bonds as investors sought safe-haven assets. More recently, as some markets have gradually relaxed quarantine measures, investor sentiment has begun to improve.
- Emerging East Asia's LCY bond market expanded to USD16.3 trillion at the end of March, growing 4.2% quarter-on-quarter and 14.0% year-on-year. Government bonds dominated the region's bond market, accounting for 60.6% of the region's total outstanding bonds at the end of the first quarter of 2020.
- Under the ASEAN+3 Multi-Currency Bond Issuance Framework, two new corporate bonds were issued in Cambodia in April.[2] RMA (Cambodia) Plc. issued a 5-year KHR80 billion bond and Prasac Microfinance Institution Plc. raised KHR127.2 billion from the sale of a 3-year bond. Both issues were guaranteed by the Credit Guarantee and Investment Facility.

Risks to Financial Stability

- Risks remain heavily tilted to the downside due to uncertainty about COVID-19 and its economic effects.
- Other risks include rising trade tensions between the People's Republic of China and the United States and financial volatility due to capital outflows from emerging markets.

Special Section: COVID-19 and Financial Sector

- This issue of the *Asia Bond Monitor* includes a special section with discussion boxes that explore how the financial sector can help fund the fight against COVID-19.
- Two boxes discuss the use of pandemic bonds and social bonds to mobilize private sector resources to mitigate the negative economic impact on developing Asia of COVID-19 and other disasters.[3]
- Another box examines how financial technology can reach vulnerable groups during high-stress periods and promote inclusiveness and resilience.
- The final box discusses the role of the government in designing market-specific policies to ensure the smooth functioning of the financial sector as a provider of liquidity during the pandemic.

Theme Chapter: Financial Architecture and Innovation

- The theme chapter investigates the link between financial architecture and innovation by summarizing a study on whether banks or capital markets are more conducive to innovation.
- The study finds that a market-based financial system is more conducive to innovation than intermediary-based financial system, while also highlighting the importance of developing a well-functioning financial system in promoting innovation.

---

[1] Emerging East Asia comprises the People's Republic of China; Hong Kong, China; Indonesia; the Republic of Korea; Malaysia; the Philippines; Singapore; Thailand; and Viet Nam.
[2] ASEAN+3 comprises the 10 member economies of the Association of Southeast Asian Nations (ASEAN) plus the People's Republic of China, Japan, and the Republic of Korea.
[3] Developing Asia comprises the 46 developing member economies of the Asian Development Bank.

Executive Summary

Global investment sentiment waned amid the sharp economic downturn triggered by the coronavirus disease (COVID-19). The governments and central banks of many economies launched fiscal stimulus packages and eased monetary policies to mitigate the economic impact of COVID-19.

Emerging East Asian markets shifted to a more accommodative monetary environment, leading to a decline in short-term interest rates.[1] The 2-year bond yield in nearly all regional markets trended downward between 28 February and 29 May. On the other hand, long-term interest rates, proxied by the 10-year bond yield, diverged based on economy-specific trends.

The outbreak of COVID-19 soured investment sentiment in emerging East Asia. Equity markets suffered losses and currencies depreciated against the United States dollar for most markets in the region during the review period. Credit spreads widened for nearly all markets as risk aversion heightened. Global investors flocked to safe-haven assets, pushing down the share of foreign holdings in most of the region's local currency (LCY) bond markets.

More recently, as some governments have gradually eased quarantine measures, investment sentiment has somewhat recovered, leading to a recovery in some markets.

However, the risks to the global outlook remain heavily tilted to the downside. Uncertainty about the trajectory of COVID-19 is the overriding risk factor. Other risk factors include trade tensions between the People's Republic of China and the United States and financial volatility due to capital outflows from emerging markets.

Emerging East Asia's local currency bonds outstanding climbed to USD16.3 trillion in the first quarter of 2020.

LCY bonds outstanding in emerging East Asian markets expanded in the first quarter (Q1) of 2020, reaching a total of USD16.3 trillion at the end of March, with growth accelerating to 4.2% quarter-on-quarter (q-o-q) and 14.0% year-on-year (y-o-y) from 2.4% q-o-q and 12.6% y-o-y in the fourth quarter of 2019.

Government bonds outstanding, which dominate the region's bond market, rose to USD9.9 trillion and accounted for 60.6% of the region's aggregate bond stock at the end of March. Corporate bonds reached USD6.4 trillion, or 39.4% of the total.

The People's Republic of China remained home to the largest bond market in the region, accounting for 76.6% of the region's total bond stock at the end of March. The share of the region's second-largest bond market in the Republic of Korea stood at 12.5%. Bond markets in member economies of the Association of Southeast Asian Nations (ASEAN) accounted for an aggregate 9.1% share.[2]

As a share of gross domestic product, emerging East Asia's LCY bonds outstanding rose to 87.8% at the end of March, up from 83.2% at the end of December and 80.2% at the end of March 2019.

Total LCY bond issuance in the region reached USD1,671.5 billion in Q1 2020, growing 19.7% q-o-q and 22.1% y-o-y. Government bond issuance reached USD918.9 billion, growing 32.9% q-o-q and 12.6% y-o-y. Corporate bond issuance reached USD752.5 billion, which represented q-o-q growth of 6.8% and y-o-y growth of 36.2%.

Under an initiative to strengthen bond market linkages among ASEAN+3 markets, two new corporate bonds were issued in Cambodia through the ASEAN+3 Multi-Currency Bond Issuance Framework in April.[3] RMA (Cambodia) Plc., a retail and distribution company, raised KHR80 billion from the sale of a 5-year bond. The issuance marked Cambodia's first bond guaranteed by the Credit Guarantee and Investment Facility and the first issuance by a nonfinancial corporation. Also in April, Prasac Microfinance Institution Plc. raised KHR127.2 billion from the sale of a 3-year bond, the largest

---

[1] Emerging East Asia comprises the People's Republic of China; Hong Kong, China; Indonesia; the Republic of Korea; Malaysia; the Philippines; Singapore; Thailand; and Viet Nam.
[2] LCY bond statistics for the Association of Southeast Asian Nations include the markets of Indonesia, Malaysia, the Philippines, Singapore, Thailand, and Viet Nam.
[3] ASEAN+3 comprises the 10 member economies of ASEAN plus the People's Republic of China, Japan, and the Republic of Korea.

corporate issuance to date in Cambodia. The issuance was the second bond in Cambodia to be guaranteed by the Credit Guarantee and Investment Facility.

The June issue of the *Asia Bond Monitor* includes a special section on how the financial sector can help fund the fight against COVID-19 and a theme chapter on the relationship between financial architecture and innovation.

Box 1: COVID-19—Impact on Capital Markets

Box 1 explains how the outbreak of COVID-19 has caused volatility and dried up liquidity in capital markets. This box discusses the disruptive impact of the pandemic on global financial markets—especially primary, secondary, and repo markets. Although central bank interventions have helped, greater coordination among central banks and more systematic solutions could have led to better outcomes.

Special Section on COVID-19 and the Financial Sector

Box 2: Pandemic Bonds—An Option for Fighting COVID-19

Box 2 explores the negative impact of COVID-19 on public finances caused by increased spending and falling revenues. Governments can mobilize more resources by issuing pandemic bonds to finance pandemic-related expenditures. At a broader level, the bond market is likely to play a significant role in bridging governments' financing gaps.

Box 3: Social Bonds and the COVID-19 Crisis

This box discusses the rising attention directed to social bonds in 2020 in response to the COVID-19 pandemic. Aggregate issuance of social bonds had reached nearly USD12 billion by 12 May, compared to USD16 billion raised in all of 2019. This box documents the major social and sustainability bond issuances in 2020 to date. These bonds have funded projects that support health services, unemployment alleviation, and small and medium-sized enterprises.

Box 4: Fintech for Inclusive Growth and Pandemic Resilience

The financial sector can promote inclusive growth and broaden access to financial services by capitalizing on financial technology (fintech). This box discusses how fintech can provide financial services to financially underserved and vulnerable groups amid the COVID-19 pandemic. Improved coordination between policy makers and the fintech sector is needed to better support households and businesses, and to provide liquidity.

Box 5: Financing Firms During the COVID-19 Pandemic

This box explains how the COVID-19 pandemic has seriously disrupted financial markets and therefore firms' ability to obtain financing. While a well-functioning financial system can lessen the impact of COVID-19 on the finances of firms, it alone is not sufficient. Adjustments to credit provision can help, such as keeping borrowing costs low and delaying repayments, but these measures must also be balanced against financial stability. Governments can contribute to financial stability through liquidity provision and by reconsidering government finances.

Theme Chapter on Financial Architecture and Innovation

The theme chapter examines the link between financial architecture and innovation. It highlights the importance of a sound and efficient financial system in fostering a viable innovation environment. The theme chapter features a study, summarized in a discussion box, that explores whether financial intermediaries (e.g., banks) or capital markets (e.g., equity and debt markets) are more conducive to innovation. Using a global sample, the study finds that a market-based financial system is more conducive to innovation, measured by both innovation quantity and quality. The evidence thus strengthens the case for developing a well-balanced financial system in the region.

Global and Regional Market Developments

Bond yields diverge in emerging East Asia amid continued weak risk appetite and a dim economic outlook.

Between 28 February and 29 May, global investment sentiment remained subdued in both developed and emerging markets. The yields on 2-year local currency government bonds fell in the United Kingdom (UK) and the United States (US), as well as in most emerging East Asian markets where policy rates have recently been adjusted.[1] The yields on 10-year government bonds posted a mixed picture, reflecting the respective fundamentals of individual economies. The weak

economic outlook and uncertain progress in fighting the coronavirus disease (COVID-19) has cast a shadow on global financial conditions (**Table A**).

In emerging East Asia, the 2-year government bond yield fell in most markets between 28 February and 29 May, while movements in 10-year bond yields diverged. The declines in 2-year bond yields were largely driven by central banks' monetary policy measures, including lowering key policy rates and adjusting reserve requirement ratios (**Table B**). The 2-year bond yield fell the most in the Philippines and Singapore, shedding 133 basis points (bps) and 103 bps, respectively. Both

Table A: Changes in Global Financial Conditions

	2-Year Government Bond (bps)	10-Year Government Bond (bps)	5-Year Credit Default Swap Spread (bps)	Equity Index (%)	FX Rate (%)
Major Advanced Economies					
United States	(75)	(50)	–	3.0	–
United Kingdom	(35)	(26)	10	(7.7)	(3.7)
Japan	10	16	2	3.1	0.1
Germany	11	16	11	(2.6)	0.7
Emerging East Asia					
China, People's Rep. of	(41)	(4)	4	(1.0)	(2.0)
Hong Kong, China	(48)	(38)	–	(12.1)	0.5
Indonesia	83	40	64	(12.8)	(2.0)
Korea, Rep. of	(37)	4	(7)	2.1	(1.8)
Malaysia	(42)	(2)	27	(0.6)	(3.0)
Philippines	(133)	(116)	15	(14.0)	0.7
Singapore	(103)	(56)	–	(16.6)	(1.4)
Thailand	(25)	9	15	0.2	(0.9)
Viet Nam	(40)	28	111	(2.0)	(0.2)
Select European Markets					
Greece	47	26	32	(9.4)	0.7
Ireland	17	28	13	(8.0)	0.7
Italy	37	43	44	(17.2)	0.7
Portugal	(7)	18	35	(9.1)	0.7
Spain	8	22	35	(18.6)	0.7

( ) = negative, – = not available, bps = basis points, FX = foreign exchange.
Notes:
1. Data reflect changes between 28 February and 29 May 2020.
2. A positive (negative) value for the FX rate indicates the appreciation (depreciation) of the local currency against the United States dollar.
Sources: Bloomberg LP and Institute of International Finance.

---

[1] Emerging East Asia comprises the People's Republic of China; Hong Kong, China; Indonesia; the Republic of Korea; Malaysia; the Philippines; Singapore; Thailand; and Viet Nam.

Table B: Policy Rate Changes

Economies	Policy Rate 31-Dec-2019 (%)	Rate Changes (%)					Policy Rate 31-May-2020 (%)	Year-to-Date Change in Policy Rates (basis points)
		Jan-2020	Feb-2020	Mar-2020	Apr-2020	May-2020		
United States	1.75			↓1.50			0.25	↓ 150
Euro Area	(0.50)						(0.50)	
Japan	(0.10)						(0.10)	
China, People's Rep. of	4.35						4.35	
Indonesia	5.00		↓ 0.25	↓0.25			4.50	↓ 50
Korea, Rep. of	1.25			↓0.50		↓0.25	0.50	↓ 75
Malaysia	3.00	↓ 0.25		↓0.25		↓0.50	2.00	↓ 100
Philippines	4.00		↓ 0.25	↓0.50	↓0.50		2.75	↓ 125
Thailand	1.25		↓ 0.25	↓0.25		↓0.25	0.50	↓ 75
Viet Nam	6.00			↓1.00		↓0.50	4.50	↓ 150

( ) = negative.
Note: Data as of 31 May 2020.
Sources: Various central bank websites.

markets also saw declines in their 10-year yields during the review period. The Bangko Sentral ng Pilipinas has been one of the most aggressive central banks in the region in terms of easing monetary policy, reducing policy rates by 125 bps and the reserve requirement ratio by 200 bps year-to-date through 31 May. The People's Republic of China (PRC); Malaysia; and Hong Kong, China also recorded declines in their 2-year and 10-year yields but to a lesser extent. The PRC reduced a number of key interest rates during the review period. On 29 March, the rate on the 7-day repurchase rate was lowered by 20 bps to 2.20%. The rate on the medium-term lending facility was lowered by 20 bps to 2.95% on 15 April, and the rate on the 1-year loan prime rate was cut by 20 bps to 3.85% on 19 April. Malaysia also cut its overnight policy rate by a cumulative 100 bps from 1 January through 31 May.

The Republic of Korea, Thailand, and Viet Nam saw declines in their 2-year yields and increases in their 10-year yields during the review period. Gains in yields at the longer-end of the curve were mostly driven by investor concerns over government finances and an expanded bond supply in the wake of COVID-19. In Thailand, the government passed its largest COVID-19 stimulus package to date on 31 May, which was valued at THB1.9 trillion. Indonesia was the sole exception to the regional trend, with 2-year and 10-year yields increasing by 83 bps and 40 bps, respectively. The uptick in yields in Indonesia was largely driven by a market sell-off as foreign investors dumped government bonds amid heightened global market uncertainties due to the COVID-19 outbreak. Investors had also been expecting additional rate cuts in April and May that did not materialize.

Further contributing to the uptick in 10-year government bond yields in some emerging East Asian markets was a downgrade of the sovereign rating outlook by major rating agencies. In April, S&P Global downgraded Indonesia's sovereign rating outlook to negative from stable and Thailand's from positive to stable. Fitch Ratings revised downward its sovereign rating outlook for Viet Nam from positive to stable in April. As the COVID-19 pandemic halted economic activities globally, all emerging East Asian economies posted much lower growth rates (or contractions) in the first quarter (Q1) of 2020, with the growth outlook expected to further decline in the second and third quarters of the year.

Advanced economies have been among the hardest hit economies globally. Between 28 February and 29 May, all major advanced economies adopted easing monetary stances and introduced fiscal stimulus schemes to mitigate the negative impact of COVID-19 on the economy. In the US, the Federal Reserve deviated from its original course after leaving the policy rate unchanged at its January meeting. As risks from the continued spread of COVID-19 heightened, the Federal Reserve announced an emergency rate cut of 50 bps in the federal funds rate on 3 March, which was well before the regularly scheduled Federal Open Market Committee monetary policy meeting on 17–18 March. Citing the negative impact of COVID-19 containment efforts on consumer sentiment and behavior, as well as the economy, the Federal Reserve reduced the federal funds rate by an additional 100 bps to between 0% and 0.25% on 15 March. In addition to interest rate cuts, the Federal Reserve also implemented measures to ease financial turmoil caused by COVID-19, including purchasing additional assets of at least USD500 billion and facilitating credit to households and businesses via a reduction in the primary credit rate at its discount window. On 17–18 March, the Federal Reserve established lending facilities for commercial paper, money markets, and primary credit dealers to ease funding demands and improve market liquidity. The Federal Reserve also engaged in coordinated actions with other central banks such as the Bank of Canada, Bank of Japan (BOJ), European Central Bank (ECB), and Swiss National Bank to provide liquidity via US dollar swap lines by reducing the rates charged.

US economic data warranted the Federal Reserve's concern. Gross domestic product (GDP) contracted 5.0% year-on-year (y-o-y), based on a revised estimate, in Q1 2020 after gaining 2.1% y-o-y in the previous quarter. Labor markets were also hit hard, with the unemployment rate soaring to 14.7% in April from 4.4% in March. Nonfarm payrolls showed a reduction of 20.7 million jobs in April, following a decline of only 1.4 million in March and a net gain of 251,000 in February. More recently, the job market rebounded in May with the unemployment rate slipping to 13.3% and nonfarm payrolls showing an increase of 2.5 million jobs. As a result of the supply and (related) demand shock, the Personal Consumption Expenditure inflation rate fell to 0.5% in April from 1.3% in March.

In the euro area, the ECB followed suit. During its 12 March meeting, the ECB left unchanged its policy rates but announced an asset purchase program worth EUR120 billion for the remainder of the year. The ECB enacted these measures on 18 March, establishing a EUR750 billion Pandemic Emergency Purchase Programme that removed prior restrictions limiting the ECB's asset purchases to at most one-third of the outstanding sovereign bonds of a given market. Judging these measures to be sufficient, existing monetary policy measures were left unchanged at the ECB's 30 April meeting. However, worsening economic conditions led the ECB to increase the volume of purchases under the program to EUR1,350 billion on 4 June. The euro area economy was hit hard by COVID-19, with GDP for Q1 2020 falling 3.1% y-o-y after gaining 1.0% in the previous quarter. Inflation also fell to an estimated 0.1% in May from 0.3% in April. In addition, the June economic forecast showed that the euro area's GDP is expected to decline 8.7% y-o-y in 2020 from a previous forecast of 0.8% growth in March.

In Japan, the BOJ also enacted easing measures in the form of increased asset purchases. On 16 March, the BOJ left both the monetary policy rate and government bond purchases unchanged but announced an increase

of JPY2.0 trillion in asset purchases of commercial paper and corporate bonds and of JPY6.0 trillion and JPY90 billion in purchases of exchange-traded funds and Japanese real estate investment trusts, respectively. On 27 April, acknowledging the worsening economic impact of COVID-19, the BOJ introduced more aggressive measures at its monetary policy meeting. While the interest rate target remained unchanged at 0%, purchases of commercial paper and corporate bonds were more than doubled to JPY20 trillion, and the upper limit on the purchase of 10-year government bonds was lifted. On 22 May, the BOJ announced that it would continue purchasing commercial paper and corporate bonds until March 2021, which is later than the previously announced deadline of September 2020. The GDP growth forecast for fiscal year 2020 was revised downward to between –5.0% and –3.0% from growth of between 0.8% and 1.1%. Japan's GDP in Q1 2020 contracted by 2.2% y-o-y after falling 7.2% y-o-y in the previous quarter.

Other than monetary measures, advanced economies also introduced fiscal stimulus programs to help mitigate the impact of COVID-19. In the US, the Coronavirus Aid, Relief, and Economic Security Act was signed on 27 March, introducing a USD2.0 trillion package that includes direct payments to households. On 27 April, another USD484 billion package aimed at small businesses and hospitals was signed. In the euro area, the European Commission unveiled a proposed EUR750 billion stimulus package on 30 May. In Japan, the government announced a number of support measures on 6 April totaling JPY108 trillion.

The monetary and fiscal policies introduced in response to the COVID-19 pandemic largely shaped bond yield patterns in advanced economies. Between 28 February and 29 May, the 10-year government bond yield declined in the UK and the US, while it rose in Germany and Japan. In March, all advanced economies witnessed a spike in the 10-year government bond yield, driven by deficit concerns in response to the fiscal stimulus measures announced in the US. Markets gradually returned to normal shortly thereafter (**Figure A**). In the case of Germany and Japan, yields ended the review period slightly higher as both the ECB and the BOJ focused largely on asset purchase programs to guide interest rates.

The outbreak of COVID-19 has caused a steep decline in global economic development. The Asian Development Bank (ADB) estimates the global economic impact of COVID-19, excluding the impact of policy measures, at

Figure A: 10-Year Government Bond Yields in Major Advanced Economies (% per annum)

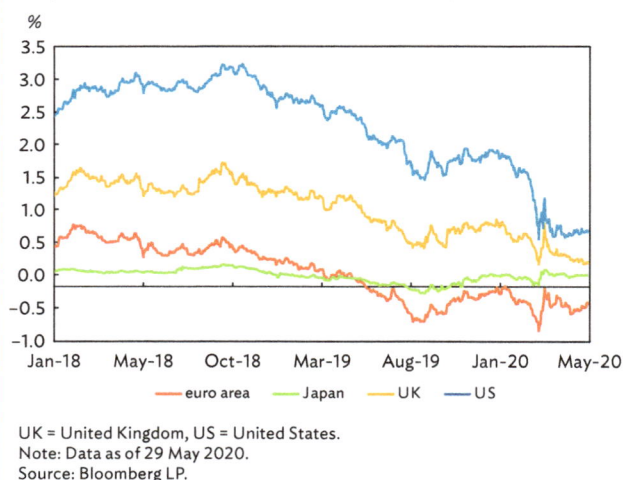

UK = United Kingdom, US = United States.
Note: Data as of 29 May 2020.
Source: Bloomberg LP.

Figure B: Changes in Equity Indexes in Emerging East Asia

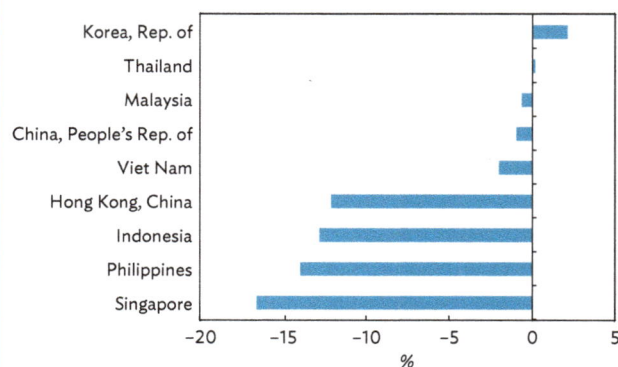

Note: Changes between 28 February and 29 May 2020.
Source: Bloomberg LP.

Figure C: Capital Flows into Equity Markets in Emerging East Asia

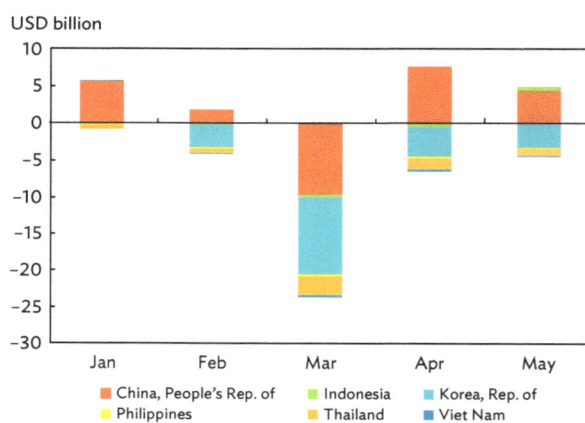

USD = United States dollar.
Source: Institute of International Finance.

between USD5.8 trillion and USD8.8 trillion (6.4%–9.7% of global GDP).[2] The potential economic impact on Asia and the Pacific is estimated at USD1.7 trillion (6.2% of regional GDP) under a 3-month containment scenario and USD2.5 trillion (9.3% of regional GDP) under a 6-month containment scenario. As discussed, global governments and central banks have launched massive stimulus packages to mitigate the negative impact of COVID-19 on the economy.

The huge economic losses caused by COVID-19 and the continued uncertainty surrounding its containment significantly restricted investment appetite in financial markets. Most equity markets in emerging East Asia posted losses during the review period on heightened risk aversion, with the largest declines recorded in Singapore (–16.6%), the Philippines (–14.0%), and Indonesia (–12.8%) (**Figure B**). Equity markets in the Republic of Korea and Thailand posted slight gains on the back of improved investor sentiment due to effective containment of COVID-19 in the case of the Republic of Korea and a partial lifting of lockdown measures in Thailand on 17 May. March saw the largest outflow across the region's equity markets, with all markets posting outflows (**Figure C**).

During the review period, nearly all emerging East Asian currencies weakened vis-à-vis the US dollar on the back of subdued investment sentiment (**Figure D**). The Malaysian ringgit saw the largest decline at 3.0% amid

capital outflows and a slump in oil prices. The Philippine peso and Hong Kong dollar bucked the regional trend, appreciating 0.7% and 0.5%, respectively, versus the US dollar during the review period. The strengthening of the peso was supported by a stronger balance-of-payments surplus and increased gross international reserves. In 2019, the balance-of-payments surplus in the Philippines reached USD7.8 billion, or the equivalent of 2.2% of GDP, the highest level since 2012. At the end of April 2020, gross international reserves climbed to USD90.9 billion, or the equivalent of 8 months of goods and services. Recently, regional currencies have recovered

---

[2] Asian Development Bank. 2020. Policy Brief No. 133. https://www.adb.org/sites/default/files/publication/604206/adb-brief-133-updated-economic-impact-covid-19.pdf.

somewhat as investor sentiment slightly improves. This has created challenges for markets such as Thailand, as it seeks a weaker Thai baht to improve exports and attract tourists.

Heightened uncertainty and subdued investment appetite not only led to a climb in the regions' risk premiums but also caused concerns regarding debt refinancing and a rise in financing costs. Credit default

swap spreads in emerging East Asia rocketed upward in March and were largely volatile at their higher levels in April before falling slightly in May (**Figure E**). The CBOE Volatility Index and the EMBIG spread also showed similar patterns, with large spikes in March followed by volatility at elevated levels (**Figures F** and **G**). **Box 1** describes the rise of risk premiums in financial markets in more detail.

Figure D: Changes in Month-End Spot Exchange Rates vs. the United States Dollar

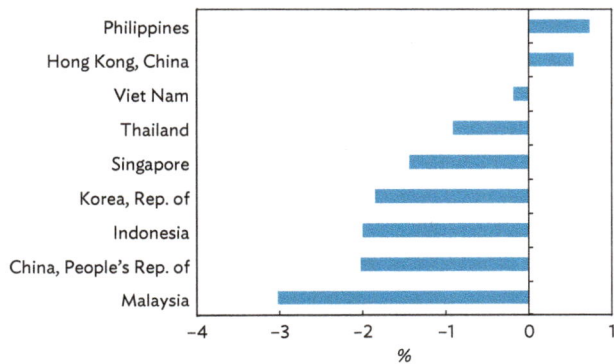

Notes:
1. Changes between 28 February and 29 May 2020.
2. A positive (negative) value for the foreign exchange rate indicates the appreciation (depreciation) of the local currency against the United States dollar.
Source: Bloomberg LP.

Figure E: Credit Default Swap Spreads in Select Asian Markets (senior 5-year)

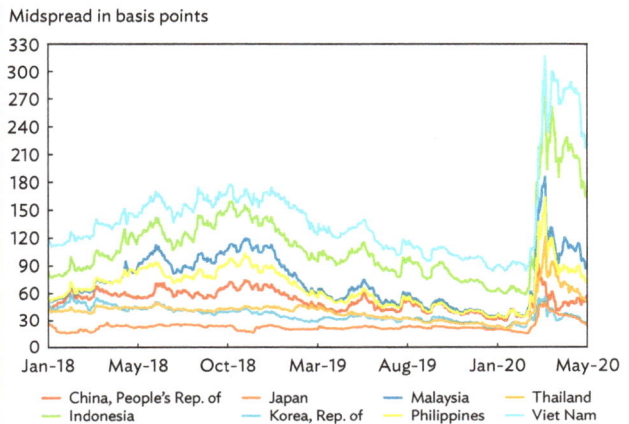

USD = United States dollar.
Notes:
1. Based on USD-denominated sovereign bonds.
2. Data as of 29 May 2020.
Source: Bloomberg LP.

Figure F: United States Equity Volatility and Emerging Market Sovereign Bond Spread

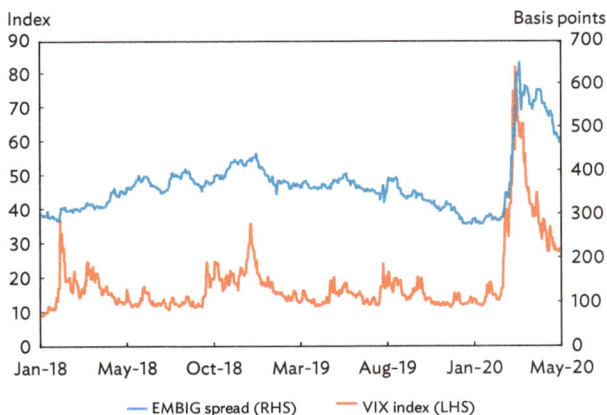

EMBIG = Emerging Markets Bond Index Global, LHS = left-hand side, RHS = right-hand side, VIX = Chicago Board Options Exchange Volatility Index.
Note: Data as of 29 May 2020.
Source: Bloomberg LP.

Figure G: JP Morgan Emerging Markets Bond Index Sovereign Stripped Spreads

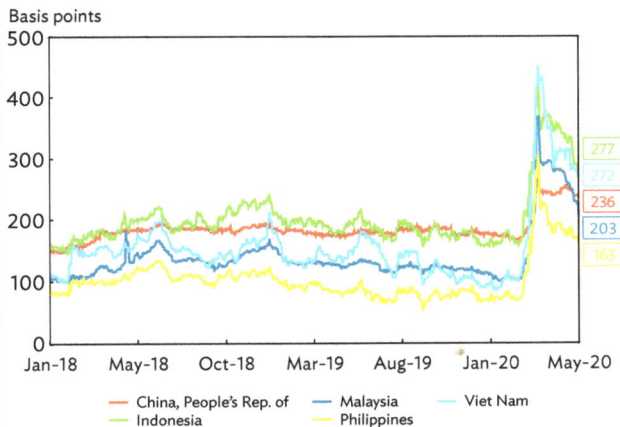

USD = United States dollar.
Notes:
1. Based on USD-denominated sovereign bonds.
2. Data as of 29 May 2020.
Source: Bloomberg LP.

Box 1: COVID-19—Impact on Capital Markets

From a market perspective, the coronavirus disease (COVID-19) has caused enormous volatility and provided the ultimate test of the resilience of primary, secondary, and repurchase agreement (repo) markets.[a] In early March, there were days when the normally robust primary markets were simply shut for business and when secondary bond market liquidity evaporated in both the credit and rates segments. On those days, for anything but the most liquid bonds, dealer bids were scarce and offers were in short supply unless the dealer already owned inventory. The situation was exacerbated by many regulated entities adjusting to operating from split locations as they moved part of their critical teams to disaster recovery sites to ensure business continuity. Coincidentally, this scenario occurred shortly after the publication of the International Capital Market Association's (ICMA) latest study on secondary markets, *Time to Act*, which highlighted the fact that, despite the changes in market structure and the move toward electronic trading, secondary markets remain dealer-centric and moves to further limit the ability of dealers to assume risk positions only contribute to the fragility of liquidity in stressed markets (**Figure B1**).

The progressive and substantial actions of central banks in the middle of March, particularly the reintroduction and expansion of quantitative easing measures with substantial bond purchase programs, were the catalyst to restarting primary markets, allowing confidence to return and the markets to reopen. From the middle of March onward, issuance volumes picked up, starting with the highest-grade issuers (e.g., sovereigns, supranationals, and agencies) and followed by corporates, both financial and nonfinancial. Strong institutional investor demand led to record volumes of new issuance shortly before the middle of April. These central bank interventions also provided support to secondary markets, easing liquidity concerns. However, liquidity remains a challenge, particularly for lower-grade structurally illiquid bonds.

The repo market is a critical funding tool, particularly in times of stress, and has been arguably the most robust element of the financial market, remaining operational throughout and generally performing well in the face of high trading volumes. Nevertheless, dealer capacity to take on new clients was constrained, with the result being that certain categories of buy-side firms found it problematic to access the repo market. Supply constraints were also evident as counterparties withdrew from lending securities unless it was part of their core business, as explained in more detail in ICMA's recent study on this topic.

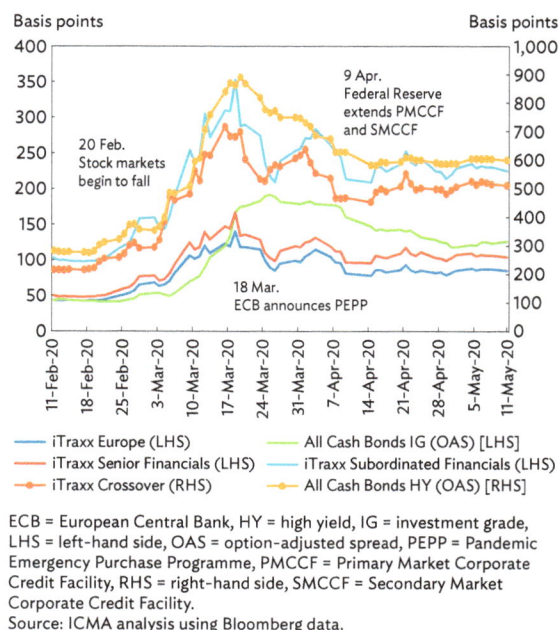

Figure B1: Euro-Denominated Corporate Credit Spreads

ECB = European Central Bank, HY = high yield, IG = investment grade, LHS = left-hand side, OAS = option-adjusted spread, PEPP = Pandemic Emergency Purchase Programme, PMCCF = Primary Market Corporate Credit Facility, RHS = right-hand side, SMCCF = Secondary Market Corporate Credit Facility.
Source: ICMA analysis using Bloomberg data.

The mixture of central bank monetary policy responses and fiscal measures from governments has been designed to ensure that there is sufficient liquidity available in the real economy, particularly for small and medium-sized enterprises, to bridge the temporary cash flow constraints of otherwise healthy companies, minimize unemployment with furloughs and other schemes, and support individuals. As the crisis became deeper and more prolonged, the clamor for government help from large companies in hard-hit sectors intensified; support has often been forthcoming in response.

One problem is that there has not been a globally coordinated response to the crisis, and the piecemeal policy responses have increased market participant nervousness and likely contributed to volatility. Unsurprisingly, the current environment generates enormous challenges and uncertainties for ICMA's buy- and sell-side members, who play a critical role in ensuring liquidity reaches those most in need. However, it has been very positive that the remote working arrangements implemented by many of our members have allowed them to work effectively during the crisis.

---

[a] This box was written by Martin Scheck, Chief Executive of the International Capital Market Association.

continued on next page

Box 1: COVID-19—Impact on Capital Markets   *continued*

The economic impacts of the pandemic are beginning to become evident. The main questions being just how severely growth will be damaged, what is the long-term outlook for unemployment, what will be the related social impacts—and, of course, who ultimately will "pay the bill." One can certainly expect rates to remain lower for even longer and, while it is evident that economic activity has declined significantly during the government-imposed lockdowns, it is not at all clear to what extent, and how quickly, economic activity will pick up as many economies start to ease their current restrictions.

The impact of COVID-19 on capital markets has been the overarching concern for ICMA, and we have responded with a range of activities designed to keep markets open and operating efficiently, while assisting our members on a day-to-day basis. An important initiative has been to review the timetables of consultation papers and regulatory implementation that were already in progress and to work with our members and the appropriate authorities to have these measures postponed where needed. This was particularly important for the European Union Securities Financing Transaction Regulation implementation deadline, which is set to introduce an extensive reporting regime for repo and other securities financing instruments. Following ICMA's intervention, the European Securities and Markets Authority provided a 3-month forbearance on the implementation date. Similarly, the consultations for the European Securities and Markets Authority's Markets in Financial Instruments Directive and Associated Regulation have been postponed, as have the deadlines of many other regulatory bodies. Given that it is not clear how quickly the

crisis will abate, discussions are ongoing with respect to all appropriate timelines for these and other consultations and implementations.

In the market for EUR-denominated commercial paper, where ICMA has provided its members with standard form documentation for many years, following confirmation from the Bank of England that it would accept commercial paper with documentation based on ICMA's Euro Commercial Paper standard, for the period of the crisis we have chosen to make this documentation available to all participants whether or not they are ICMA members. We have also recommended to the European Central Bank that it include asset-backed commercial paper in its asset purchase program.

Sustainability remains an intense focus for the market and for ICMA. There has been an increase in the issuance of social bonds that reference the Social Bond Principles, which ICMA manages, to raise funds to respond to the social and economic impacts of the COVID-19 pandemic; we expect this market segment to grow. We also foresee that as future environmental, social, and governance reporting becomes more complex and far-reaching under a range of different regulations, it will impact most of our member categories as a topic of increased focus during 2020 and beyond.

In conclusion, the COVID-19 pandemic has presented enormous challenges and reminded us of the fragility of markets in times of great stress. The capital markets have a vital role to play in facilitating the flow of liquidity during these trying times. It is important that they remain open for business.

Foreign holdings of local currency government bonds declined in most emerging East Asian markets during the review period, as global investors shifted to safe-haven assets (**Figure H**). The largest decline in foreign holdings was seen in Indonesia, where the foreign holdings' share dropped from 38.6% at the end of December to 32.7% at the end of March. Indonesia's financial market was routed by a sell-off, leading to record-high capital outflows from the bond market in March on heightened risk aversion. A similar market sell-off was observed in Malaysia with the foreign holdings' share falling from 25.3% at the end of December to 22.2% at the end of March. The foreign holdings' share in the PRC remained stable during Q1 2020. More recently, investor

sentiment has improved over optimism that economic growth will recover as markets began unwinding quarantine measures.

Overall, risk to the region remains titled toward the downside. The regional outlook has been weakened by ongoing uncertainty regarding the containment of COVID-19, a risk that also hovers over the global economy and financial markets. In addition to COVID-19, trade tensions between the PRC and the US have escalated again, casting further uncertainty on the global economic outlook. Global oil prices also contribute to the uncertainty given ongoing geopolitical risks and tensions in the Middle East.

**Figure H: Foreign Holdings of Local Currency
Government Bonds in Select Asian Markets** (% of total)

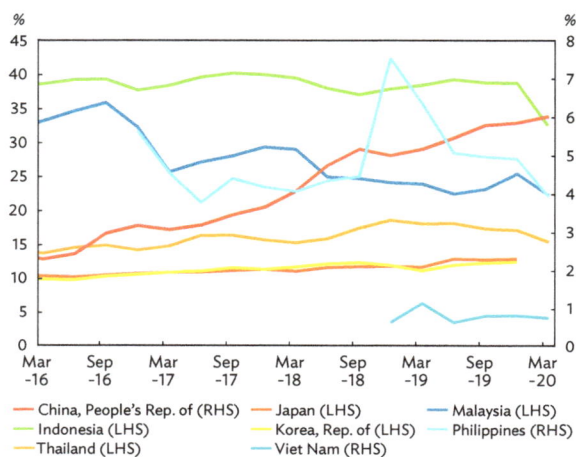

LHS = left-hand side, RHS = right-hand side.
Note: Data as of 31 March 2020 except for Japan and the Republic of Korea
(31 December 2019).
Source: *AsianBondsOnline*.

Economic Outlook

The world is facing an unprecedented public health crisis caused by COVID-19. Although the outbreak initially only affected the PRC and other Asian economies in December 2019 and January 2020, it soon spread to all corners of the world in a matter of weeks. Although some regions and economies were hit harder by the virus than others, no region or economy has been immune from its devastating impact on public health. As the global public health situation went from bad to worse, the World Health Organization declared COVID-19 a global pandemic on 11 March. As of 25 May, the number of confirmed cases and deaths had reached 5,304,772 and 342,029, respectively.[3] The US, the world's largest economy, emerged as the biggest hot spot, with almost one-third of global cases and 30% of global deaths. Other hard-hit countries include Brazil, the Russian Federation, several major Western European countries, Turkey, and India. COVID-19 has inflicted untold human misery, pain, and suffering around the world.

While the immediate impact of COVID-19 is on global public health, it has dealt an equally severe blow to the world economy. There is firm consensus that the current

global economic downturn caused by the pandemic will be much worse than the Great Recession that followed the global financial crisis of 2008–2009. That recession reduced global output by around 1%, which marked the first and only contraction of the world economy in the postwar period. The current downturn is likely to be the biggest negative global economic shock since the Great Depression of the late 1920s and 1930s. Like the public health crisis, the economic crisis is widely viewed as a once-in-a-century crisis.

The bulk of the economic costs of COVID-19 do not stem directly from those who are infected by the disease or succumbed to it. Rather, they are the consequences of the travel restrictions, lockdowns, widespread closures, isolation, and other social distancing measures put in place by governments to contain the disease. Precautionary personal behavior, such as staying at home to minimize the risk of infection, is adding to the gloom. Above all, public health restrictions have severely disrupted the production of goods and services, and their transportation. The result has been a massive supply-side shock that is forcing firms and industries to produce far below their capacity.

Global growth forecasts are being sharply downgraded. According to the International Monetary Fund's (IMF) *World Economic Outlook April 2020*, the world economy grew by an estimated 2.9% in 2019 and is projected to contract by 3.0% in 2020 before rebounding to expand 5.8% in 2021. As late as January 2020, the IMF had forecast global growth in 2020 of 3.3%. The downward revision of 6.3 percentage points in just 3 months reflects the scale and speed of the deterioration of the global economic outlook due to the rapid spread of COVID-19 and the concomitant social distancing restrictions. The IMF's forecast of 5.8% growth in 2021 reflects an optimistic underlying assumption of a V-shaped recovery, which is predicated on a sharp yet short downturn. While there is no cause for undue pessimism, the highly uncertain and unpredictable nature of this pandemic implies that the world may be heading instead for a U-shaped, or even an L-shaped, recovery.

According to the IMF's World Economic Outlook April 2020, the output of advanced economies, which grew by 1.7% in 2019, will shrink by 6.1% in

3 World Health Organization. COVID-19 Situation Report—126. 2020. https://www.who.int/docs/default-source/coronavirus/situation-reports/20200525-covid-19-sitrep-126.pdf?sfvrsn=887dbd66_2.

2020 before bouncing back to expand 4.5% in 2021. The corresponding figures for emerging markets and developing countries are 3.7%, −1.0%, and 6.6%, respectively. The IMF is downgrading growth forecasts for all the major economies that it tracks, underscoring the global nature of the downturn. Global trade, which was already slowing before the COVID-19 outbreak due to trade tensions, is projected to contract by 11.0% in 2020 after growing by 0.9% in 2019. Next year, in line with the expected global economic recovery, global trade is forecast to expand by 8.4%.

Developing Asia is feeling the economic pain too.[4] ADB's *Asian Development Outlook 2020* released in April 2020 forecast the region's economy to grow by 2.2% in 2020 and 6.2% in 2021, after expanding by 5.2% in 2019. By comparison, ADB's *Asian Development Outlook 2019 Supplement* released in December 2019 had forecast a 2020 growth rate of 5.2%, representing a full 3-percentage-point decline in the April 2020 forecast. The PRC, which grew by 6.1% in 2019, is projected to expand by only 2.3% in 2020, before rebounding to growth of 7.3% in 2021. The 2019 growth estimate and 2020 and 2021 growth forecasts for the 10 members of the Association of Southeast Asian Nations are 4.4%, 1.0%, and 4.7%, respectively. The Republic of Korea is projected to grow by 1.3% in 2020 and 2.3% in 2021, after growing by 2.0% in 2019. The growth figures for Hong Kong, China are −1.2% in 2019 and a projected −3.3% in 2020 and 3.5% in 2021. There is a fairly good chance that developing Asia's growth, likely to be the slowest since 1998, will be even lower than ADB's April forecasts. This is primarily because the global outlook has further deteriorated since the publication of the *Asian Development Outlook 2020* due to the global spread of the pandemic and the resultant severe downturns in Europe and the US.

COVID-19 remains the overarching source of uncertainty in the global and regional economic picture. The trajectory of the economic outlook over the next 2 years will be determined to a large extent by the trajectory of the pandemic. In particular, as economies in Asia and elsewhere gradually reopen, there are widespread concerns about a second wave of COVID-19 that could trigger the reintroduction of travel bans, lockdowns, and other social distancing restrictions. A virulent second wave could stop reopening in its tracks and take the world

back to square one. If, on the other hand, COVID-19 recedes on its own, or a safe and effective vaccine is developed and made widely available in record time, it is likely that life would return rapidly to the "pre-COVID-19 normal" and the global economy would experience a robust V-shaped recovery. To sum up, the evolution of the COVID-19 pandemic, which is the huge cloud of uncertainty hanging over the world economy, will have a big say in how the economies of Asia and the world actually perform in 2020 and 2021.

Risks to Economic Outlook and Financial Stability

By far the biggest source of risks to the global and regional economic outlook, which are heavily tilted to the downside, is COVID-19. Until the pandemic is brought under control, it will hover like a dark cloud over the global economic outlook. The IMF's sharp downgrade of the 2020 global growth forecast and the ADB's sharp downgrade of developing Asia's 2020 growth forecast already factor in the pronounced effect of the negative supply shocks on economic activity. However, there is a fairly good chance that global output may shrink by more than 3.0% in 2020 and developing Asia's output may expand by less than 2.2% due to COVID-19. That is, the pandemic may yet inflict more damage on the economy than expected for a number of reasons. Given the uncertain and unpredictable nature of the outbreak, along with COVID-19's high degree of contagiousness, economists may be underestimating the risk it poses to the economy and society. After all, the pandemic has engulfed the entire world in a few months and shows little sign of receding any time soon.

Above all, the risk is that the COVID-19 pandemic could turn out to be more persistent than expected, and it may not stabilize or recede even with the advent of summer in the Northern Hemisphere. We cannot rule out the possibility that the effect of the public health crisis on the world economy and global financial markets is more potent and persistent than is currently being assumed. For example, the pandemic may leave a powerful imprint on consumer behavior for a long time to come. Individuals typically save more during times of uncertainty, and the current COVID-19 environment is about as uncertain as it gets. Therefore, even as

---

[4] Developing Asia refers to the 46 developing member economies of the Asian Development Bank.

economies around the world reopen, consumers may be reluctant to open their wallets, weakening aggregate demand and dampening the momentum of economic recovery. And, if reopening leads to second waves of new infections and deaths, the reimposition of lockdowns may be inevitable. Even under more benign scenarios, which assume that the pandemic will be contained in the foreseeable future, negative long-term consequences are entirely possible. For example, supply chains may have been significantly disrupted due to widespread business closures. Equally serious, given the sheer magnitude of the COVID-19 shock, it will take some time for consumer and business confidence to recover. Yet, improved confidence is vital for kickstarting consumption, investment, and overall economic activity.

While the pandemic is the paramount source of downside risks, a wide range of second-tier risks remain, from natural hazards to geopolitical events. The biggest second-tier risk is global trade tensions, in particular the trade conflict between the PRC and the US. The PRC–US trade conflict appeared to ease at the beginning of the year when the two sides reached a Phase 1 trade deal on 15 January 2020. In exchange for the US cutting tariffs on some Chinese imports, the PRC pledged to buy more American agricultural, manufacturing, and energy products and services, in addition to addressing some US complaints about intellectual property practices. The US pledged to cut by 50% the tariffs it had imposed on 1 September 2019 on USD120 billion worth of goods imported from the PRC. The PRC's commitment to buying more US exports was sizable. For example, the PRC committed itself to buying an additional USD77.7 billion more in US manufacturing products over a 2-year period (2020–2021). However, it is unclear whether the PRC will be able to purchase so many goods and services from the US in these difficult economic times, although in recent days officials have repeatedly reaffirmed the PRC's commitment to meet these targets. More ominously, COVID-19 itself has seriously strained PRC–US relations with the two sides becoming increasingly more aggressive in their rhetoric. Furthermore, the growing hostility is threatening to escalate the trade conflict into a broader economic and technological conflict. For example, the US has imposed restrictions on exports of vital components to the PRC tech giant Huawei. In addition, the main US federal government pension fund has halted plans to invest in PRC equities.

In addition to the tangible deterioration of the global trade environment, which will adversely affect the economic prospects of ASEAN+3 countries, severe financial turmoil and financial crises also cannot be discounted. Global financial conditions have tightened significantly since February, increasing demand for safe-haven assets, which has been especially painful for emerging markets and developing economies, many of which are also dealing with the widening spread of COVID-19. Some emerging economies with weak fundamentals are already in financial distress. For instance, Argentina defaulted on its debt on 22 May, although it was continuing to negotiate with its creditors.

Movements in global equity markets, exchange rates, bond spreads, and volatility indexes have been pronounced, while emerging Asian markets experienced a surge in capital outflows in March. Heightened financial volatility and a sudden halt in capital flows into the region cannot be ruled out. The decade-long rise in regional debt, primarily private but some of it public, exacerbates the risk from volatile capital flows. Small and medium-sized firms may be susceptible to tightening financial conditions and a worsening economic environment.

Finally, COVID-19 is likely to leave long-lasting, or even permanent, scars on the world economy. Above all, the pandemic will give impetus to anti-globalization forces that were already gathering momentum before the outbreak, as evident in growing trade protectionism and rising trade tensions. Globalization, in particular the dramatic expansion of international trade made possible by technological progress and trade liberalization, has been perhaps the single most powerful driver of economic growth in the postwar period. However, COVID-19 dramatically highlights the fact that globalization is at best a mixed blessing. After all, close and growing transport linkages among the global community of countries helped to spread the pandemic like a wildfire across the world. More concretely, the pandemic has underscored the vulnerability of global supply chains to trade and transport disruptions. In the current environment of weak confidence and heightened uncertainty, upside risks to the global outlook are few and far between. In particular, the widespread availability of a safe and effective vaccine would fast-forward economic recovery and our return to normality.

Bond Market Developments in the First Quarter of 2020

Size and Composition

Emerging East Asia's local currency bond market expanded in the first quarter of 2020 to reach a size of USD16.3 trillion at the end of March.

Local currency (LCY) bonds outstanding in emerging East Asia amounted to USD16.3 trillion at the end of March, up from USD15.6 trillion (in current terms) at the end of December.[5] Overall growth quickened to 4.2% quarter-on-quarter (q-o-q) in the first quarter (Q1) of 2020 from 2.4% q-o-q in the fourth quarter (Q4) of 2019 (**Figure 1a**). The region's bond market growth was tempered by the risk-off sentiment affecting emerging markets, which was brought about by the slowdown in the global economy and the onset of the coronavirus disease (COVID-19) during the quarter.

The majority of the region's nine markets posted moderate q-o-q growth in Q1 2020, with the fastest growth seen in Viet Nam and the Philippines. Hong Kong, China and Thailand experienced negative q-o-q growth during the review period. Compared with Q4 2019, the q-o-q growth rate accelerated in five of the region's nine bond markets.

On a year-on-year (y-o-y) basis, the region's LCY bond market grew at a faster pace of 14.0% in Q1 2020 versus 12.6% in Q4 2019 (**Figure 1b**). All nine emerging East Asian markets posted positive y-o-y growth in Q1 2020, led by the People's Republic of China (PRC)

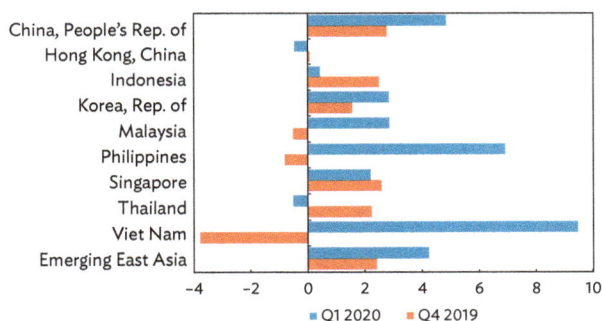

Figure 1a: Growth of Local Currency Bond Markets in the Fourth Quarter of 2019 and First Quarter of 2020 (q-o-q, %)

q-o-q = quarter-on-quarter, Q1 = first quarter, Q4 = fourth quarter.
Notes:
1. Calculated using data from national sources.
2. Growth rates are calculated from local currency base and do not include currency effects.
3. Emerging East Asia growth figures are based on 31 March 2020 currency exchange rates and do not include currency effects.
4. For Singapore, corporate bonds outstanding are based on *AsianBondsOnline* estimates.
Sources: People's Republic of China (CEIC); Hong Kong, China (Hong Kong Monetary Authority); Indonesia (Bank Indonesia; Directorate General of Budget Financing and Risk Management, Ministry of Finance; and Indonesia Stock Exchange); Republic of Korea (*EDAILY BondWeb* and The Bank of Korea); Malaysia (Bank Negara Malaysia); Philippines (Bureau of the Treasury and Bloomberg LP); Singapore (Monetary Authority of Singapore, Singapore Government Securities, and Bloomberg LP); Thailand (Bank of Thailand); and Viet Nam (Bloomberg LP and Vietnam Bond Market Association).

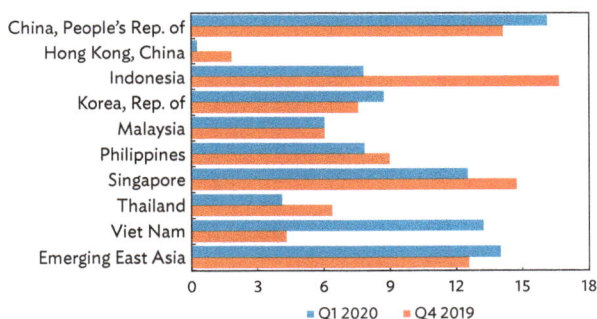

Figure 1b: Growth of Local Currency Bond Markets in the Fourth Quarter of 2019 and First Quarter of 2020 (y-o-y, %)

Q1 = first quarter, Q4 = fourth quarter, y-o-y = year-on-year.
Notes:
1. Calculated using data from national sources.
2. Growth rates are calculated from local currency base and do not include currency effects.
3. Emerging East Asia growth figures are based on 31 March 2020 currency exchange rates and do not include currency effects.
4. For Singapore, corporate bonds outstanding are based on *AsianBondsOnline* estimates.
Sources: People's Republic of China (CEIC); Hong Kong, China (Hong Kong Monetary Authority); Indonesia (Bank Indonesia; Directorate General of Budget Financing and Risk Management, Ministry of Finance; and Indonesia Stock Exchange); Republic of Korea (*EDAILY BondWeb* and The Bank of Korea); Malaysia (Bank Negara Malaysia); Philippines (Bureau of the Treasury and Bloomberg LP); Singapore (Monetary Authority of Singapore, Singapore Government Securities, and Bloomberg LP); Thailand (Bank of Thailand); and Viet Nam (Bloomberg LP and Vietnam Bond Market Association).

[5] Emerging East Asia comprises the People's Republic of China; Hong Kong, China; Indonesia; the Republic of Korea; Malaysia; the Philippines; Singapore; Thailand; and Viet Nam.

and Viet Nam. The LCY bond markets of the PRC, the Republic of Korea, and Viet Nam recorded faster y-o-y growth in Q1 2020 than in Q4 2019. Malaysia's y-o-y growth was steady between the two quarters, while the region's remaining markets experienced a slowdown in y-o-y growth in Q1 2020.

The PRC remained the region's leader in terms of bond market size, with outstanding bonds of USD12.5 trillion at the end of March. The PRC's share of the regional bond market increased to 76.6% at the end of March from 76.1% at the end of December. The PRC's overall bond market growth accelerated to 4.9% q-o-q in Q1 2020 from 2.8% q-o-q in Q4 2019.

The PRC's government bond segment recorded 3.5% q-o-q growth in Q1 2020, up from 2.0% q-o-q in Q4 2019. Growth in the outstanding government bond stock was supported by the issuance of Treasury and other government bonds, which rose 68.2% q-o-q in Q1 2020.

Growth in the PRC's corporate bond stock rose to 7.3% q-o-q in Q1 2020 from 4.1% q-o-q in Q4 2019, bolstered by strong issuance, which accelerated to 10.7% q-o-q in Q1 2020 from 1.7% q-o-q in Q4 2019. On a y-o-y basis, the PRC's bond market expanded 16.1% in Q1 2020, up from 14.1% in the prior quarter.

The Republic of Korea's LCY bond market was the second-largest in the region at the end of March at USD2.0 trillion. Growth in the bond market increased to 2.8% q-o-q in Q1 2020 from 1.6% q-o-q in Q4 2019. However, its share of the regional total slipped to 12.5% in Q1 2020 from 12.7% in the previous quarter. Government bonds rose 4.2% q-o-q, bolstered by strong issuance, which accelerated 45.4% q-o-q, largely driven by Korea Treasury Bonds. In Q1 2020, the Government of the Republic of Korea sold more bonds than in the previous quarter as it frontloaded expenditures for 2020 and raised funds to finance the government's stimulus program to counter the impact of COVID-19. The stock of corporate bonds posted a modest 1.9% q-o-q hike in Q1 2020, down from 2.7% q-o-q in Q4 2019. On an annual basis, the Republic of Korea's bond market growth rose to 8.7% y-o-y in Q1 2020 from 7.6% y-o-y in Q4 2019.

The size of the LCY bond market in Hong Kong, China was little changed at the end of March at USD291.0 billion. Overall, the bond market contracted 0.5% q-o-q in Q1 2020, driven by a decline in outstanding government bonds. The stock of government bonds contracted 1.1% q-o-q in Q1 2020, largely driven by a decline in the stock of Hong Kong Special Administrative Region bonds due to maturities. The stock of Exchange Fund Bills posted weak 0.4% q-o-q growth in Q1 2020, while the stock of Exchange Fund Notes was unchanged on zero growth. The corporate bond segment recorded marginal 0.2% q-o-q growth in Q1 2020. On a y-o-y basis, the bond market of Hong Kong, China barely grew at 0.3% in Q1 2020. The weak growth in Hong Kong, China's bond market stemmed from an economic contraction brought about by the combined effects of prolonged political protests, softening global demand, and the onset of COVID-19.

The aggregate amount of LCY bonds outstanding of the member economies of the Association of Southeast Asian Nations (ASEAN) stood at USD1.5 trillion at the end of March.[6] Overall growth inched up to 2.0% q-o-q in Q1 2020 from 1.2% q-o-q in Q4 2019. The total government bond stock reached USD1.0 trillion at the end of March, while corporate bonds stood at USD469.3 billion. Thailand, Malaysia, and Singapore remained the three largest bond markets in the ASEAN space.

Thailand's LCY bonds outstanding amounted to USD402.1 billion at the end of March. The 0.5% q-o-q contraction in Q1 2020 reversed the 2.2% q-o-q gain posted in the previous quarter. The global exodus from emerging markets impacted Thailand during the quarter, resulting in heightened volatility and tight liquidity in the domestic bond market. In March, the Bank of Thailand tapered its bond issuances and called off some offerings to improve market liquidity. Government bonds outstanding declined 1.0% q-o-q during the review period due to contractions in the outstanding stock of Bank of Thailand bonds and state-owned enterprise and other bonds, which outpaced the growth in government bonds and Treasury bills. The stock of outstanding corporate bonds posted marginal growth of 0.8% q-o-q in Q1 2020, down from 1.6% q-o-q in the previous quarter. Weak investor confidence dented demand for corporate bonds during the review period, resulting in a 12.5% q-o-q

---

[6] LCY bond statistics for ASEAN include the markets of Indonesia, Malaysia, the Philippines, Singapore, Thailand, and Viet Nam.

drop in corporate issuance. The y-o-y growth rate in the Thai bond market eased to 4.1% in Q1 2020 from 6.4% in Q4 2019.

The outstanding amount of Malaysia's LCY bonds totaled USD353.6 billion at the end of March, with growth rebounding to 2.9% q-o-q in Q1 2020 from –0.5% q-o-q in Q4 2019. Growth was supported by strong issuance of government bonds, particularly Treasury and other government bonds, which rose 72.7% q-o-q in Q1 2020. The growth of outstanding corporate bonds picked up, rising to 1.7% q-o-q in Q1 2020 from 0.7% q-o-q in Q4 2019. On a y-o-y basis, Malaysia's LCY bond market expanded 6.0% in Q1 2020.

The largest *sukuk* (Islamic bond) market in emerging East Asia is that of Malaysia, where about 61.5% of total LCY bonds outstanding comprise *sukuk*. At the end of Q1 2020, 45.2% of outstanding government bonds were structured following Islamic principles, while 79.6% of corporate bonds were *sukuk*.

At the end of March, Singapore's LCY bond market amounted to USD328.5 billion as growth dipped to 2.2% q-o-q in Q1 2020 from 2.6% q-o-q in Q4 2019. The slowdown in growth stemmed from the weaker growth of outstanding government bonds in Q1 2020 compared with the previous quarter. The corporate bond stock grew 1.7% q-o-q, the same pace recorded in Q4 2019. On an annual basis, Singapore's bond market growth eased to 12.5% y-o-y in Q1 2020 from 14.7% y-o-y in Q4 2019.

The outstanding amount of Indonesia's LCY bonds stood at USD203.8 billion at the end of March, with growth decelerating to 0.4% q-o-q in Q1 2020 from 2.5% q-o-q in Q4 2019. The stock of government bonds rose only 0.6% q-o-q and the corporate bond stock contracted 0.5% q-o-q. Indonesia's bond market was also largely affected by investors' risk-off sentiment due to COVID-19, lowering demand for both government and corporate bonds. On a y-o-y basis, Indonesia's LCY bond market growth moderated to 7.8% in Q1 2020 from 16.6% in Q4 2019.

The Philippines' LCY bond market reached a size of USD140.2 billion at the end of March, as growth rebounded to 6.9% q-o-q in Q1 2020 from –0.8% q-o-q in Q4 2019. The stock of government bonds posted

7.5% q-o-q growth in Q1 2020, reversing the 2.1% q-o-q decline in the previous quarter. Growth in the stock of corporate bonds rose to 5.0% q-o-q in Q1 2020 from 4.0% q-o-q in Q1 2019. Annual bond market growth in the Philippines eased to 7.9% y-o-y in Q1 2020 from 9.0% y-o-y in Q4 2019.

The LCY bond market in Viet Nam posted the highest growth in the region during the review period, albeit coming from a low base. Overall growth rebounded to 9.5% q-o-q in Q1 2020 from –3.8% q-o-q in the previous quarter. The growth stemmed from a rise in the government bond stock, which increased 10.5% q-o-q in Q1 2020, reversing the 3.9% q-o-q drop in Q4 2019. The stock of corporate bonds contracted 1.7% q-o-q in Q1 2019. On a y-o-y basis, Viet Nam's bond market expanded 13.2% in Q1 2020, up from 4.3% in Q4 2019.

At the end of March, government bonds continued to account for the majority of emerging East Asia's total LCY bond stock, representing a 60.6% share. In nominal terms, the outstanding amount of government bonds climbed to USD9.9 trillion on growth of 3.3% q-o-q and 12.3% y-o-y (**Table 1**). Accounting for the largest shares of the regional government bond market were the PRC and the Republic of Korea. Together, the two markets accounted for 88.2% of emerging East Asia's total government bond stock.

ASEAN economies accounted for 10.3% of aggregate government bonds outstanding in emerging East Asia at the end of Q1 2020. Among ASEAN economies, Thailand had the largest LCY government bond market at the end of March at a size of USD285.6 billion. The next largest markets were those of Singapore and Malaysia, with outstanding government bonds totaling USD205.9 billion and USD186.0 billion, respectively. Indonesia's government bond stock stood at USD176.7 billion at the end of March. The Philippines and Viet Nam continued to have the smallest government bond stocks at USD109.0 billion and USD53.3 billion, respectively.

LCY corporate bonds outstanding in emerging East Asia reached USD6.4 trillion at the end of March. On a q-o-q basis, growth in corporate bonds outstanding accelerated to 5.7% in Q1 2020 from 3.5% in the previous quarter. The faster growth rate was driven mostly by growth in

Table 1: Size and Composition of Local Currency Bond Markets

	Q1 2019		Q4 2019		Q1 2020		Growth Rate (LCY-base %)				Growth Rate (USD-base %)			
							Q1 2019		Q1 2020		Q1 2019		Q1 2020	
	Amount (USD billion)	% share	Amount (USD billion)	% share	Amount (USD billion)	% share	q-o-q	y-o-y	q-o-q	y-o-y	q-o-q	y-o-y	q-o-q	y-o-y
China, People's Rep. of														
Total	11,325	100.0	12,090	100.0	12,464	100.0	3.0	16.7	4.9	16.1	5.6	9.1	3.1	10.1
Government	7,309	64.5	7,753	64.1	7,886	63.3	2.5	16.1	3.5	13.8	5.0	8.5	1.7	7.9
Corporate	4,015	35.5	4,337	35.9	4,577	36.7	4.1	17.8	7.3	20.3	6.7	10.1	5.5	14.0
Hong Kong, China														
Total	287	100.0	291	100.0	291	100.0	1.1	8.5	(0.5)	0.3	0.9	8.5	0.05	1.6
Government	148	51.6	152	52.2	151	51.9	(0.6)	1.1	(1.1)	0.7	(0.9)	1.1	(0.6)	2.0
Corporate	139	48.4	139	47.8	140	48.1	3.0	17.8	0.2	(0.2)	2.8	17.8	0.7	1.1
Indonesia														
Total	217	100.0	239	100.0	204	100.0	8.7	18.7	0.4	7.8	9.8	14.4	(14.6)	(5.9)
Government	187	86.2	207	86.6	177	86.7	9.6	21.0	0.6	8.4	10.7	16.7	(14.5)	(5.4)
Corporate	30	13.8	32	13.4	27	13.3	3.0	5.9	(0.5)	4.4	4.0	2.1	(15.4)	(8.8)
Korea, Rep. of														
Total	2,006	100.0	2,083	100.0	2,032	100.0	1.7	4.2	2.8	8.7	(0.4)	(2.4)	(2.4)	1.3
Government	820	40.9	824	39.5	814	40.1	1.9	1.7	4.2	6.6	(0.3)	(4.7)	(1.1)	(0.7)
Corporate	1,186	59.1	1,259	60.5	1,218	59.9	1.7	5.9	1.9	10.2	(0.5)	(0.8)	(3.3)	2.7
Malaysia														
Total	353	100.0	363	100.0	354	100.0	2.9	7.6	2.9	6.0	4.1	1.8	(2.6)	0.2
Government	188	53.1	189	52.1	186	52.6	3.6	8.7	3.9	4.9	5.0	2.8	(1.6)	(0.9)
Corporate	165	46.9	174	47.9	168	47.4	2.0	6.4	1.7	7.3	3.3	0.7	(3.7)	1.3
Philippines														
Total	125	100.0	131	100.0	140	100.0	8.0	17.8	6.9	7.9	8.0	17.0	6.8	11.8
Government	99	79.0	101	77.4	109	77.8	8.8	16.2	7.5	6.2	8.8	15.4	7.4	10.1
Corporate	26	21.0	30	22.6	31	22.2	5.4	24.4	5.0	14.0	5.4	23.5	4.9	18.2
Singapore														
Total	306	100.0	340	100.0	329	100.0	3.1	8.3	2.2	12.5	3.7	4.7	(3.3)	7.3
Government	188	61.5	212	62.5	206	62.7	4.5	11.1	2.5	14.6	5.1	7.5	(3.0)	9.3
Corporate	118	38.5	127	37.5	123	37.3	0.9	4.0	1.7	9.2	1.4	0.6	(3.7)	4.1
Thailand														
Total	399	100.0	446	100.0	402	100.0	1.6	10.9	(0.5)	4.1	30.1	43.4	(9.8)	0.9
Government	287	72.0	318	71.4	286	71.0	1.4	11.1	(1.0)	2.7	27.0	38.0	(10.2)	(0.5)
Corporate	111	28.0	127	28.6	117	29.0	2.3	10.3	0.8	7.9	39.0	59.5	(8.6)	4.5
Viet Nam														
Total	52	100.0	54	100.0	58	100.0	0.8	0.5	9.5	13.2	0.8	(1.2)	7.3	11.1
Government	47	90.9	49	91.8	53	92.6	0.9	(2.4)	10.5	15.4	0.9	(4.1)	8.3	13.2
Corporate	5	9.1	4	8.2	4	7.4	(0.1)	43.7	(1.7)	(8.5)	(0.2)	41.3	(3.6)	(10.2)
Emerging East Asia														
Total	15,069	100.0	16,036	100.0	16,272	100.0	2.9	14.1	4.2	14.0	5.2	7.9	1.5	8.0
Government	9,273	61.5	9,805	61.1	9,868	60.6	2.6	13.9	3.3	12.3	5.1	7.8	0.6	6.4
Corporate	5,796	38.5	6,231	38.9	6,404	39.4	3.4	14.4	5.7	16.8	5.3	8.0	2.8	10.5
Japan														
Total	10,597	100.0	10,966	100.0	11,079	100.0	0.2	1.9	0.04	1.4	(0.8)	(2.3)	1.03	4.5
Government	9,881	93.2	10,180	92.8	10,282	92.8	0.3	1.8	0.01	0.9	(0.8)	(2.4)	1.0	4.1
Corporate	717	6.8	786	7.2	797	7.2	0.1	3.5	0.4	7.9	(0.9)	(0.8)	1.4	11.3

( ) = negative, LCY = local currency, q-o-q = quarter-on-quarter, Q1 = first quarter, Q4 = fourth quarter, USD = United States dollar, y-o-y = year-on-year.

Notes:
1. For Singapore, corporate bonds outstanding are based on *AsianBondsOnline* estimates.
2. Corporate bonds include issues by financial institutions.
3. Bloomberg LP end-of-period LCY–USD rates are used.
4. For LCY base, emerging East Asia growth figures are based on 31 March 2020 currency exchange rates and do not include currency effects.
5. Emerging East Asia comprises the People's Republic of China; Hong Kong, China; Indonesia; the Republic of Korea; Malaysia; the Philippines; Singapore; Thailand; and Viet Nam.

Sources: People's Republic of China (CEIC); Hong Kong, China (Hong Kong Monetary Authority); Indonesia (Bank Indonesia; Directorate General of Budget Financing and Risk Management, Ministry of Finance; and Indonesia Stock Exchange); Republic of Korea (*EDAILY BondWeb* and The Bank of Korea); Malaysia (Bank Negara Malaysia); Philippines (Bureau of the Treasury and Bloomberg LP); Singapore (Monetary Authority of Singapore, Singapore Government Securities, and Bloomberg LP); Thailand (Bank of Thailand); Viet Nam (Bloomberg LP and Vietnam Bond Market Association); and Japan (Japan Securities Dealers Association).

the PRC's corporate bond sector, which rose 7.3% q-o-q in Q1 2020. Seven out of the nine markets in emerging East Asia posted positive q-o-q growth in the corporate bond stock; Indonesia and Viet Nam posted contractions in the stock of their corporate bonds. The PRC and the Republic of Korea account for a majority of emerging East Asia's corporate bond sector with a combined share of 90.5% at the end of March. ASEAN economies accounted for 7.3% of emerging East Asia's corporate bond stock. Within ASEAN, Malaysia had the largest corporate bond market, followed by Singapore.

Emerging East Asia's total LCY bond market constituted 87.8% of the region's gross domestic product (GDP) at the end of March, expanding from 83.2% at the end of December and 80.2% in March 2019 (**Table 2**). The respective percentage shares of government and corporate bonds to GDP were higher at the end of Q1 2020 compared with the end of Q4 2019: the government bonds-to-GDP ratio climbed to 53.2% from 50.9%, while the corporate bonds-to-GDP ratio rose to 34.6% from 32.3%. The higher bond-to-GDP ratios can be attributed to an increase in the region's bond market size in Q1 2020 as regional GDP contracted due to the impact of COVID-19.

The bond markets of the Republic of Korea and Malaysia had the highest bonds-to-GDP ratios in the region, both of which exceeded 100% of their GDP, while Indonesia had the smallest at 20.8%. All emerging East Asian economies saw increases in their bonds-to-GDP ratios between Q4 2019 and Q1 2020 except for Indonesia and Thailand, where the ratios declined.

By segment, Singapore had the highest government bonds-to-GDP ratio in the region at 58.0%, while Indonesia had the smallest at 18.0%. The Republic of Korea had the largest corporate bonds-to-GDP share at 80.0%, while in Viet Nam this share was only 1.6%.

Foreign Investor Holdings

Foreign ownership of LCY government bonds declined in Q1 2020.

Emerging East Asia's foreign investor holdings share at the end of Q1 2020 declined from the end of Q4 2019 in all markets except for the PRC, where a minimal increase was observed (**Figure 2**). With uncertainty surrounding

Table 2: Size and Composition of Local Currency Bond Markets (% of GDP)

	Q1 2019	Q4 2019	Q1 2020
China, People's Rep. of			
Total	81.3	85.0	90.1
Government	52.5	54.5	57.0
Corporate	28.8	30.5	33.1
Hong Kong, China			
Total	78.7	79.1	80.0
Government	40.6	41.3	41.5
Corporate	38.1	37.8	38.5
Indonesia			
Total	20.4	20.9	20.8
Government	17.6	18.1	18.0
Corporate	2.8	2.8	2.8
Korea, Rep. of			
Total	125.2	130.2	133.5
Government	51.2	51.5	53.5
Corporate	74.0	78.7	80.0
Malaysia			
Total	104.6	104.5	107.3
Government	55.6	54.4	56.4
Corporate	49.0	50.1	50.9
Philippines			
Total	35.4	34.1	36.3
Government	28.0	26.3	28.2
Corporate	7.5	7.7	8.1
Singapore			
Total	81.7	90.1	92.6
Government	50.2	56.3	58.0
Corporate	31.4	33.8	34.5
Thailand			
Total	76.5	78.4	78.2
Government	55.1	56.0	55.6
Corporate	21.4	22.4	22.7
Viet Nam			
Total	21.3	20.6	22.3
Government	19.4	18.9	20.6
Corporate	1.9	1.7	1.6
Emerging East Asia			
Total	80.2	83.2	87.8
Government	49.3	50.9	53.2
Corporate	30.8	32.3	34.6
Japan			
Total	214.3	215.1	215.6
Government	199.8	199.7	200.1
Corporate	14.5	15.4	15.5

GDP = gross domestic product, Q1 = first quarter, Q4 = fourth quarter.
Notes:
1. Data for GDP are from CEIC.
2. For Singapore, corporate bonds outstanding are based on *AsianBondsOnline* estimates.
Sources: People's Republic of China (CEIC); Hong Kong, China (Hong Kong Monetary Authority); Indonesia (Bank Indonesia; Directorate General of Budget Financing and Risk Management, Ministry of Finance; and Indonesia Stock Exchange); Republic of Korea (*EDAILY BondWeb* and The Bank of Korea); Malaysia (Bank Negara Malaysia); Philippines (Bureau of the Treasury and Bloomberg LP); Singapore (Monetary Authority of Singapore, Singapore Government Securities, and Bloomberg LP); Thailand (Bank of Thailand); Viet Nam (Bloomberg LP and Vietnam Bond Market Association); and Japan (Japan Securities Dealers Association).

Figure 2: Foreign Holdings of Local Currency Government Bonds in Select Asian Markets (% of total)

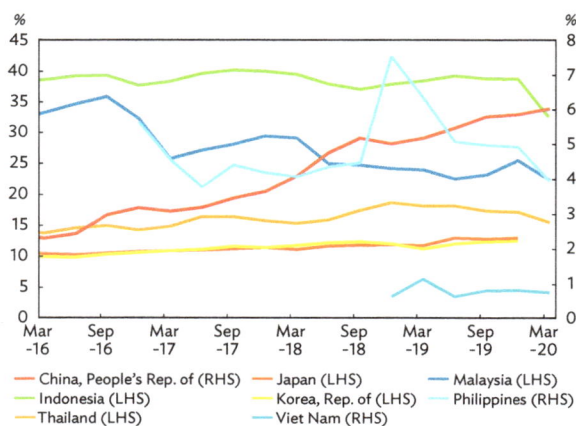

LHS = left-hand side, RHS = right-hand side.
Note: Data as of 31 March 2020 except for Japan and the Republic of Korea (31 December 2019).
Source: *AsianBondsOnline*.

the financial and economic environment, foreign investors have been cautious with their asset holdings, which was evident in the observed retreat of foreign funds from Southeast Asian economies during Q1 2020.

In the PRC, the foreign holdings share of government bonds increased slightly to 6.0% at the end of March from 5.8% at the end of December 2019. The increase can be attributed to market optimism as the PRC recovers from the impact of the COVID-19 pandemic. Investor interest in the PRC's bond market continued to be supported by the inclusion of its government bonds in the Bloomberg Barclays Global Aggregate Index and in the J.P. Morgan's Government Bond Index–Emerging Markets Global Diversified Index, as well as by being on the watchlist for inclusion in FTSE Russell's World Government Bond Index.

Indonesia's foreign holdings' share fell to 32.7% at the end of March, its lowest level since December 2013. The share of bonds held by foreigners declined by 5.9 percentage points from the end of December 2019, making it the largest drop in the region in Q1 2020 and the largest quarterly drop in Indonesia's foreign holdings' share since such data became available. The fall in foreign holdings was mainly due to the reflexive risk reduction of investors

on the back of market routs caused by the pandemic. At the same time, Indonesia continued to have the highest foreign holdings' share in the region.

In Malaysia, the share of government bonds held by foreign investors dropped to 22.2% at the end of March from 25.3% at the end of December. The fall in foreign holdings can be traced to the perceived risks brought about by the negative impacts of COVID-19 and tumbling oil prices, as well as profit-taking by investors over fears caused by the short-lived political turmoil during Q1 2020. Investors took some respite from the announcement that the FTSE Russell's World Government Bond Index would keep Malaysia on the watchlist. Malaysia has the region's second-largest share of foreign-held government bonds.

In Thailand, the share of foreign holdings fell to 15.3% at the end of March from 17.0% at the end of the preceding quarter. The decline in foreign ownership was mainly due to investor profit-taking as the Bank of Thailand loosened its monetary policy by cutting its key rate to shore up the domestic economy. The record-low policy rate has prompted bond yields to fall, making them unattractive to foreign investors.

Foreign investors reduced their holdings share of Philippine government bonds to 3.9% at the end of March from 4.9% at the end of December. Despite moderating inflation since the start of 2020, the foreign holdings' share still declined. Foreign investor decisions were induced by the aggressive interest rate cuts of the Bangko Sentral ng Pilipinas, which pulled yields down.

Foreign ownership of sovereign debt in Viet Nam fell in Q1 2020, albeit only marginally. The share of foreign holders was at 0.7% at the end of March, down from 0.8% at the end of December. Having only a small bond market, Viet Nam's foreign holdings' share is the smallest in the region.

Meanwhile, the Republic of Korea's share of foreign holdings increased to 12.3% at the end of December from 12.2% at the end of September. The share has been on a gradual uptrend since March 2019. Higher yields in the Republic of Korea's bond market and fiscal strength are seen as the factors behind increasing foreign interest.

Foreign Bond Flows

Foreign funds flowed out of most emerging East Asian markets in January–April.

Most economies in the region for which data are available registered net outflows of foreign funds during Q1 2020 with the exception of the PRC and the Republic of Korea (**Figure 3**). For markets that experienced net outflows during the review period, the outflows began mainly in February in the wake of the COVID-19 outbreak, with the largest outflows seen in March. The fund withdrawal by foreign investors was underlain by risk aversion and profit-taking as yields in those markets declined due to interest rate cuts by central banks.

Foreign investor interest in the PRC's LCY bond market remained strong throughout Q1 2020, with net monthly inflows that continued into April. Inflows in the PRC market totaled USD11.5 billion during Q1 2020, which was slightly higher than total inflows of USD10.8 billion in Q4 2019. In April, foreign investors poured an additional USD6.4 billion in the debt market, bringing the total fund inflows in the first 4 months of the year to USD17.8 billion.

Indonesia saw net foreign fund outflows of USD9.1 billion from its government bond market in Q1 2020, far exceeding the foreign inflows of USD2.2 billion in Q4 2019. Additional outflows of USD0.1 billion in April resulted in year-to-date outflows of USD9.2 billion in the first 4 months of the year, the largest cumulative foreign bond outflows among all markets in the region during the review period.

Malaysia also registered outflows in Q1 2020 after experiencing net inflows in the previous quarter. Total foreign outflows in Q1 2020 amounted to USD3.9 billion, compared with inflows of USD3.3 billion in Q4 2019, as falling oil prices highlighted concerns about the government's finances. Including outflows in April, the total amount of funds withdrawn by foreign investors from the bond market in the first 4 months of the year amounted to USD4.3 billion.

In the Philippines and in Thailand, bond sell-offs by foreign investors in Q4 2019 continued into Q1 2020. In Q4 2019, the Philippines and Thailand experienced net outflows of USD0.2 billion each. In Q1 2020, Thailand's net outflows amounted to USD3.1 billion,

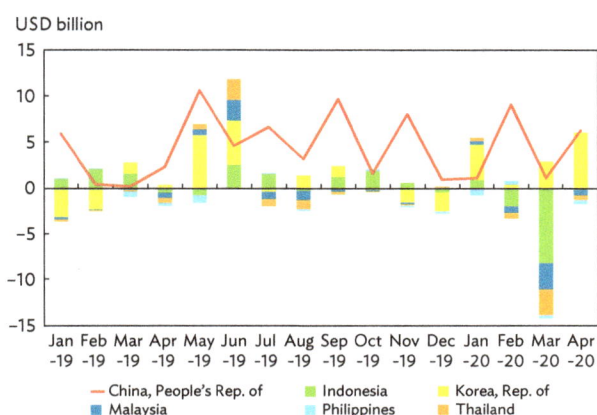

Figure 3: Foreign Bond Flows in Select Emerging East Asian Economies

USD = United States dollar.
Notes:
1. The Republic of Korea and Thailand provided data on bond flows. For the People's Republic of China, Indonesia, Malaysia, and the Philippines, month-on-month changes in foreign holdings of local currency government bonds were used as a proxy for bond flows.
2. Data as of 30 April 2020.
3. Figures were computed based on 30 April 2020 exchange rates to avoid currency effects.
Sources: People's Republic of China (*Wind Information*); Indonesia (Directorate General of Budget Financing and Risk Management, Ministry of Finance); Republic of Korea (Financial Supervisory Service); Malaysia (Bank Negara Malaysia); Philippines (Bureau of the Treasury); and Thailand (Thai Bond Market Association).

while the Philippines' quarterly outflows were more modest at USD0.7 billion. Outflows continued in April in both markets at USD0.4 billion for the Philippines and USD0.6 billion for Thailand.

The opposite trend was seen in the Republic of Korea as foreign investors flocked to its government bond market in Q1 2020, bringing in a total of USD7.3 billion during the quarter and reversing the previous quarter's USD3.7 billion of net outflows. The trend continued into April, with foreign inflows in the Republic of Korea's bond market from January to April totaling USD13.4 billion.

LCY Bond Issuance

Emerging East Asia's aggregate LCY bond sales reached USD1.7 trillion in Q1 2020, buoyed by increased issuance volumes in nearly all markets.

LCY bond issuance in emerging East Asia climbed to USD1,671.5 billion in Q1 2020 on growth of 19.7% q-o-q after a contraction of 9.6% q-o-q in Q4 2019 (**Table 3**).

Table 3: Local-Currency–Denominated Bond Issuance (gross)

	Q1 2019		Q4 2019		Q1 2020		Growth Rate (LCY-base %) Q1 2020		Growth Rate (USD-base %) Q1 2020	
	Amount (USD billion)	% share	Amount (USD billion)	% share	Amount (USD billion)	% share	q-o-q	y-o-y	q-o-q	y-o-y
China, People's Rep. of										
Total	869	100.0	834	100.0	1,075	100.0	31.2	30.6	29.0	23.7
Government	443	50.9	297	35.7	491	45.7	68.2	17.2	65.3	11.0
Central Bank	0	0.0	0	0.0	0	0.0	–	–	–	–
Treasury and Other Govt.	443	50.9	297	35.7	491	45.7	68.2	17.2	65.3	11.0
Corporate	426	49.1	536	64.3	584	54.3	10.7	44.5	8.8	36.9
Hong Kong, China										
Total	136	100.0	128	100.0	136	100.0	5.0	(1.4)	5.5	(0.1)
Government	104	76.3	109	85.2	108	79.7	(1.8)	2.9	(1.3)	4.3
Central Bank	103	76.2	109	84.6	108	79.4	(1.4)	2.9	(0.8)	4.2
Treasury and Other Govt.	0.3	0.2	0.8	0.6	0.3	0.2	(61.5)	19.0	(61.3)	20.6
Corporate	32	23.7	19	14.8	28	20.3	44.3	(15.3)	45.0	(14.2)
Indonesia										
Total	26	100.0	21	100.0	20	100.0	13.7	(11.6)	(3.4)	(22.8)
Government	25	94.2	19	88.3	19	94.3	21.4	(11.4)	3.2	(22.7)
Central Bank	7	28.3	8	39.2	7	34.5	0.3	8.0	(14.7)	(5.7)
Treasury and Other Govt.	17	65.9	10	49.2	12	59.8	38.2	(19.8)	17.5	(29.9)
Corporate	2	5.8	2	11.7	1	5.7	(44.9)	(14.3)	(53.2)	(25.1)
Korea, Rep. of										
Total	163	100.0	196	100.0	197	100.0	6.1	30.0	0.6	21.2
Government	71	43.4	60	30.5	82	41.8	45.4	25.1	37.9	16.5
Central Bank	32	19.6	29	14.6	30	15.2	10.7	1.2	5.0	(5.7)
Treasury and Other Govt.	39	23.9	31	15.9	52	26.6	77.3	44.6	68.2	34.7
Corporate	92	56.6	136	69.5	115	58.2	(11.1)	33.9	(15.7)	24.7
Malaysia										
Total	25	100.0	20	100.0	21	100.0	10.7	(10.1)	4.8	(15.1)
Government	15	58.5	9	43.5	12	56.2	42.9	(13.8)	35.2	(18.5)
Central Bank	5	19.2	3	14.6	2	11.0	(16.4)	(48.5)	(20.8)	(51.3)
Treasury and Other Govt.	10	39.3	6	28.9	10	45.1	72.7	3.2	63.5	(2.5)
Corporate	10	41.5	12	56.5	9	43.8	(14.1)	(5.0)	(18.7)	(10.2)
Philippines										
Total	14	100.0	7	100.0	17	100.0	128.6	18.0	128.4	22.3
Government	13	92.0	5	71.9	14	83.0	163.9	6.4	163.7	10.4
Central Bank	0	0.0	0	0.0	0	0.0	–	–	–	–
Treasury and Other Govt.	13	92.0	5	71.9	14	83.0	163.9	6.4	163.7	10.4
Corporate	1	8.0	2	28.1	3	17.0	38.4	149.6	38.3	158.8
Singapore										
Total	112	100.0	130	100.0	125	100.0	1.3	17.5	(4.1)	12.0
Government	108	96.7	128	98.4	122	97.7	0.6	18.7	(4.8)	13.2
Central Bank	103	92.0	103	79.3	101	80.9	3.2	3.3	(2.3)	(1.5)
Treasury and Other Govt.	5	4.8	25	19.1	21	16.9	(10.4)	316.7	(15.2)	297.2
Corporate	4	3.3	2	1.6	3	2.3	44.9	(19.4)	37.2	(23.1)
Thailand										
Total	85	100.0	79	100.0	72	100.0	1.1	(12.2)	(8.3)	(14.9)
Government	70	82.7	66	83.7	62	85.9	3.7	(8.8)	(5.9)	(11.6)
Central Bank	65	76.6	59	74.8	56	77.9	5.2	(10.8)	(4.6)	(13.5)
Treasury and Other Govt.	5	6.1	7	8.9	6	8.1	(8.9)	15.9	(17.4)	12.3
Corporate	15	17.3	13	16.3	10	14.1	(12.5)	(28.6)	(20.7)	(30.8)

continued on next page

Table 3 *continued*

	Q1 2019		Q4 2019		Q1 2020		Growth Rate (LCY-base %)		Growth Rate (USD-base %)	
							Q1 2020		Q1 2020	
	Amount (USD billion)	% share	Amount (USD billion)	% share	Amount (USD billion)	% share	q-o-q	y-o-y	q-o-q	y-o-y
Viet Nam										
Total	6	100.0	22	100.0	7	100.0	(66.6)	27.7	(67.3)	25.2
Government	6	96.5	22	99.2	7	100.0	(66.4)	32.3	(67.0)	29.8
Central Bank	3	44.5	20	88.5	6	80.4	(69.7)	130.6	(70.3)	126.2
Treasury and Other Govt.	3	52.0	2	10.8	1	19.6	(39.1)	(51.8)	(40.3)	(52.7)
Corporate	0.2	3.5	0.2	0.8	0	0.0	(100.0)	(100.0)	(100.0)	(100.0)
Emerging East Asia										
Total	1,435	100.0	1,439	100.0	1,671	100.0	19.7	22.1	16.2	16.4
Government	853	59.4	716	49.8	919	55.0	32.9	12.6	28.4	7.7
Central Bank	318	22.1	330	23.0	310	18.6	(2.0)	0.5	(6.1)	(2.4)
Treasury and Other Govt.	535	37.3	385	26.8	609	36.4	62.4	20.1	58.0	13.7
Corporate	582	40.6	723	50.2	753	45.0	6.8	36.2	4.1	29.3
Japan										
Total	385	100.0	418	100.0	383	100.0	(9.4)	(3.5)	(8.5)	(0.5)
Government	362	94.1	376	89.9	356	92.9	(6.3)	(4.6)	(5.4)	(1.7)
Central Bank	0	0.0	20	4.8	0	0.0	(100.0)	–	(100.0)	–
Treasury and Other Govt.	362	94.1	356	85.0	356	92.9	(1.0)	(4.6)	0.01	(1.7)
Corporate	23	5.9	42	10.1	27	7.1	(36.4)	15.3	(35.8)	18.9

( ) = negative, – = not applicable, LCY = local currency, q-o-q = quarter-on-quarter, Q1 = first quarter, Q4 = fourth quarter, USD = United States dollar, y-o-y = year-on-year.
Notes:
1. Corporate bonds include issues by financial institutions.
2. Bloomberg LP end-of-period LCY–USD rates are used.
3. For LCY base, emerging East Asia growth figures are based on 31 March 2020 currency exchange rates and do not include currency effects.
Sources: People's Republic of China (CEIC); Hong Kong, China (Hong Kong Monetary Authority); Indonesia (Bank Indonesia; Directorate General of Budget Financing and Risk Management, Ministry of Finance; and Indonesia Stock Exchange); Republic of Korea (*EDAILY BondWeb* and The Bank of Korea); Malaysia (Bank Negara Malaysia); Philippines (Bureau of the Treasury and Bloomberg LP); Singapore (Singapore Government Securities and Bloomberg LP); Thailand (Bank of Thailand and ThaiBMA); Viet Nam (Bloomberg LP and Vietnam Bond Market Association); and Japan (Japan Securities Dealers Association).

The q-o-q growth stemmed largely from higher bond sales of Treasury bonds and other government bonds and a modest increase in corporate bond issuance. On the other hand, the issuance of central bank instruments slowed from Q4 2019 as central banks focused on monetary easing. Six out of nine LCY bond markets in the region posted faster q-o-q issuance growth during the quarter. On a q-o-q basis, only the bond markets of the Republic of Korea, Singapore, and Viet Nam registered a slowdown in issuance, with Viet Nam posting a contraction during the quarter.

On an annual basis, overall growth in LCY bond issuance in emerging East Asia accelerated to 22.1% y-o-y in Q1 2020 from 12.5% y-o-y in Q4 2019. All bond market segments contributed to the y-o-y hike in issuance during the quarter. Most markets, however, registered slower y-o-y growth or even contractions in issuance in Q1 2020 compared with Q4 2019, particularly in Indonesia; Singapore; Thailand; Viet Nam; and Hong Kong, China.

In Q1 2020, more than half of the region's LCY bond issuance was accounted for by government bonds. LCY government bond issuance totaled USD918.9 billion, up 32.9% q-o-q and 12.6% y-o-y. Of this amount, 66.2% comprised Treasury and other government bonds. The governments of the PRC, Indonesia, the Republic of Korea, Malaysia, and the Philippines were the most active in issuing Treasury and other government bonds in Q1 2020, due mostly to frontloading policies and increased financing needs to fund stimulus packages and recovery efforts in response to the COVID-19 pandemic. In contrast, lower issuance volumes for Treasury and other government bonds were noted in Singapore; Thailand; Viet Nam; and Hong Kong, China.

The region's issuance of central bank instruments slowed in Q1 2020 versus Q4 2019. Total issuance from central banks tallied USD310.3 billion, a 2.0% q-o-q contraction from 1.6% q-o-q growth in the prior quarter. On a y-o-y basis, the aggregate issuance volume of central banks slumped from growth of 10.2% in Q4 2019 to only 0.5% in Q1 2020.

New corporate debt from emerging East Asia totaled USD752.5 billion in Q1 2020, up 6.8% q-o-q and 36.2% y-o-y. Six out of nine markets posted slower q-o-q growth in corporate bond issuance during the quarter. However, the region's overall issuance level was lifted by a surge in the issuance of corporate bonds in the PRC, which accounted for 77.6% of the region's new corporate debt during Q1 2020.

The PRC continued to account for nearly 65% of the region's aggregate bond sales in Q1 2020, up from about 59% of the total in the previous quarter. The total issuance volume reached USD1,075.1 billion as q-o-q growth rebounded to 31.2% q-o-q after declining 17.2% q-o-q in Q4 2019. Government bonds buoyed growth, particularly local government bonds as the State Council pushed for an acceleration in the issuance and use of local government special bonds to support key projects. A bond quota of CNY1.8 trillion was announced by the Ministry of Finance in February, and about CNY1.6 trillion had been tapped by local governments at the end of March. The corporate bond segment also contributed to the overall growth in issuance but to a lesser extent. New corporate debt issued during the quarter climbed 10.7% q-o-q following the government's relaxation of rules for issuing bonds through a registration-based application with the China Securities Regulatory Commission, as well as an increase in short-term instruments amid falling interest rates. On a y-o-y basis, overall bond issuance climbed 30.6% in Q1 2020, up from 11.1% in the previous quarter.

In the Republic of Korea, new bond sales totaled USD197.4 billion in Q1 2020, up 6.1% from Q4 2019. Overall growth was capped by a decline in issuance of corporate bonds during the quarter. Government bond issuance rose 45.4% q-o-q, a turnaround from a decline of 9.0% q-o-q in Q4 2019, buoyed by strong issuance of Treasury securities. The government continued to adopt a frontloading issuance policy, aiming to sell more than half of its planned issuance for 2020 during the first half of the year to bolster the economy. The passage of the supplemental budget, which will be largely extended for COVID-19 stimulus programs and social aid, also warranted an increase in government borrowing. Central bank issuance edged higher on growth of 10.7% q-o-q. In contrast, issuance of corporate bonds dropped

11.1% q-o-q due to tight credit conditions, particularly in March. Some corporates in the Republic of Korea failed to meet their targeted bond issuance amounts amid a tight credit environment as investors sought higher rates to compensate for the economic uncertainty brought about by the COVID-19 pandemic. On an annual basis, the Republic of Korea's bond issuance surged 30.0% in Q1 2020.

LCY bond issuance in Hong Kong, China totaled USD135.6 billion in Q1 2020 on a 5.0% q-o-q expansion during the quarter. Government bonds, which account for nearly 80% of total issuance, dragged down overall issuance growth during the quarter. Total government bond issuance reached USD108.0 billion, down 1.8% q-o-q on lower sales of Exchange Fund Bills, Exchange Fund Notes, and Hong Kong Special Administrative Region bonds. Corporate bond sales were more active on growth of 44.3% q-o-q in Q1 2020 after a contraction of 18.9% q-o-q in the preceding quarter. On a y-o-y basis, LCY bond issuance in Hong Kong, China was down 1.4% in Q1 2020.

Aggregate bond issuance among ASEAN member economies reached USD263.4 billion in Q1 2020, representing a 15.8% share of the regional total. The q-o-q growth, while marginal at 0.8% in Q1 2020, was an improvement from a decline of 0.3% in the previous quarter. On a y-o-y basis, however, ASEAN economies' issuance total moderated to 3.0% from 24.3% in the same period.

The Philippines posted the fastest q-o-q growth in the region as its issuance more than doubled in Q1 2020. On a q-o-q basis, LCY bond issuance in Indonesia, Malaysia, and Thailand picked up in Q1 2020 after contracting in the prior quarter. On the other hand, q-o-q bond sales in Singapore moderated in Q1 2020 and contracted in Viet Nam. In terms of total issuance amounts, the most active markets in the ASEAN space in Q1 2020 were Singapore, Thailand, and Malaysia.

Total bonds sales in Singapore reached USD125.0 billion in Q1 2020, with overall q-o-q growth moderating to 1.3% from 2.8% in the preceding quarter. Government bond issuance was capped by the decline in sales of Singapore Government Securities bills and bonds. Issuance of Monetary Authority of Singapore bills grew by a modest 3.2% q-o-q. Corporate bond issuance in Q1 2020 was more active, rising 44.9% over the previous quarter.

A number of firms tapped the debt market during the quarter, with a huge volume coming from state-owned firms and higher-rated corporates. On an annual basis, bond issuance slowed from 28.2% y-o-y growth in Q4 2019 to 17.5% y-o-y in Q1 2020.

In Thailand, overall LCY bond issuance rebounded, gaining 1.1% q-o-q to USD72.2 billion after a 2.1% q-o-q contraction in the previous quarter. The gains were driven solely by government bond issuance, which grew 3.7% q-o-q to USD62.1 billion as a result of a 5.2% q-o-q increase in the issuance of central bank bonds (from a decline of 3.3% q-o-q in the previous quarter), more than offsetting the 8.9% q-o-q decline in Treasury and other government bonds. Thai corporate bond issuance continued to be weak as the ongoing pandemic curtailed demand and companies shied away from taking on more debt. Corporate bond issuance in Thailand fell 12.5% q-o-q to USD10.2 billon after declining 7.5% q-o-q in Q4 2019. On an annual basis, issuance fell 12.2% y-o-y in Q1 2020.

In Malaysia, LCY bond issuance tallied USD21.4 billion in Q1 2020, rising 10.7% q-o-q after contracting 1.2% in Q4 2019. Government bond issuance rebounded 42.9% q-o-q as the government ramped up its issuance of Treasury instruments during the quarter to help fund the budget deficit amid falling global crude prices that acted as a drag on government revenues. Issuance by the central bank declined 16.4% q-o-q in Q1 2020 following a 41.9% q-o-q hike in Q4 2019. Corporate bond issuance became less active during the quarter, despite a low-interest-rate environment. Compared with Q1 2019, overall growth in issuance fell 10.1% in Q1 2020.

LCY bond issuance in Indonesia climbed to USD20.4 billion in Q1 2020 with growth rebounding to 13.7% q-o-q following a decline of 15.2% q-o-q in Q4 2019. Government bond issuance drove much of the growth as the government continued to adopt a frontloading policy as in past years. Aside from weekly auctions of Treasury bills and bonds, the government also issued through private placements of select issues of Treasury bonds and bookbuilding for retail *sukuk* (Islamic bonds) during the quarter. Central bank bills also rose by a marginal 0.3% q-o-q. Corporate bond issuance continued to slow down, as the volume of new issuance contracted

44.9% in Q1 2020 after declining 22.6% in Q4 2019. On a y-o-y basis, Indonesia's bond issuance was down 11.6% in Q1 2020.

LCY bond issuance in the Philippines surged 128.6% q-o-q in Q1 2020 to reach USD17.1 billion. The strong growth was largely driven by increased government bond issuance during the quarter. Amid flush liquidity in the market, the government took advantage and accepted a higher volume of bids during the weekly Treasury auctions. In addition, it also raised PHP310.8 billion from the sale of Retail Treasury Bonds in February. Corporate bond issuance also rose during the quarter but to a lesser extent. On an annual basis, LCY bond issuance growth quickened to 18.0% y-o-y from 0.1% y-o-y in the previous quarter.

In Viet Nam, LCY bond issuance fell sharply by 66.6% q-o-q to USD7.2 billion in Q1 2020. Government bond issuance fell 66.4% q-o-q as the volume of issuance for both Treasuries and central bank bills declined during the quarter. There was no issuance in Q1 2020 of either government-guaranteed bonds or corporate bonds. On a y-o-y basis, overall growth in issuance eased to 27.7% in Q1 2020.

Two corporate bonds with guarantees from the Credit Guarantee and Investment Facility were issued in Cambodia in April. The issuance also utilized the ASEAN+3 Multi-Currency Bond Issuance Framework. RMA (Cambodia) Plc., a retail and distribution company, sold a KHR80 billion 5-year bond. RMA (Cambodia) Plc.'s issuance marked the first Credit Guarantee and Investment Facility-guaranteed bond and the first issuance by a nonfinancial company in Cambodia. In the same month, Prasac Microfinance Institution Plc. raised KHR127.2 billion from the sale of a 3-year bond. To date, Prasac Microfinance's Plc. issuance is the largest corporate bond issue from Cambodia.

Cross-Border Bond Issuance

Cross-border bond issuance in emerging East Asia reached USD2.4 billion in Q1 2020.

Intraregional bond issuance in emerging East Asia reached USD2.4 billion in Q1 2020, a 12.5% q-o-q increase from USD2.2 billion in Q4 2019 but a 57.5% y-o-y

---

[7] For the discussion on cross-border issuance, emerging East Asia comprises Cambodia; the People's Republic of China; Hong Kong, China; Indonesia; the Republic of Korea; the Lao People's Democratic Republic; Malaysia; the Philippines; Singapore; Thailand; and Viet Nam.

Figure 4: Origin Economies of Intra-Emerging East Asian Bond Issuance in the First Quarter of 2020

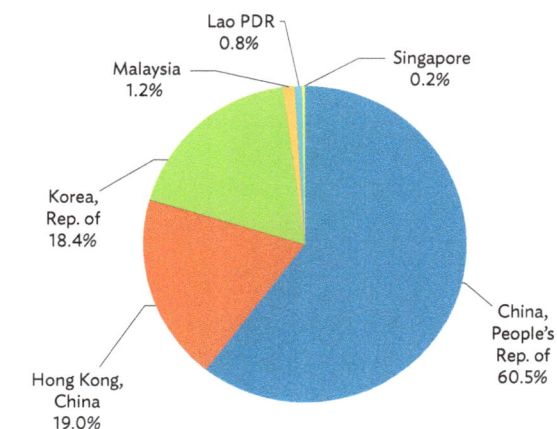

Lao PDR 0.8%
Malaysia 1.2%
Singapore 0.2%
Korea, Rep. of 18.4%
China, People's Rep. of 60.5%
Hong Kong, China 19.0%

Lao PDR = Lao People's Democratic Republic.
Source: *AsianBondsOnline* calculations based on Bloomberg LP data.

decline from Q1 2019.[7] Institutions from six economies issued cross-border bonds in Q1 2020, led by the PRC; Hong Kong, China; and the Republic of Korea. The PRC continued to have the largest aggregate issuance volume at USD1.5 billion and a share of 60.5% (**Figure 4**). Hong Kong, China and the Republic of Korea registered shares of 19.0% and 18.4%, respectively. Other economies that issued cross-border bonds were Malaysia, the Lao People's Democratic Republic, and Singapore.

Intraregional bond issuances in the PRC rose 8.2% q-o-q to USD1.5 billion in Q1 2020. Nearly a third of the bond issuers in the region in Q1 2020 came from the PRC. The region's top two issuers in Q1 2020, who also had the two single-largest bond issuances during the quarter, were from the PRC. Bank of China and Bank of Communications issued USD516.0 million and USD361.3. million, respectively; both of these 2-year bonds were denominated in Hong Kong dollars. The remaining eight institutions from the PRC that issued cross-border bonds in Q1 2020 accounted for aggregate issuance of USD590.8 million. These bonds were denominated in Hong Kong dollars, Malaysian ringgit, and Singapore dollars.

Three institutions from Hong Kong, China issued CNY-denominated cross-border bonds in Q1 2020 totaling USD461.1 million on a 37.1% q-o-q increase from the previous quarter. Visari Investment Holding raised USD333.3 million worth of 5-year bonds, government-owned Hong Kong Mortgage Corporation issued USD126.4 million of 1-year bonds, and KGI International sold USD1.4 million of 2-year bonds.

In the Republic of Korea, cross-border bond issuances in Q1 2020 reached USD445.6 million, a 79.1% q-o-q increase from the previous quarter. The majority of these issuances came from state-owned institutions, led by Korea Development Bank, which raised the equivalent of USD269.8 million in various currencies: Indonesian rupiah (USD96.3 million), Thai baht (USD91.6 million), Hong Kong dollars (USD46.6 million), and Chinese yuan (USD35.3 million). Korea Resources, a mining company, had the single-largest issuance in the Republic of Korea during the quarter, raising USD64.5 million worth of HKD-denominated 5-year bonds. Other state-owned institutions that issued cross-border bonds were Export–Import Bank of Korea (USD41.3 million) and Korea National Oil (USD20.6 million). The only private firm was Kookmin Bank, which issued USD49.4 million worth of 2-year bonds denominated in Hong Kong dollars.

Malayan Banking was the sole issuer of cross-border bonds in Malaysia, raising USD28.2 million of CNY-denominated 5-year bonds. In the Lao People's Democratic Republic, Nam Ngum 2 Power, a hydroelectric power plant operator, raised USD18.3 million worth of THB-denominated bonds.

In Singapore, three institutions issued cross-border bonds with an aggregate volume of USD5.4 million: Credit Suisse (USD4.0 million), DBS Bank (USD1.3 million), and Nomura International Fund (USD0.1 million).

The top 10 issuers of cross-border bonds in the region had an aggregate volume of USD2.3 billion and accounted for 92.8% of the regional total. The list mainly comprised firms from the PRC, with six companies issuing the equivalent of USD1.5 billion denominated in Hong Kong dollars, Malaysian ringgit, and Singapore dollars. Two companies each were from Hong Kong, China (USD459.4 million) and the Republic of Korea (USD340.9 million). The top two issuers were again from the PRC: Bank of China and Bank of Communications.

The Hong Kong dollar remained the predominant currency of cross-border bonds in emerging East Asia in Q1 2020 with an aggregate issuance amount of USD1.1 billion and a share of 46.0% of the regional total (**Figure 5**). Firms that issued in this currency were

Figure 5: Currency Shares of Intra-Emerging East Asian Bond Issuance in the First Quarter of 2020

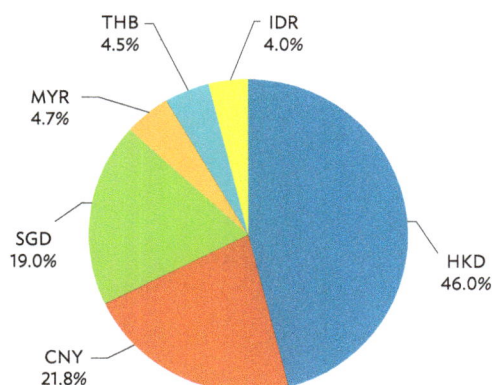

CNY = Chinese yuan, HKD = Hong Kong dollar, IDR = Indonesian rupiah, MYR = Malaysian ringgit, SGD = Singapore dollar, THB = Thailand baht.
Source: *AsianBondsOnline* calculations based on Bloomberg LP data.

from the PRC, the Republic of Korea, and Singapore. The Chinese yuan was the second most widely used currency, totaling USD528.7 million and comprising a share of 21.8%. Other cross-border issuance currencies were the Singapore dollar (19.0%, USD460.6 million); Malaysian ringgit (4.7%, USD115.2 million); Thai baht (4.5%, USD109.9 million); and Indonesian rupiah (4.0%, USD96.3 million).

G3 Currency Bond Issuance

Total G3 currency bond issuance in emerging East Asia amounted to USD112.5 billion in January–April.

The value of G3 currency bonds issued in emerging East Asia from January to April totaled USD112.5 billion, a decrease of 3.9% y-o-y from USD117.1 billion in the same period in 2019 (**Table 4**).[8] The contraction was driven by lower G3 issuance in the PRC; Singapore; Thailand; and Hong Kong, China.

During the review period, 91.7% of all G3 currency bonds issued were denominated in US dollars, while 7.6% were in euros, and 0.7% were in Japanese yen. In January–April, a total of USD103.2 billion worth of bonds denominated in US dollars was issued in emerging East Asia, representing a decline of 5.0% y-o-y. The equivalent of USD8.5 billion

of EUR-denominated bonds were issued during the review period, a surge of 49.9% y-o-y, as more economies issued such bonds. Bonds issued in Japanese yen totaled USD0.8 billion, a decline of 72.1% y-o-y from a high base as Malaysia had a significant issuance of samurai bonds in March 2019.

The PRC continued to dominate all economies in the issuance of G3 currency bonds, totaling USD64.6 billion during the January–April period and mainly supported by its issuance in US dollars. This was followed by Indonesia with USD13.8 billion and Malaysia with USD9.7 billion, both issuing mainly in US dollars as well.

In the first 4 months of 2020, G3 currency bond issuance increased on a y-o-y basis in Indonesia (117.5%), Malaysia (71.9%), the Philippines (20.9%), and the Republic of Korea (3.4%). Issuance of G3 currency bonds in January–April declined on a y-o-y basis in Hong Kong, China (−43.7%); Thailand (−21.3%); the PRC (−14.6%); and Singapore (−7.5%).

The PRC accounted for 57.4% of all G3 currency issuance in emerging East Asia in January–April, issuing USD62.3 billion in US dollars and the equivalent of USD2.2 billion in euros. In January, real estate developer Scenery Journey issued USD-denominated callable bonds in two tranches worth USD2.0 billion each and with tenors of 3 years and 4 years and coupon rates of 11.5% and 12.0%, respectively. Proceeds from the bonds will be used to refinance existing obligations and for general corporate purposes. Bank of China issued a USD2.8 billion perpetual callable bond with a 3.6% coupon rate. This came after the PRC's central bank encouraged banks at the start of last year to replenish their capital through perpetual bond issuances. It also relaxed rules to allow perpetual bonds as qualified collateral for various lending facilities.

The Republic of Korea accounted for an 8.6% share of all G3 currency bonds issued during the review period: USD7.1 billion in US dollars and the equivalent of USD2.5 billion in euros. The Export–Import Bank of Korea issued six USD-denominated bonds totaling USD1.1 billion with tenors ranging from 2 years to 5 years and carrying various coupon rates. It also had a dual-tranche offering with a USD0.7 billion 3-year

---

[8] G3 currency bonds are denominated in either euros, Japanese yen, or US dollars.

Table 4: G3 Currency Bond Issuance

2019			January–April 2020		
Issuer	Amount (USD billion)	Issue Date	Issuer	Amount (USD billion)	Issue Date
China, People's Rep. of	**225.2**		**China, People's Rep. of**	**64.6**	
Tencent Holdings 3.975% 2029	3.0	11-Apr-19	Bank of China 3.6% Perpetual	2.8	4-Mar-20
People's Republic of China (Sovereign) 0.125% 2026	2.2	12-Nov-19	Scenery Journey 11.5% 2022	2.0	24-Jan-20
People's Republic of China (Sovereign) 1.950% 2024	2.0	3-Dec-19	Scenery Journey 12.0% 2023	2.0	24-Jan-20
Others	218.0		Others	57.7	
Hong Kong, China	**31.9**		**Hong Kong, China**	**6.8**	
Celestial Miles 5.75% Perpetual	1.0	31-Jan-19	AIA Group 3.375% 2030	1.0	7-Apr-20
Hong Kong, China (Sovereign) 2.50% 2024	1.0	28-May-19	Elect Global Investments 4.100% Perpetual	0.9	3-Mar-20
AIA Group 3.60% 2029	1.0	9-Apr-19	Sino Pharmaceutical 0.000% 2025	0.8	17-Feb-20
Others	28.9		Others	4.1	
Indonesia	**22.4**		**Indonesia**	**13.8**	
Perusahaan Penerbit SBSN Sukuk 4.45% 2029	1.3	20-Feb-19	Indonesia (Sovereign) 3.85% 2030	1.7	15-Apr-20
Indonesia (Sovereign) 1.40% 2031	1.1	30-Oct-19	Indonesia (Sovereign) 4.20% 2050	1.7	15-Apr-20
Indonesia (Sovereign) 3.70% 2049	1.0	30-Oct-19	Indonesia (Sovereign) 2.85% 2030	1.2	14-Jan-20
Others	19.0		Others	9.3	
Korea, Rep. of	**29.4**		**Korea, Rep. of**	**9.6**	
Republic of Korea (Sovereign) 2.500% 2029	1.0	19-Jun-19	Korea Housing Finance 0.01000% 2025	1.1	5-Feb-20
Export–Import Bank of Korea 0.375% 2024	0.8	26-Mar-19	Export–Import Bank of Korea 0.82900% 2025	0.8	27-Apr-20
LG Display 1.500% 2024	0.7	22-Aug-19	Korea Development Bank 2.04175% 2023	0.8	18-Feb-20
Others	26.8		Others	7.0	
Lao People's Democratic Republic	**0.2**		**Lao People's Democratic Republic**	**0.0**	
Malaysia	**13.7**		**Malaysia**	**9.7**	
Malaysia (Sovereign) 0.530% 2029	1.8	15-Mar-19	Petronas Capital 4.55% 2050	2.8	21-Apr-20
Resorts World Las Vegas 4.625% 2029	1.0	16-Apr-19	Petronas Capital 3.50% 2030	2.3	21-Apr-20
Others	10.9		Others	4.7	
Philippines	**6.7**		**Philippines**	**2.9**	
Philippines (Sovereign) 3.750% 2029	1.5	14-Jan-19	Philippines (Sovereign) 0.7% 2029	0.7	3-Feb-20
Philippines (Sovereign) 0.875% 2027	0.8	17-May-19	Philippines (Sovereign) 0.0% 2023	0.7	3-Feb-20
Others	4.4		Others	1.6	
Singapore	**9.7**		**Singapore**	**4.3**	
DBS Group 2.85% 2022	0.8	16-Apr-19	DBS Group Holdings 3.30% Perpetual	1.0	27-Feb-20
BOC Aviation 3.50% 2024	0.8	10-Apr-19	BOC Aviation 3.25% 2025	1.0	29-Apr-20
Others	8.2		Others	2.3	
Thailand	**6.4**		**Thailand**	**0.8**	
Bangkok Bank/Hong Kong 3.733% 2034	1.2	25-Sep-19	PTTEP Treasury 2.993% 2030	0.4	15-Jan-20
Kasikornbank 3.343% 2031	0.8	2-Oct-19	TMB Bank 0.250% 2021	0.2	24-Mar-20
Others	4.4		Others	0.2	
Viet Nam	**1.0**		**Viet Nam**	**0.0**	
Emerging East Asia Total	**346.4**		**Emerging East Asia Total**	**112.5**	
Memo Items:			Memo Items:		
India	**21.9**		**India**	**8.4**	
Indian Oil Corporation 4.75% 2024	0.9	16-Jan-19	Adani Electricity 3.949% 2030	1.0	12-Feb-20
Others	21.0		Others	7.4	
Sri Lanka	**4.9**		**Sri Lanka**	**0.1**	
Sri Lanka (Sovereign) 7.55% 2030	1.5	28-Jun-19	Sri Lanka (Sovereign) 5.93% 2021	0.02	22-Jan-20
Others	3.4		Others	0.1	

USD = United States dollar.
Notes:
1. Data exclude certificates of deposits.
2. G3 currency bonds are bonds denominated in either euros, Japanese yen, or US dollars.
3. Bloomberg LP end-of-period rates are used.
4. Emerging East Asia comprises Cambodia; the People's Republic of China; Hong Kong, China; Indonesia; the Republic of Korea; the Lao People's Democratic Republic; Malaysia; the Philippines; Singapore; Thailand; and Viet Nam.
5. Figures after the issuer name reflect the coupon rate and year of maturity of the bond.
Source: *AsianBondsOnline* calculations based on Bloomberg LP data.

USD-denominated bond and a USD0.8 billion 5-year EUR-denominated green bond. Proceeds from the USD-denominated tranche will be used for general funding purposes, while those from the EUR-denominated bond will be utilized for extending loans to green projects. Korea Development Bank issued eight USD-denominated bonds totaling USD2.2 billion with tenors of 3–6 years and varying coupon rates.

Hong Kong, China accounted for a 6.0% share of G3 currency bond issuance in January–April. By currency, USD5.7 billion was issued in US dollars, and EUR-denominated and JPY-denominated bonds amounted to USD0.9 billion and USD0.2 billion, respectively. Financial services company AIA Group issued USD1.0 billion of 10-year callable USD-denominated bonds with a coupon rate of 3.375%. Under its global medium-term note and securities program, proceeds from the issuance will be used for general corporate purposes. Elect Global Investments also sold bonds in US dollars: a USD0.9 billion perpetual callable bond with a 4.1% coupon rate.

G3 currency bond issuance among ASEAN member economies increased 57.0% y-o-y to USD31.5 billion in January–April from USD20.1 billion in the same period in 2019 as Indonesia, Malaysia, and the Philippines ramped up issuance during the period. As a share of emerging East Asia's total, ASEAN's G3 currency bond issuance accounted for 28.0% during the review period, up from 17.1% during the same period in 2019. Indonesia and Malaysia led all ASEAN members in terms of G3 currency bond issuance, followed by Singapore, the Philippines, and Thailand, with issuances amounting to USD4.3 billion, USD2.9 billion, and USD0.8 billion, respectively.

Indonesia's G3 currency bond issuance in January–April accounted for 12.3% of the total in emerging East Asia, comprising USD12.7 billion in US dollars and the equivalent of USD1.1 billion in euros. In January, the Government of Indonesia issued USD3.1 billion worth of dual-currency bonds in three tranches, two of which were in US dollars (10-year and 30-year tenors) and one in euros (7-year tenor). Taking advantage of stable market conditions and positive investor sentiment, proceeds from the issuance will be used for general budgetary purposes. In April, the Government of Indonesia sold the first global bond in response to the COVID-19 pandemic. Proceeds from the issuance will be used to

finance the government's measures to fight the impact of the pandemic. The issuance totaled USD4.3 billion in USD-denominated bonds with three tranches in tenors of 10.5 years, 30.5 years, and 50 years. State-owned oil and natural gas corporation Pertamina issued two dual-tranche USD-denominated callable bonds totaling USD3.0 billion, with tenors ranging from 10 years to 40 years, to refinance capital expenditures and for general corporate purposes. Proceeds from the 11-year and 40-year tenors will also be used to fund a tender offer to buy back the state-owned firm's senior notes due in May 2021 and extend the company's debt maturity profile.

G3 currency bonds issued in Malaysia accounted for 8.6% of emerging East Asia's total, including USD-denominated bonds worth USD9.1 billion and JPY-denominated bonds worth USD0.6 billion. State-owned oil company Petronas Capital raised USD6.0 billion through three tranches of USD-denominated callable bonds. The tranches have tenors of 10 years, 30 years, and 40 years, and coupon rates of 3.5%, 4.55%, and 4.8%, respectively. Proceeds from the issuance will be used for general corporate purposes. In February, Maybank issued three USD-denominated bonds with tenors of 2 years, 3 years, and 40 years totaling USD0.5 billion. The 40-year tenor was a zero-coupon callable bond. During the same month, Maybank also sold samurai bonds in three tranches of 10-year, 30-year, and 40-year tenors to expand its investor base.

Singapore's share of G3 currency bond issuance in emerging East Asia was 3.8% in January–April, comprising USD4.2 billion in US dollars and the equivalent of USD0.1 billion in euros. Global aircraft operating company BOC Aviation expanded its USD-denominated bonds with two 5-year callable bonds totaling USD1.4 billion and with coupon rates of 2.625% and 3.25%. Proceeds from both issuances will be used for new capital expenditure, general corporate purposes, and debt financing. DBS Group Holdings raised USD1.0 billion through issuance of a perpetual callable bond with a coupon rate of 3.3%.

The Philippines accounted for a 2.6% share of total G3 currency bonds issued in emerging East Asia during the January–April period, comprising bonds denominated in US dollars and euros amounting to USD1.6 billion and USD1.3 billion, respectively. In February, the Government of the Philippines issued two tranches of EUR-denominated bonds worth USD1.3 billion and with tenors of 3 years and 9 years and coupon rates of 0.0% and 0.7%, respectively. The issuance diversifies the government's funding sources. SMC Global Power issued a USD-denominated callable perpetual bond worth USD0.6 billion with a coupon rate of 5.7%. Proceeds from the issuance will be used for the development of battery energy storage projects and for general corporate purposes.

During the January–April period, 0.7% of all G3 currency bonds issued in the region were from Thailand, comprising USD0.5 billion worth of bonds denominated in euros and USD0.4 billion in US dollars. TMP Bank issued two EUR-denominated 1-year bonds totaling USD0.5 billion with a 0.25% coupon each. Oil and gas producer PTTEP sold USD0.4 billion of 10-year callable bonds denominated in US dollars. Proceeds will be used for general corporate purposes.

Monthly G3 currency issuance trends from January to April 2020 reversed those observed from January to April 2019 (**Figure 6**). Declining G3 issuances in January–April 2020 from the PRC; Hong Kong, China; Indonesia; and the Philippines weighed on the regional trend. The downtrend reflected weak global conditions amid uncertainties caused by the COVID-19 pandemic.

Figure 6: G3 Currency Bond Issuance in Emerging East Asia

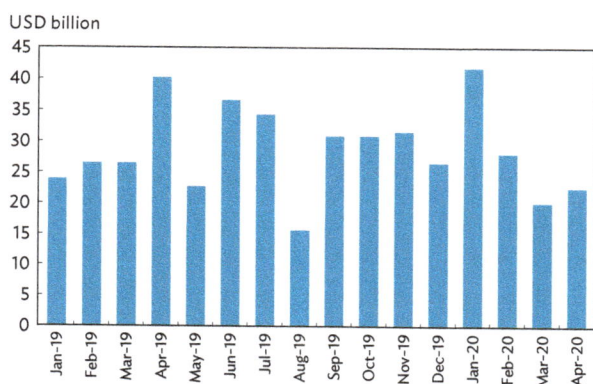

USD billion

USD = United States dollar.
Notes:
1. Emerging East Asia comprises Cambodia; the People's Republic of China; Hong Kong, China; Indonesia; the Republic of Korea; the Lao People's Democratic Republic; Malaysia; the Philippines; Singapore; Thailand; and Viet Nam.
2. G3 currency bonds are bonds denominated in either euros, Japanese yen, or US dollars.
3. Figures were computed based on 30 April 2020 currency exchange rates and do not include currency effects.
Source: *AsianBondsOnline* calculations based on Bloomberg LP data.

Government Bond Yield Curves

Government bond yields in emerging East Asia fell at the shorter-end of the curve for nearly all markets as governments sought to mitigate the economic impact of COVID-19, while in a number of markets yields rose at the longer-end over rising risk aversion and the potential deterioration of government finances.

Between 28 February and 29 May, the ongoing impact of COVID-19 and efforts to minimize the spread led to a deterioration in economic growth across the region, with most economies contracting. To manage the economic impact and calm financial markets, regional economies have eased both monetary and fiscal policy.

Among advanced economies, the United States (US) Federal Reserve was the most aggressive, implementing a cut of 50 basis points (bps) on 3 March ahead of its scheduled 17–18 March meeting. An additional 100-bps cut was announced on 15 March. Other measures were initiated by the government and the Federal Reserve, including a US Treasury-bond-buying program of at least USD500 billion and measures to ease the financing strain on corporates and households.

In the euro area, the European Central Bank did not adjust its policy rates, but it announced a EUR120 billion asset purchase program on 18 March. It also launched the EUR750 billion Pandemic Emergency Purchase Programme on 18 March that is scheduled to run for the duration of 2020. Subsequently, on 4 June, the ECB increased the volume of purchases under the program to EUR1,350 billion.

In Japan, the Bank of Japan (BOJ) likewise did not adjust policy rates but instead engaged in additional asset purchases. On 16 March, the BOJ increased its purchase of (i) corporate bonds and commercial paper by JPY2.0 trillion, (ii) exchange-traded funds by JPY6.0 trillion, and (iii) Japan real-estate investment trusts by JPY90 billion. On 27 April, the BOJ more than doubled its purchase of corporate bonds and commercial paper to JPY20 trillion and removed existing limits on the purchase of 10-year government bonds.

The economic impacts of COVID-19 and efforts to mitigate these effects have not been limited to advanced economies; emerging East Asian economies have also pursued a number of policy measures. As the pandemic's impact has been global, yield movements in most economies have moved similarly. In particular, 2-year yields in emerging East Asia have moved largely in tandem with and in response to US yield movements, declining steadily over the period in review (**Figure 7a**). Spikes were noted in March, coinciding with aggressive US stimulus measures and a sharp decline in oil prices. This largely increased uncertainty, raising investor risk aversion and highlighting concerns that stimulus measures could result in worsening fiscal deficits. However, after March, yield movements largely trended downward. The region's

exception to this trend was Indonesia, with its 2-year yield rising between 28 February and 29 May (**Figure 7b**). Bank Indonesia has generally not been as aggressive in easing monetary policy as its regional peers.

The 10-year yield movements in emerging East Asia also trended downward during the review period, but the March spike in 10-year yields was even more pronounced across the region. In addition, while 10-year yields trended downward after March, in some markets—such as the Republic of Korea, Thailand, and Viet Nam—they remained elevated (**Figure 8a** and **Figure 8b**). Similar to its

---

Figure 7a: 2-Year Local Currency Government Bond Yields

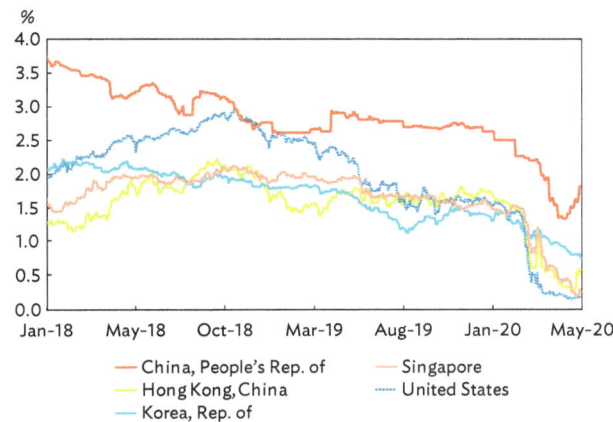

Note: Data as of 29 May 2020.
Source: Based on data from Bloomberg LP.

Figure 7b: 2-Year Local Currency Government Bond Yields

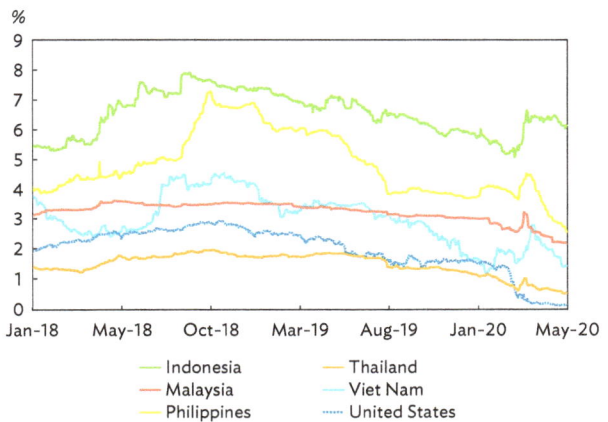

Note: Data as of 29 May 2020.
Source: Based on data from Bloomberg LP.

Figure 8a: 10-Year Local Currency Government Bond Yields

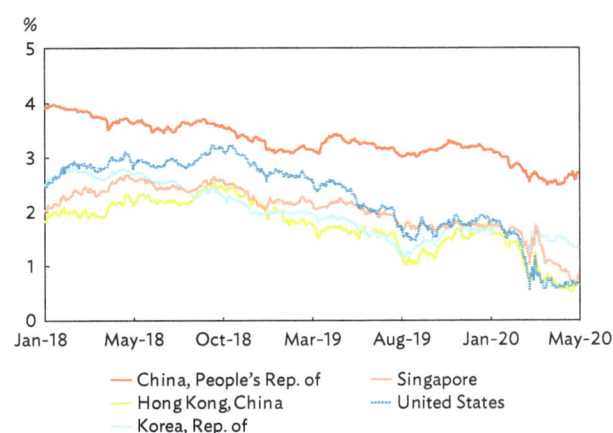

Note: Data as of 29 May 2020.
Source: Based on data from Bloomberg LP.

Figure 8b: 10-Year Local Currency Government Bond Yields

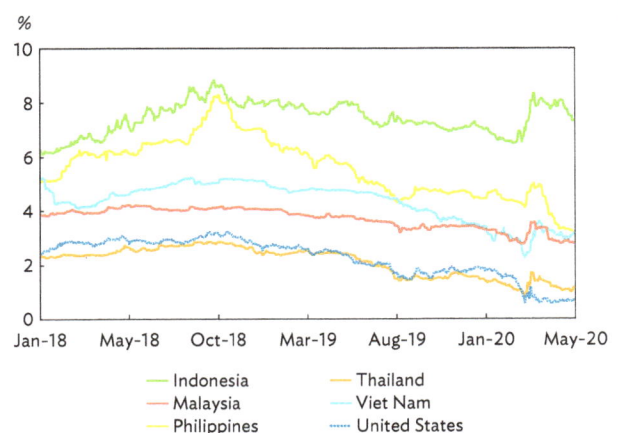

Note: Data as of 29 May 2020.
Source: Based on data from Bloomberg LP.

2-year yield movement, Indonesia's 10-year yield trended upward during the review period.

Many of the region's benchmark yield curves moved similarly to one another during the review period (**Figure 9**). The entire yield curve shifted downward between 28 February and 29 May in the Philippines; Singapore; and Hong Kong, China, while in the PRC, only the 30-year tenor rose. Yields fell at the shorter-end of the curve but rose for longer tenors in the Republic of Korea, Malaysia, Thailand, and Viet Nam. In Indonesia, the yield curve rose for all tenors.

Aggressive policy rate reductions and rising risk aversion at the longer-end of the yield curve led to a widening in the 2-year versus 10-year yield spread in all emerging East Asian markets except Indonesia (**Figure 10**).

With demand falling as a result of the effects of COVID-19, inflation declined in all markets in emerging East Asia (**Figure 11a** and **Figure 11b**). The Republic of Korea slipped into deflation with consumer prices declining 0.3% y-o-y in May after 0.1% y-o-y growth in April. In Malaysia, inflation came in below zero in March at −0.2% y-o-y and fell further to −2.9% y-o-y in April. Other markets which posited deflation in consumer prices were Singapore (−0.7%) in April and Thailand (−3.0%) in May.

Weak demand and subdued inflation have largely been supportive of emerging East Asian central banks' easing measures. More worrisome has been the economic impact of COVID-19, which was exacerbated by community quarantine measures implemented to reduce transmission. These measures have affected consumer sentiment and led to reductions in consumer demand and pending investment, and impacted supply chains and production.

In emerging East Asia, only four markets showed positive y-o-y GDP growth in Q1 2020: Indonesia, the Republic of Korea, Malaysia, and Viet Nam. And in these markets, economic growth slowed notably. In Indonesia, GDP growth eased to 3.0% y-o-y in Q1 2020 from 5.0% y-o-y in Q4 2019. The Republic of Korea's GDP growth slowed to 1.4% y-o-y in Q1 2020 from 2.3% y-o-y in the previous quarter. In Malaysia, GDP growth slowed to 0.7% y-o-y in Q1 2020 from 3.6% y-o-y in Q4 2019. In Viet Nam, GDP growth moderated to 3.8% y-o-y in Q1 2020 from 7.0% y-o-y in Q4 2019. The economies that showed the largest contractions in GDP during Q1 2020 were

Hong Kong, China (−8.9% y-o-y) and the PRC (−6.8% y-o-y). Thailand also saw a contraction in GDP of −1.8% y-o-y in Q1 2020. The smallest declines in GDP were seen in the Philippines and Singapore, where GDP contracted 0.2% y-o-y and 0.7% y-o-y, respectively, in Q1 2020.

The pandemic's impact also led to a downgrade in the ratings outlook for a number of markets. In April, S&P Global downgraded the outlook of Indonesia to negative from stable and of Thailand to stable from positive. Also in April, Fitch Ratings downgraded the outlook of Malaysia to negative from stable and of Viet Nam to stable from positive, while in May its outlook for the Philippines was revised downward to stable from positive. In June, S&P Global downgraded the outlook of Japan to stable from positive.

Central banks in the region have been forced to ease monetary policy to help boost economic output and reduce financial market volatility. For example, the People's Bank of China (PBOC) reduced a number of key interest rates to lower borrowing costs and prime the economy. On 29 March, the PBOC reduced its 7-day repurchase rate by 20 bps to 2.20%, and it lowered the rate it charges on its medium-term lending facility by 20 bps to 2.95% on 15 April. On 19 April, the PBOC reduced the rate on the 1-year loan prime rate by 20 bps to 3.85%.

Among central banks in the region, the Bangko Sentral ng Pilipinas has been among the most active in taking aggressive action, with a year-to-date cumulative reduction in the policy rate of 125 bps (**Figure 12a**). The Bangko Sentral ng Pilipinas reduced its policy rate by 25 bps on 6 February; 50 bps on 19 March; and engaged in another 50 bps reduction on 16 April, bringing the overnight reverse repurchase facility rate to 2.75%.

In the Republic of Korea, the Bank of Korea reduced by 25 bps its policy rate on 25 May, after leaving rates unchanged during its 9 April meeting, due to economic weakness and declining inflation. Bank Negara Malaysia has implemented a cumulative reduction in its key policy rate of 100 bps in response to the economic downturn. Bank Negara Malaysia implemented a 25-bps cut to its overnight policy rate on 22 January and again on 3 March. This was followed by a 50-bps cut on 5 May, lowering the rate to 2.0%.

Figure 9: Benchmark Yield Curves—Local Currency Government Bonds

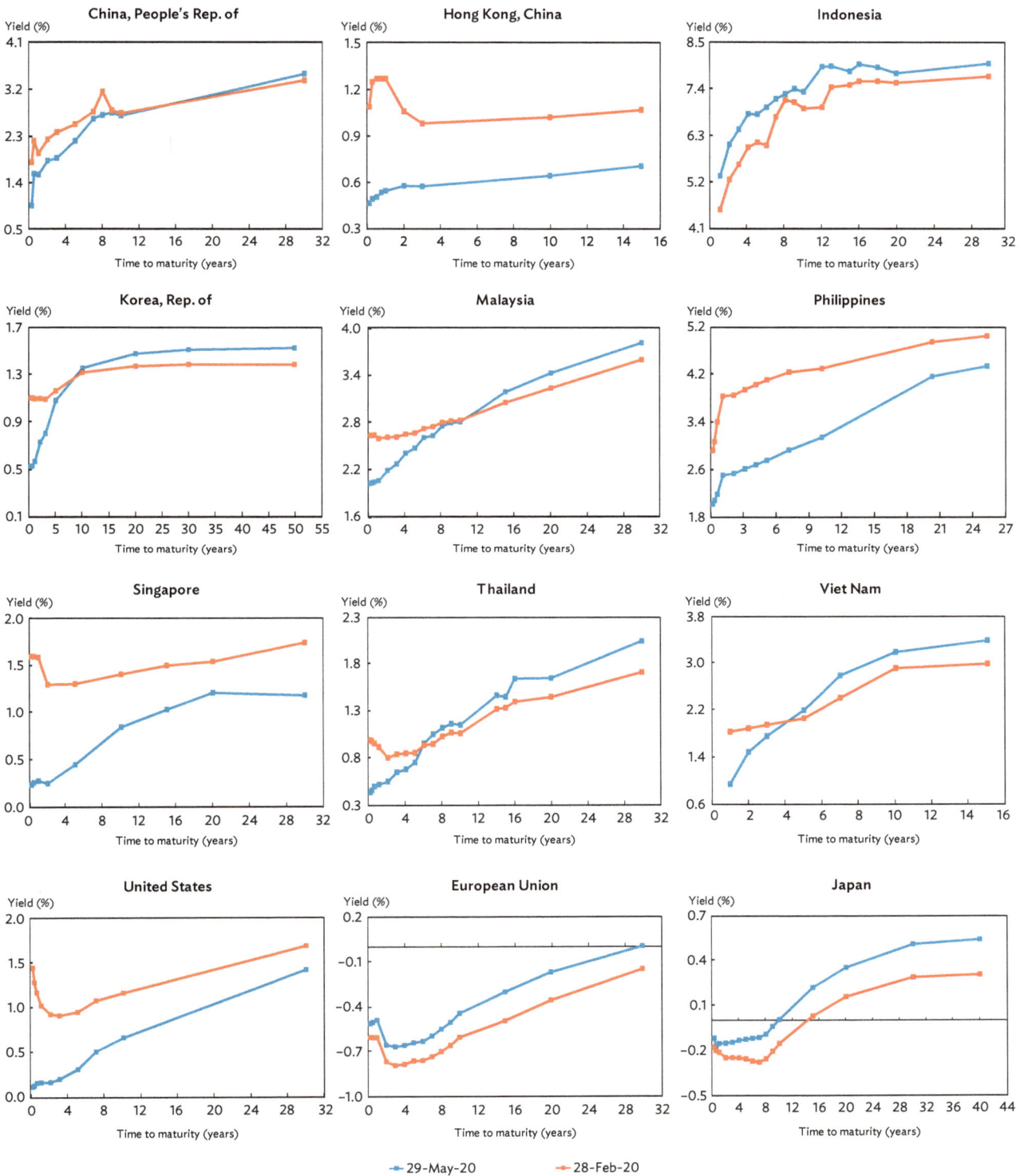

China, People's Rep. of

Hong Kong, China

Indonesia

Korea, Rep. of

Malaysia

Philippines

Singapore

Thailand

Viet Nam

United States

European Union

Japan

29-May-20   28-Feb-20

Sources: Based on data from Bloomberg LP and Thai Bond Market Association.

Figure 10: Yield Spreads between 2-Year and 10-Year Government Bonds

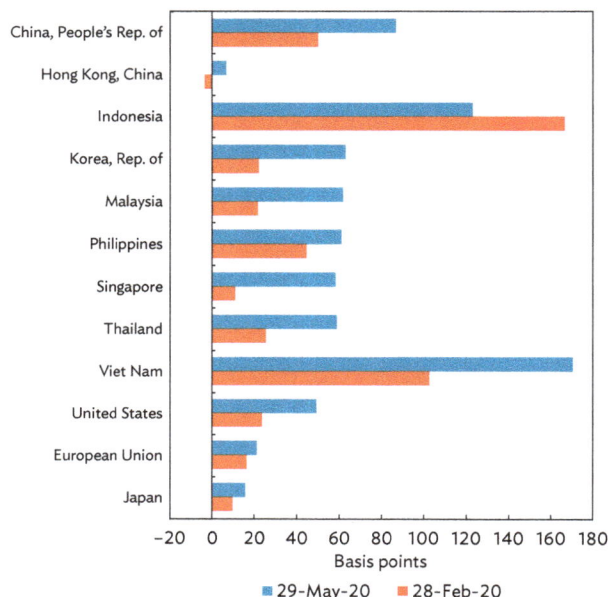

Source: Based on data from Bloomberg LP.

In Thailand, the central bank reduced its policy rate by 25 bps on 5 February and another 25 bps in a special meeting on 20 March, which was earlier than its originally scheduled meeting on 25 March. The Bank of Thailand again reduced its policy rate by an additional 25 bps on 20 May.

Indonesia was the only market in the region that experienced a consistent rise in yields over the review period. This was largely due to the central bank's relatively tamer policy rate reductions compared to others in the region. Bank Indonesia reduced its policy rate by 25 bps on 20 February and by another 25 bps on 19 March, but it has largely left policy rates unchanged since then (**Figure 12b**). On the other hand, the State Bank of Vietnam was the most aggressive central bank in the region in terms of rate reductions with a cumulative reduction of 150 bps through the end of May, reducing its policy rate by 100 bps on 16 March and by another 50 bps on 13 May.

Figure 11a: Headline Inflation Rates

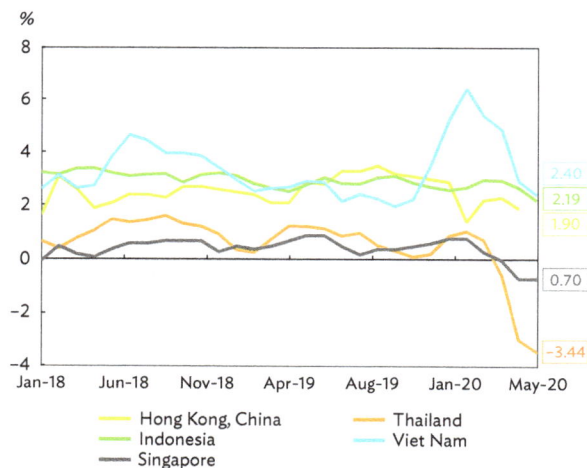

Note: Data as of May 2020 except for Hong Kong, China (April 2020).
Source: Based on data from Bloomberg LP.

Figure 11b: Headline Inflation Rates

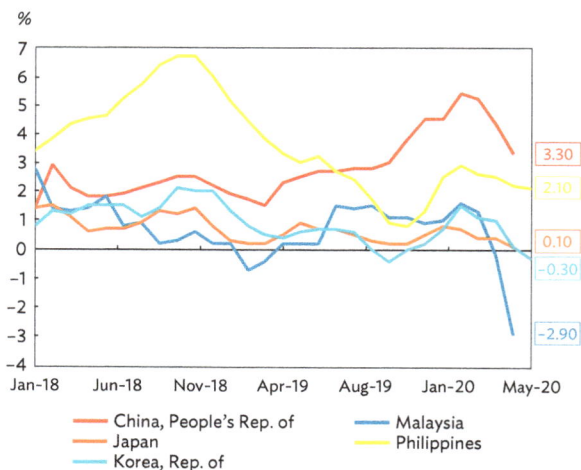

Note: Data as of May 2020 except for the People's Republic of China, Japan, and Malaysia (April 2020).
Source: Based on data from Bloomberg LP.

Figure 12a: Policy Rates

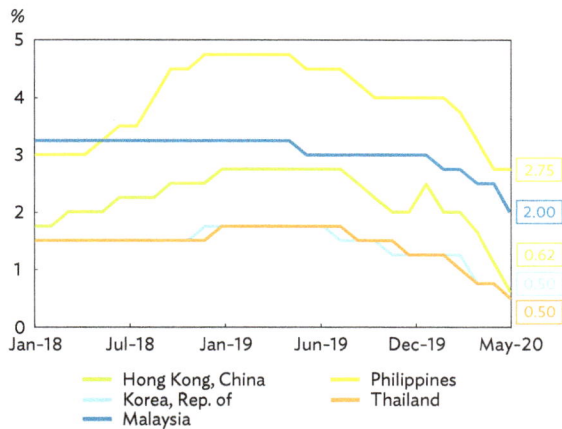

Note: Data as of 29 May 2020.
Source: Based on data from Bloomberg LP.

Figure 12b: Policy Rates

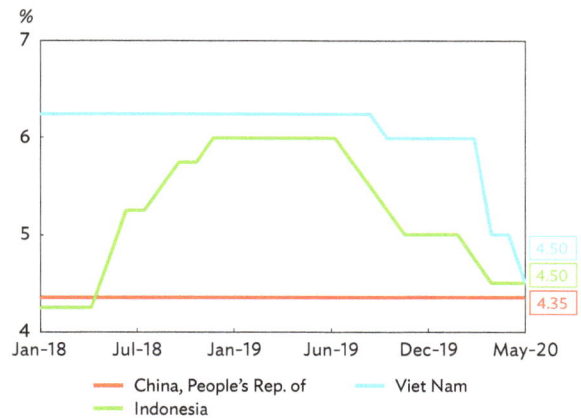

Note: Data as of 29 May 2020.
Source: Based on data from Bloomberg LP.

The AAA-rated corporate versus government yield spread widened in all markets on rising risk aversion that resulted in a flight to safety for most investors.

The AAA-rated corporate versus government yield spread widened between 28 February and 15 May in all markets for which data are available (**Figure 13a**). This was largely the result of a flight to safety by investors as the economic impact of COVID-19 led to repayment concerns.

For lower-rated credit spreads, movements were mixed. The spread between lower-rated and AAA-rated corporate bonds widened in the PRC and the Republic of Korea for all tenors, but only rose at the shorter-end of the curve in Malaysia and Thailand (**Figure 13b**).

Figure 13a: Credit Spreads—Local Currency Corporates Rated AAA vs. Government Bonds

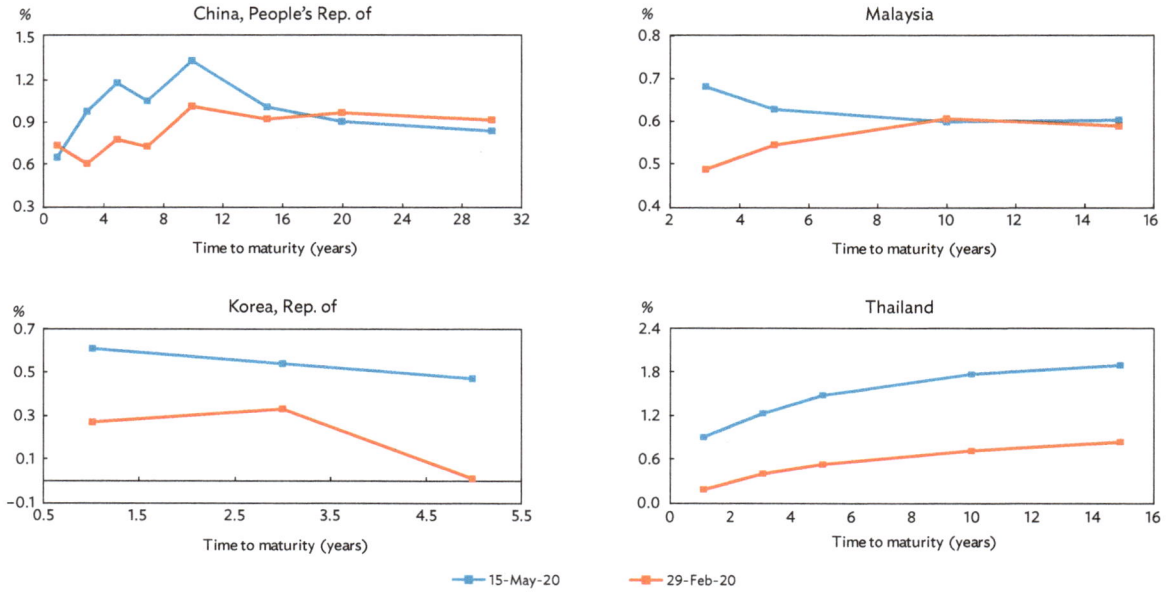

Notes:
1. Credit spreads are obtained by subtracting government yields from corporate indicative yields.
2. For Malaysia, data on corporate bonds yields are as of 29 February 2020 and 14 May 2020.
Sources: People's Republic of China (Bloomberg LP), Republic of Korea (*EDAILY BondWeb*), Malaysia (Bank Negara Malaysia), and Thailand (Bloomberg LP).

Figure 13b: Credit Spreads—Lower-Rated Local Currency Corporates vs. AAA

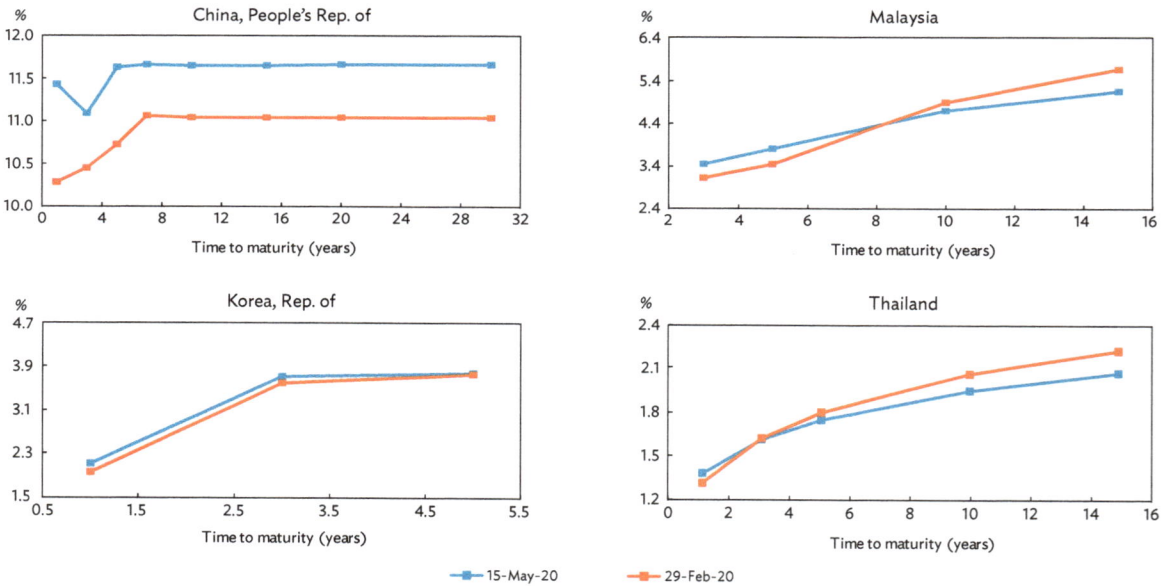

Notes:
1. For the People's Republic of China and the Republic of Korea, credit spreads are obtained by subtracting corporate indicative yields rated AAA from corporate indicative yields rated BBB+.
2. For Malaysia, data on corporate bonds yields are as of 29 February 2020 and 14 May 2020.
Sources: People's Republic of China (Bloomberg LP), Republic of Korea (*EDAILY BondWeb*), Malaysia (Bank Negara Malaysia), and Thailand (Bloomberg LP).

Policy and Regulatory Developments

People's Republic of China

National Development and Reform Commission Eases Bond Issuance Regulations

In March, the National Development and Reform Commission launched a registration-based system for the public issuance of enterprise and corporate bonds to replace the previous approval-based corporate and enterprise bond issuance system. Starting 1 March, the National Development and Reform Commission began registering the issuance of enterprise bonds if a firm's average distributable profits over the last 3 years were enough to cover 1 year of interest. The new system was expected to reduce the issuance period of enterprise bonds to 2 weeks from 2–6 months.

People's Bank of China Reduces Reserve Requirement Ratios for Small Banks

In April, the People's Bank of China announced a reduction in the reserve requirement ratio for small banks by a total of 100 basis points (bps), a 50-bps cut each on 15 April and 15 May. The reductions released a total of around CNY400 billion into the domestic economy, which has been negatively impacted by the outbreak of COVID-19. The People's Bank of China has stepped up its policy easing measures since February, cutting the benchmark leading rate and encouraging banks to offer cheap loans to firms hit hardest by the pandemic.

Hong Kong, China

Hong Kong Monetary Authority Reduces Countercyclical Capital Buffer to 1.0%

On 16 March, the Hong Kong Monetary Authority (HKMA) reduced its countercyclical buffer to 1.0% from 2.0% amid worsening economic conditions brought about by the coronavirus disease (COVID-19) outbreak. The move was intended to release additional funds that would allow banks to extend credit to support financing needs in the domestic economy, particularly for sectors and individuals affected by the downturn. The countercyclical buffer is an integral part of the Basel III regulatory capital framework designed to increase the resilience of the banking sector during periods of excess credit growth.

Hong Kong Monetary Authority Reduces Issuance of Exchange Fund Bills by HKD20.0 billion in April–May

On 9 April, the HKMA announced a reduction in the issuance of Exchange Fund Bills (EFBs), which was aimed at raising Hong Kong dollar liquidity in the interbank market. The HKMA reduced the issue size of 91-day EFBs by HKD5.0 billion in each of the tenders held on 21 April, 28 April, 5 May, and 12 May. The combined reduction lowered the issuance of EFBs by a total of HKD20.0 billion.

Hong Kong Monetary Authority Introduces a Temporary US Dollar Liquidity Facility

On 22 April, the HKMA announced the introduction of a temporary US dollar liquidity facility that will provide US dollar liquidity assistance to licensed banks through competitive tenders of 7-day repurchase transactions. Starting 6 May, the HKMA began conducting a tender once per week. Eligible banks can submit a bid of at least USD100 million or multiples thereof. The HKMA intends to maintain the facility, which currently has USD10.0 billion of available funds, until 30 September. It will also consider market conditions and revise arrangements as necessary.

Indonesia

Otoritas Jasa Keuangan Issues Regulations for the Issuance of Debt Securities Through Private Placements

In March, Otoritas Jasa Keuangan (OJK) issued regulations for the issuance of debt instruments, including *sukuk*, through private placements. The regulations, which are set to became effective in June, placed the legality of instruments issued through private placements similar to that of bonds and provide investor protections. Under the regulations, firms that undertake issuance of debt securities—in particular, medium-term notes or *sukuk*—through a private placement will be required to (i) file for registration with OJK, (ii) obtain an investment grade from an OJK-certified credit rating agency for persons outside the scope of public companies, (iii) avail the services of an arranger and monitoring agent, and (iv) limit the buying of medium-term notes to professional investors.

Bank Indonesia Lowers Reserve Requirement Ratios

In April, Bank Indonesia announced a 200-bps reduction in the rupiah reserve requirement ratio for conventional commercial banks and a 50-bps cut for Islamic banks and Islamic business units. The adjustment in reserve requirement ratios took effect in May and formed part of Bank Indonesia's accommodative macroprudential policy stance to stimulate bank intermediation and mitigate the economic impact of COVID-19.

Bank Indonesia to Purchase Government Bonds in the Primary Market

In April, Bank Indonesia commenced its participation in the weekly auctions of the government to purchase Treasury instruments. Previously, Bank Indonesia was only allowed to purchase bonds from the secondary market. The regulation, in lieu of Law 1/2020 that was passed in March, allows the central bank to participate in the weekly auctions as a noncompetitive bidder. Bank Indonesia and the Ministry of Finance set a limit on the central bank's bond purchases at 30% for Shari'ah Treasury auctions and 25% for conventional Treasury auctions. Bank Indonesia's purchase of government bonds in the primary market is only allowed when the market is unable to absorb the offers.

Republic of Korea

The Bank of Korea Announces Measures to Boost Market Liquidity

On 26 March, the Bank of Korea announced measures to support market liquidity and stabilize financial markets. This included the conduct of weekly repo auctions for a period of 3 months. It also expanded the range of institutions eligible for the auctions from five to 16 nonbanks, eligible securities will now include eight bonds issued by public organizations, and eligible collateral has been extended to eight bonds issued by public organizations and bank debentures.

The Bank of Korea Launches Corporate Bond-Backed Lending Facility

On 16 April, the Bank of Korea launched the Corporate Bond-Backed Lending Facility to allow banks and non-bank financial institutions that can provide high-rated corporate bonds as collateral to access credit from the central bank. The facility will have a ceiling of KRW10 trillion and a term of 3 months; this can be adjusted after an assessment of financial market conditions.

National Assembly Passes KRW12.2 Trillion Supplementary Budget

On 30 April, the National Assembly passed the government's second supplementary budget, which was revised upward to KRW12.2 trillion from KRW7.6 trillion. As part of the government's financial support package, funds will be used to aid sectors affected by the COVID-19 pandemic, particularly financing of the household emergency relief program. KRW8.8 trillion will be sourced from spending restructuring, and the remaining KRW3.4 trillion will be raised via debt issuance.

Malaysia

Bank Negara Malaysia Decreases Statutory Reserve Requirement

On 19 March, Bank Negara Malaysia decreased the statutory reserve requirement ratio from 3.0% to 2.0%. Principal dealers can now include up to a total of MYR1.0 billion worth of Malaysian Government Securities and Government Investment Issues in the computation of their reserves. On 5 May, the central bank allowed all banking institutions to do the same, although no cap on the total amount was mentioned. The measures are expected to release MYR46.0 billion worth of liquidity into Malaysia's banking system to support financial activities in the market.

FTSE Russell Keeps Malaysia on Its Watchlist

On 2 April, FTSE Russell decided to keep Malaysia on its watchlist during its interim March review, saying it would continue to monitor Malaysia for a possible downgrade. To avoid being removed from the FTSE Russell World Government Bond Index, Malaysia has been given 6 months to improve its market conditions. Since its placement on the watchlist last year, Malaysia has implemented regulations to improve bond and foreign exchange liquidity conditions. The decision on whether or not to exclude Malaysia from the benchmark index is expected during FTSE Russell's annual review in September.

Philippines

Bangko Sentral ng Pilipinas Cuts Reserve Requirement Ratio to Support the Economy amid COVID-19

The Bangko Sentral ng Pilipinas (BSP) announced a cut to the reserve requirement ratio (RRR) of universal and commercial banks by 200 bps on 24 March, effective on 3 April. According to the central bank, the RRR cut was intended to encourage banks to lend to the retail and corporate sectors, and to ensure that there is enough liquidity to support economic activities amid the COVID-19 pandemic. The Monetary Board has authorized the Governor of the BSP to reduce the RRR by as much as 400 bps in 2020. The BSP will assess the pandemic's ongoing impact on the domestic economy to determine the timing and extent of possible further reductions. The possibility of extending the RRR cut to other types of banks and non-bank financial institutions is being explored.

Bangko Sentral ng Pilipinas Announces Measures to Support Domestic Liquidity

On 10 April, the BSP announced measures to support domestic liquidity to ensure stability and the proper functioning of the financial market. Based on the BSP's statement, the measures include (i) purchases of government securities in the secondary market, (ii) a reduction of overnight reverse repurchase volumes to encourage counterparties to lend in the interbank market or to rechannel their funds into other assets such as government securities or loans, and (iii) a repurchase

agreement with the government where the BSP shall purchase government securities worth up to PHP300 billion from the Bureau of the Treasury.

Singapore

Monetary Authority of Singapore and Federal Reserve Establish Swap Facility

On 19 March, the Monetary Authority of Singapore (MAS) and the United States Federal Reserve established a USD60.0 billion swap facility to address liquidity concerns amid the COVID-19 pandemic. In place for at least 6 months, the swap facility provides stable liquidity conditions in the US dollar funding market in Singapore. It also complements MAS' management of the Singapore dollar market. Together, these measures reinforce the robustness and efficiency of Singapore's financial market.

Monetary Authority of Singapore Adjusts Regulations to Support Financial Institutions

On 7 April, MAS adjusted regulatory and supervisory measures to support financial institutions as they deal with the impact of the COVID-19 pandemic. To help financial institutions sustain their lending activities, MAS adjusted downward the net stable funding ratio requirement to 25% from 50%. It will also allow financial institutions to factor in the government's fiscal assistance and banks' relief measures in accounting loan loss allowances. As businesses focus on managing the impact of COVID-19, the implementation of Basel III reforms for Singaporean banks has been deferred for 1 year. MAS will coordinate with financial institutions for revised timelines for the submission of regulatory reports. Regular on-site inspections and supervisory visits will be suspended indefinitely; MAS assessments will focus instead on how financial institutions handle the impacts of COVID-19 on their businesses.

Thailand

Public Debt Management Office to Issue Shorter-Dated Bonds

In March, the Public Debt Management Office (PDMO) announced that it will adjust its bond issuance plan to include shorter-dated bonds amid weak demand for government bonds due to heightened uncertainties caused by the COVID-19 pandemic. The PDMO announcement came after a wave of fixed-income redemptions as alarm over COVID-19 drove investors to switch from debt instruments to cash.

Bank of Thailand Implements Measures to Stabilize Bond Market

In March, the Bank of Thailand (BOT) implemented several measures to alleviate the impact of COVID-19 on the Thai bond market. It established a mutual fund liquidity facility to provide liquidity for mutual funds through commercial banks. The BOT promised to inject about THB1.0 trillion into the bond market through the facility, which will be available until market conditions normalize. Commercial banks that buy investment units of high-quality mutual funds in money market and daily fixed-income funds can apply for liquidity support and use the underlying investment assets as collateral.

Along with the Thai Bankers' Association, the Government Savings Bank, Thai insurance providers, and the Government Pension Fund, the BOT also launched a Corporate Bond Stabilization Fund amounting to THB70 billion–THB100 billion. The fund will be used to inject liquidity into the corporate bond market by buying newly issued investment-grade bonds by corporates that cannot fully rollover maturing debt. The BOT will also continue to purchase government bonds to ensure stability in the government bond market.

Bank of Thailand Revises Bond Issuance Program

On 11 May, the BOT launched a revised bond issuance program for 2020 to accommodate the government's financing needs to fund relief measures and respond to changes in investor sentiment amid the COVID-19 pandemic. The auction days and frequency will remain as announced at the beginning of the year, but the BOT may adjust the issue sizes and will notify market participants of relevant changes at least 2 days before the auction dates. If necessary, the BOT will adjust the auction frequency of 3-month and 6-month BOT bills and of fixed-coupon bonds to accommodate the issuance schedule of Treasury bills and government bonds of comparable tenors. The ranges and minimum issue size per auction were expanded to between TH10.0 billion and THB60.0 billion for all maturities of BOT bills. The BOT will closely coordinate with the PDMO and take into consideration domestic and global market conditions in setting the issue sizes of BOT bills and bonds.

Viet Nam

State Bank of Vietnam Issues Circular on Reserve Requirements

In December, the State Bank of Vietnam issued a circular that grants credit institutions either a lower reserve requirement ratio or a reserve requirement waiver. Circular 30/2019/TT-NHNN identified cases where credit institutions would be granted a reserve requirement waiver: (i) the credit institution is placed under special control; (ii) the credit institution has not yet started its business; and (iii) the credit institution is given an approval for dissolution, issued a decision to institute bankruptcy proceedings, or issued a decision on the revocation of a business license by a competent authority. The circular also granted credit institutions that support the system restructuring a 50% reduction in the reserve requirement rate. The new circular took effect on 1 March 2020.[9]

---

[9] *Hanoi Times.* 2020. Vietnam C. Bank's New Circular to Turn USD1.73 Billion Required Reserves to Loans. 4 January.

COVID-19 and the Financial Sector

The outbreak of the coronavirus disease (COVID-19) has caused a sharp decline in global economic growth. Large-scale pandemic containment measures—lockdowns, travel restrictions, and quarantines, along with growing business closures and rising unemployment—have adversely affected both supply and demand. Business and consumer confidence have deteriorated. In response, governments around the world have launched sizable fiscal stimulus packages and central banks have aggressively eased monetary policy to mitigate the negative economic impact of COVID-19. The financial sector can ease the stress on government finances by unlocking resources from the private sector to join the fight against the pandemic. This special section discusses some of the financial sector's solutions for mobilizing private sector resources.

The global fight against COVID-19 can be viewed as a war. As war is a costly endeavor, it brings to the fore the issue of financing. Other than conventional bonds, pandemic bonds have been issued to cover extreme mortality during the pandemic. Sometimes, such bonds offer a higher yield to investors for taking higher risk. Asian governments have begun to explore the potential of pandemic bonds to finance large and growing public expenditures in response to COVID-19. On 7 April, the Government of Indonesia successfully issued its first "pandemic bond," raising over USD4.3 billion. **Box 2** discusses how, given the huge amounts of fiscal spending that will be needed to tackle the health and economic crisis, the bond market is likely to play a prominent role in funding the global war against COVID-19.

While COVID-19 slows down overall economic activity, it hits smaller businesses and poorer households disproportionately hard. Social bonds can help small and medium-sized enterprises and vulnerable groups survive the current turmoil. They are a useful tool for mobilizing resources for sectors that have a large social impact such as medical services, sanitation, small and medium-sized enterprises, housing, and gender equality. **Box 3** explores recent developments in the global social bond market amid the COVID-19 crisis.

The lockdown and social distancing prevalent during COVID-19 has restricted the normal functioning of traditional financial services. The pandemic has led to more economic activities shifting online. Financial technology (fintech) offers good solutions to deliver safe and contactless financial services while also serving financially underserved group. Thus, fintech can contribute to inclusiveness and economic resilience during the COVID-19 pandemic. **Box 4** elaborates on how fintech can effectively provide financial services, especially to underserved and vulnerable groups, amid the current environment.

While the financial sector can help finance funding needs and mitigate the wide range of risks confronting the economy during the COVID-19 shock, it too faces systematic risks that will be difficult to diversify. Policy makers need to work with the financial sector to provide liquidity in the economy and support firms. **Box 5** discusses the role of government in designing market-specific policies that can guide the financial sector to function as a liquidity provider during the pandemic.

This special section discusses the different financial instruments and technologies that can unlock private sector resources to support businesses and households during the COVID-19 pandemic. Since the pandemic poses systemic risks to the financial sector too, properly designed policy tools can mitigate these risks and effectively support the functioning of the financial sector.

Box 2: Pandemic Bonds—An Option for Fighting COVID-19

The world is in the midst of an unprecedented public health and economic crisis due to the coronavirus disease (COVID-19) outbreak.[a] As of 15 April 2020, there were almost 2 million confirmed cases and more than 125,000 fatalities worldwide.[b] Unlike a conventional war, there are no soldiers, tanks, or warships in the global fight against COVID-19. However, it is a war all the same as humanity is facing a common insidious, invisible, and formidable enemy that is ravaging health-care systems and inflicting economic pain. Doctors, nurses, other health-care workers, first responders, and medical scientists are on the frontlines of this unconventional war.

As in all past wars, governments are leading the overall war effort. They are managing and coordinating the reorganization of the economy and society to defeat the viral enemy. It is the government that determines whether community quarantines are necessary and enforces them accordingly. Many governments around the world have imposed lockdowns, from the Philippines to Italy and elsewhere. Another example is the United States (US) government ordering General Motors to make ventilators on 27 March. To do so, President Donald Trump tellingly invoked the Defense Production Act, which dates back to the Korean War. The act gives the President the authority to mandate that businesses produce goods needed for national defense (i.e., war) purposes.

The global fight against COVID-19 is clearly a war and wars are a costly endeavor, which brings to the fore the issue of financing. That is, how can countries find the resources required to fight this war? One option comes from past experiences of financing conventional wars through "war bonds," which refer to bonds issued by the government to finance military spending or other wartime expenditures. They are either retail bonds sold directly to the public or wholesale bonds traded on an exchange. Bond sale campaigns during wartime have often been accompanied by appeals to patriotism, while retail war bonds generally offered below-market yields.

One of the best-known early examples of a public war bond comes from Germany during the First World War. The bonds, which were called *Kriegsanleihe*, sought to mobilize domestic borrowing for the German war effort. Most bond buyers were large companies and institutions, such as university endowments, rather than individuals. Perhaps the best-known war bonds were those issued by the US government during the Second World War. The sale of these bonds was accompanied by intense patriotic propaganda efforts directed toward the

public. The sales campaign was hugely successful, and the bonds became a major source of funding for the US war effort. By the end of the war, 85 million Americans had purchased bonds worth USD185 billion.

The logic of using pandemic bonds to finance the fight against COVID-19 is simple and straightforward. War bonds are used to finance wars, and the fight against COVID-19 is a war, so why not use war bonds to finance the COVID-19 war? There is a large reservoir of goodwill among ordinary citizens to contribute to the global fight against the pandemic. It is difficult not to be moved when we see doctors and nurses heroically helping COVID-19 patients in overcrowded hospitals at great risk to their own safety. Similarly, most citizens are probably willing to lend a helping hand to less fortunate fellow citizens who have lost their job through no fault of their own.

To further cement the sense of solidarity that will drive people to buy pandemic bonds, governments can launch sales campaigns. Just as propaganda machines went into overdrive during war bond drives, the government can take the lead in advertising and advocating the purchase of pandemic bonds. There is no shame in engaging in propaganda to promote the social good. The proceeds from the pandemic bond sales can be used to finance various expenditures related to COVID-19. Obvious priority spending areas include strengthening health-care systems and boosting collapsing economies.

Asian governments have begun to explore the potential of pandemic bonds to finance large and growing public expenditures due to COVID-19. Most notably, on 7 April, the Government of Indonesia successfully issued its first pandemic bond, raising over USD4.3 billion. The issue included a USD1.0 billion 50-year tranche, which represents the longest-dated USD-denominated debt tranche ever issued in Asia. The government indicated that it would use part of the proceeds from the bond deal, which is the largest in the country's history, to fund its COVID-19 relief and recovery efforts. Most of the proceeds will go toward covering the country's widening fiscal deficit.

Indonesia's USD4.3 billion pandemic bond issue is not, strictly speaking, a pandemic bond since only part of the proceeds will fund COVID-19-related expenditures. However, the bond issue does illuminate a broader point. Given the huge fiscal spending required to tackle the current crisis and lay down the foundation for an economic recovery, the bond market is likely to play a prominent role in funding the global war against COVID-19 and the post-COVID-19 reconstruction effort.

---

[a] This box was written by Donghyun Park, Principal Economist in the Economic Research and Regional Cooperation Department of the Asian Development Bank.
[b] World Health Organization. COVID-19 Situation Report—86. 2020. https://www.who.int/docs/default-source/coronaviruse/situation-reports/20200415-sitrep-86-covid-19.pdf?sfvrsn=c615ea20_6.

Box 3: Social Bonds and the COVID-19 Crisis

Aggregate social bond issuance in 2020 stood at almost USD12 billion as of 12 May, compared with a total of USD16 billion in full-year 2019 (**Figure B3**).[a] Social bonds make up around 16% of total sustainable bond issuance—comprising green, social, and sustainability bonds—thus far in 2020, compared with only 6% in 2019. About 70% of social bonds issued in 2020 refer to mitigation of the impacts from the coronavirus disease (COVID-19) in their use of proceeds.

Having long been green bonds' less well-known sibling, the issuance of social bonds (and to a lesser degree sustainability bonds) is on the rise, albeit thanks to an unfortunate catalyst. Social bonds are used to finance projects that aim to address or mitigate a specific social issue and/or seek to achieve positive social outcomes directed toward a specified target population. Sustainability bonds can finance both green and social development projects.

Given the socioeconomic issues that economies around the world have been facing amid the COVID-19 pandemic, social bonds are beginning to emerge as a readily actionable mechanism for the market to respond to the social and economic consequences of the crisis. The global outbreak is a social issue that threatens the well-being of the world's population, especially the elderly and those with underlying health problems. In addition, millions of people around the world are suffering, or will be suffering, from the resulting economic downturn.

The Social Bond Principles (SBP) were published by the International Capital Market Association (ICMA) in 2017 to provide voluntary guidelines for the issuance of social bonds. They build on the use of a proceeds concept and, like the Green Bond Principles, consist of the following four pillars:

1. Use of Proceeds
2. Process for Project Evaluation and Selection
3. Management of Proceeds
4. Reporting

Any debt issuer in the international capital market can issue a social bond related to COVID-19 as long as all four core components of the SBP are recognized and the bond's proceeds go exclusively toward addressing or mitigating social issues wholly or partially emanating from the COVID-19 outbreak.

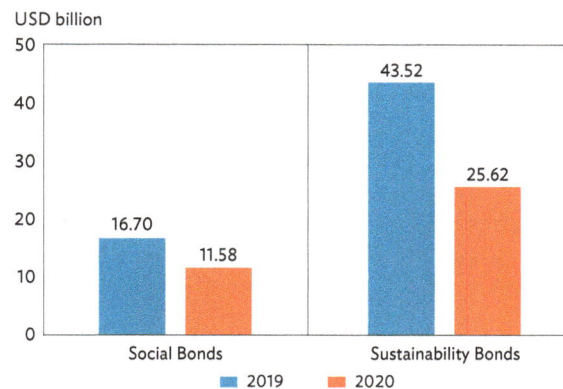

Figure B3: Social Bonds and Sustainability Bonds

USD billion

USD = United States dollar.
Note: Data for 2020 is as of 12 May 2020.
Source: International Capital Market Association analysis using Environmental Finance data.

Illustrative examples of eligible social projects include COVID-19-related health care and medical research and the development of vaccines, investment in additional medical equipment or manufacturing facilities to produce health and safety equipment and hygienic supplies, and specific projects designed to alleviate unemployment generated by the crisis. These projects can target specific groups directly impacted by the COVID-19 outbreak, although they may also seek to support a wider population affected by the economic crisis.

Sovereign, supranational, and agency issuers, who were among the first to develop the thriving green bond market, have been in the vanguard of the move toward social bond issuance. On 11 March 2020, the International Finance Corporation issued a USD1 billion 3-year social bond to "support the private sector and jobs in developing countries affected by the COVID-19 outbreak." The fact that this bond experienced exceptional global investor demand at a point when financial markets were in turmoil can be viewed as a reflection of the interest in a debt instrument that addresses the consequences of a global threat, which can be compared to the appetite for green bonds amid increased global understanding of the threat of climate change. On 27 March 2020, the African Development Bank issued the largest social bond to date in response to COVID-19: a USD3 billion 3-year bond to help alleviate the economic and social impacts of the pandemic on African livelihoods and economies called the Fight COVID-19

---

[a] This box was written by Simone Utermarck, Director of Market Practice and Regulatory Policy at the International Capital Market Association.

continued on next page

Box 3: Social Bonds and the COVID-19 Crisis   *continued*

Social Bond. On 1 April 2020, the European Investment Bank launched a SEK3 billion 3-year Sustainability Awareness Bond to combat the socioeconomic impacts of COVID-19. The proceeds from the issuance are earmarked for the European Investment Bank's lending activities that contribute to sustainability objectives, including Universal Access to Affordable Health Services (United Nations Sustainability Development Goal No. 3). In April, there were additional issuances from the Council of Europe and the World Bank, which issued the largest COVID-19-themed bond to date, an USD8 billion sustainability bond with proceeds dedicated to employment generation.

It is not just multilateral development banks that are accessing the market. Corporates and financial institutions are also issuing social and sustainability bonds. Pfizer, for example, is using bond proceeds to improve access to essential services such as health care. The Bank of China and Kookmin Bank are directing bond proceeds toward the financing of small and medium-sized enterprises affected by the virus.

There have been other bonds issued recently that are not considered social bonds, yet they seek to address the consequences of COVID-19. For example, a sovereign issue by the Government of Indonesia raised funds for general budgetary purposes. While this and other bonds may provide financing to help repair the social and economic damage caused by the pandemic, they are not aligned with SBP or Sustainability Bond Guidelines, and therefore do not fall within the ICMA definition of a social bond.

For issuers that would like to issue bonds aligned with the SBP or Sustainability Bond Guidelines, the Executive Committee of the Green Bond Principles, Social Bond Principles, and Sustainability Bond Guidelines, supported by ICMA, released a public statement in March 2020 underlining that existing guidance for social and sustainability bonds was immediately applicable to efforts addressing the COVID-19 crisis. Additional advice for issuers in the form of an updated Q&A and new case studies were also provided.

Box 4: Fintech for Inclusive Growth and Pandemic Resilience

Financial technology (fintech), or the fusion of finance and technology, has emerged as a new model for financial innovation.[a] Fintech covers a constellation of complementary technologies—including mobile networks, big data, cloud computing, distributed ledger technology, artificial intelligence, and data analytics—that jointly shape a broad swathe of operations in the financial industry. The past few years have witnessed the rapid growth of investment in fintech (**Figure B4**). Fintech has already left its imprint on a wide array of financial services, including microfinance, blockchain, payments, personal finance, digital banking, insurance, wealth management, capital markets, money transfers, and mortgages.

Fintech enhances financial inclusion and broadens access to financial services by capitalizing on technological advances. Fintech mitigates the risks and lack of information associated with underserved households and small and medium-sized enterprises (SMEs) via digital financial services and enhanced risk-assessment skills. Specialized digital banking businesses serve specific sectors and demographic groups

Figure B4: Total Investment Activity in Fintech—Venture Capital, Private Equity, and Mergers and Acquisitions

	2013	2014	2015	2016	2017	2018
Deal Count	1,132	1,543	1,925	1,893	2,165	2,196
Capital Invested (USD billion)	18.9	45.4	67.1	63.4	50.8	111.8

Source: Asian Development Bank chart based on data from Consultancy.eu. 2019. *Global FinTech Investment More than Doubled to $112 billion*. https://www.consultancy.eu/news/2390/global-fintech-investment-more-than-doubled-to-112-billion.

---

[a] This box was written by Donghyun Park (Principal Economist) and Shu Tian (Economist) in the Economic Research and Regional Cooperation Department of the Asian Development Bank.

continued on next page

Box 4: Fintech for Inclusive Growth and Pandemic Resilience *continued*

via business-to-consumer and business-to-business debit and credit extended to underbanked and unbanked individuals, households, and SMEs. In doing so, fintech not only improves the variety and efficiency of financial services, but also enhances financial inclusion. According to the Asian Development Bank (ADB) (2017), digital financial solutions can address about 40% of unmet demand for payment services and about 20% of credit requirements of poor households and small businesses in Asia.[b]

Fintech's role as a driver of financial inclusion is especially pronounced in financially underdeveloped emerging markets. Qamruzzaman and Wei (2019) document a positive association between financial innovation and financial inclusion in a sample of six South Asian countries.[c] CBInsights (2019) show that customers in emerging African markets have benefited from digital microfinance, especially mobile payments, microcredit, and saving accounts.[d] ADB plays an important role in supporting financial inclusion via fintech across developing Asia.[e] For example, ADB supported an artificial-intelligence-enabled credit score system that helped more than 8,000 SMEs in the Greater Mekong Subregion obtain credit of USD50,000 each. ADB also supported a cloud-based banking app in the Philippines and branchless banking in Indonesia, contributing to financial inclusion in member economies of the Association of Southeast Asian Nations. Asia is now a major player riding the global fintech wave, hosting 34 out of the top 100 global fintech innovators at the end of 2019.[f]

The role of fintech in improving financial inclusion comes to the fore during big economic shocks such as the COVID-19 pandemic. The poor suffer disproportionately during such shocks. Their hardship is exacerbated by lack of access to financial services, and they often do not have online bank accounts. Even in advanced economies like the United States, delivering financial assistance to the unemployed and small businesses has emerged as a major problem during the COVID-19 pandemic. The nimbleness and flexibility of fintech can mitigate such problems. For example, on 14 April 2020, PayPal and other fintech companies in the United States were approved to participate in a government program to extend loans to small businesses.

The COVID-19 crisis creates opportunities to further expand the role of fintech in financial inclusion in developing economies. Fintech can not only contribute to inclusive growth but also contribute to the economic resilience of the poor and SMEs in times of economic shock. Developing economies can harness fintech to keep the poor and SMEs connected to the financial system even in the face of a crisis such as a pandemic. In particular, fintech can unlock new sources of finance for groups that are underserved by banks and other traditional financial institutions. In addition, fintech can enable banks and lenders to extend funds more quickly and smoothly to these groups, which is critical during major economic shocks.

In developing Asia, fintech companies are coming up with innovative solutions to fund SMEs struggling to stay afloat amid COVID-19. They are providing new turn-key loan origination and underwriting platforms to allow banks and lenders to provide financing for small businesses. These platforms encompass risk assessment and insurance capabilities. Fintech also offers innovative finance solutions that are valuable to low-income groups during pandemics. For instance, the Indonesian ride-hailing delivery start-up GO-JEK offers a cash-in, cash-out platform for financial services. India's EKO, a financial transactions platform, is trying to create "human automated teller machines" out of anyone with a mobile phone and a little cash.

While financial innovation promotes financial inclusion, it also raises regulatory challenges such as cybersecurity, other technical vulnerabilities, data governance, and privacy protection. At a broader level, regulators must strike the right balance between enabling fintech innovations that benefit the poor and SMEs while also monitoring and managing the risks associated with innovation. Given the frenetic pace of innovation in the fintech sector, which is likely to pick up even more speed in the increasingly digital post-COVID-19 world, regulatory capacity must be strengthened to keep pace with change. Finally, developing economies must make digital infrastructure investments to improve the interface between the digital and nondigital economies for the poor.

---

[b] ADB. 2017. *Accelerating Financial Inclusion in Southeast Asia with Digital Finance.* https://www.adb.org/sites/default/files/publication/222061/financial-inclusion-se-asia.pdf.
[c] M. Qamruzzaman and J. Wei. 2019. Financial Innovation and Financial Inclusion Nexus in South Asian Countries: Evidence from Symmetric and Asymmetric Panel Investigation. *International Journal of Financial Studies.* 7(4). pp. 1–27.
[d] CBInsights. 2019. *Global Fintech Report Q3 2019.* https://www.cbinsights.com/research/report/fintech-trends-q3-2019/.
[e] Developing Asia comprises the 46 developing member economies of ADB.
[f] D. Ngo. 2019. *Top 100 Fintech Companies Repartition Map, 2019 Fintech100, H2 Ventures/KPMG, November 2019.* https://fintechnews.hk/10385/various/top-fintech-companies-asia/attachment/top-100-fintech-companies-repartition-map-2019-fintech100-h2-ventureskpmg-november-2019/.

Box 5: Financing Firms during the COVID-19 Pandemic

The coronavirus disease (COVID-19) outbreak has imposed a heavy toll on economic activity worldwide.[a] Because of the rapid transmission of the virus, social distancing measures have been applied to save lives and avoid the collapse of health-care systems, which in turn has led to a synchronized downfall in economic activity around the world and has had a significant impact in financial markets (**Figure B5**).

In contrast with the global financial crisis, the shock did not originate in the financial sector. This has important implications for the menu of options available for policy makers, who must be creative until the health crisis is resolved. Currently, economies are facing a combination of supply and demand shocks, as well as the interruption of relationships between firms and their stakeholders, leading to a collapse in corporate cash flows. Firms have struggled to survive as their working capital gets depleted. A firm's ability to continue operating during the pandemic shock thus depends on whether it can raise additional financing and adjust expenses. Although it alone is not enough, a well-functioning financial system can help firms stay alive and preserve their relationships with stakeholders.

Policy makers can play a role in stabilizing the economy by working with the financial sector to keep firms afloat. However, because of the unique characteristics of the current crisis, the first set of policies relates to adapting the institutional framework, while a second set is linked to the provision of credit to firms.

Adapting the Institutional Framework

Although financial systems have worked as expected, they are ill equipped to cope with a shock like COVID-19 because they are geared toward detecting idiosyncratic risk when it arises (e.g., an increased credit score of nonperforming loans). However, during the COVID-19 crisis, signaling firms in trouble would not be very informative, given that most firms have suffered a sizable and unexpected negative external shock. To the extent that financial sector stability can be preserved, allowing forbearance and avoiding undue increases in borrowing costs might be necessary.

An important margin of adjustment is choosing which firms to apply such forbearance measures to. On the one

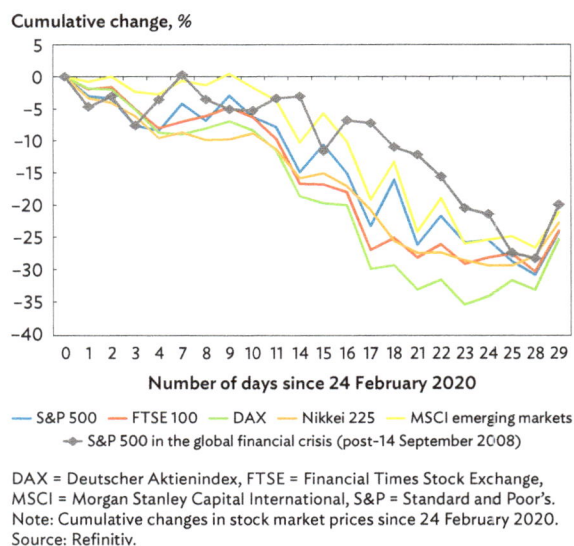

Figure B5: Decline in Global Stock Markets

Cumulative change, %

DAX = Deutscher Aktienindex, FTSE = Financial Times Stock Exchange, MSCI = Morgan Stanley Capital International, S&P = Standard and Poor's.
Note: Cumulative changes in stock market prices since 24 February 2020.
Source: Refinitiv.

hand, while universal application is easy to implement and increases the chance of survival for all firms, it creates significant risks for banks if they impose no conditions on firms. On the other hand, policies that allow for some screening of firms would probably entail smaller transfers and reduced fiscal costs, though screening could delay implementation and would not offer the same chance of survival for all existing firms.

Providing Credit to Firms

Policy makers around the world have considered several options to enhance the provision of credit to firms. Central banks have quickly responded by lowering interest rates. However, standard monetary policy measures might have limited effects during the COVID-19 outbreak because of the uncertainty surrounding the shock and measures to contain it, and limited scope to reduce already low interest rates.

Central banks have thus turned to liquidity measures, while governments have stepped in with policies that absorb the extra credit risk and transfer the increased liquidity into

---

[a]   This box was written by Sergio Schmukler, Lead Economist and Acting Research Manager for the Development Research Group of the World Bank. This text box summarizes the following World Bank publications: T. Didier, F. Huneeus, M. Larrain, and S. L. Schmukler. 2020. Financing Firms in Hibernation During the COVID-19 Pandemic. *Working Paper*. No. 9236. http://documents.worldbank.org/curated/en/818801588952012929/Financing-Firms-in-Hibernation-during-the-COVID-19-Pandemic; and T. Didier, F. Huneeus, M. Larrain, and S. L. Schmukler. 2020. Financing Firms in Hibernation During the COVID-19 Pandemic. *Research and Policy Briefs*. No. 30. http://documents.worldbank.org/curated/en/228811586799856319/Financing-Firms-in-Hibernation-During-the-COVID-19-Pandemic.

continued on next page

Box 5: Financing Firms during the COVID-19 Pandemic   *continued*

the real economy. For large companies, governments have supported financing through capital markets by, for example, purchasing corporate liabilities to be resold once the firm has recovered. For small and medium-sized enterprises (SMEs), who mostly rely on bank financing, governments have capitalized state-owned banks and/or scaled up public credit guarantee programs. Some economies with fairly well-developed capital markets have moved toward allowing the central bank or the government to engage in large-scale purchases of SME loans. Other central banks have developed lending facilities to encourage investors to purchase securities collateralized by a portfolio of SME loans. All of these measures seek to provide incentives to banks to lend to firms.

Policies aimed at transferring credit risk to the government should be designed to minimize the cost to public coffers and should benefit from two characteristics. First, scale is crucial to allow for risk diversification as not all firms and industries have been equally affected. Second, providing incentives for both creditors and debtors is also important to avoid irresponsible lending by banks and moral hazard by firms. For example, public credit guarantees should be partial so that banks have an incentive to monitor and screen borrowers. Regarding firms, their challenge is to avoid the ex-post moral hazard problem of not repaying loans.

Conclusion

Governments have limited resources so they must prioritize and evaluate the trade-offs associated with different policies. Their assistance may be needed now more than ever as banks and investors face unprecedented uncertainty.

There are stark differences between developed and developing economies regarding the scope for policy action. Economies with shallower financial markets, less fiscal space, and more constrained central banks will face greater challenges in channeling credit to struggling firms. With the rise in global risk, developing economies have faced a sudden stop in capital inflows, rising costs to issue new debt in capital markets, and a sharp depreciation of domestic currencies. These significant macroeconomic challenges, combined with the large financing needs that have arisen amid the pandemic shock, could trigger widespread sovereign debt restructurings.[a] This could be followed by widespread turbulence in the corporate sector, especially in economies where firms entered the pandemic shock with high outstanding debt levels. The liquidity issues in developing economies might thus rapidly turn into solvency problems— and not only at the firm level. Multilateral policy action, involving international financial institutions and creditor economies, could help resolve a common threat facing many developing economies.

---

[a] O. Blanchard. 2020. *What It Will Take to Save the Economy from COVID-19*. Presentation for a Peterson Institute for International Economics Webinar. 6 April; P.-O. Gourinchas and C.-T. Hsieh. 2020. The COVID-19 Default Time Bomb. *Project Syndicate*. 9 April.

Financial Architecture and Innovation

Access to finance is indispensable for innovative activity, which is inherently costly, risky, and subject to a great deal of uncertainty.[10] There is almost no way of knowing beforehand whether a particular innovation will turn out to be commercially successful. It is even more difficult to predict whether an innovator can turn his vision into a viable reality. In addition, not even the greatest inventions could take off in the absence of financing. For example, while we associate Apple with Steve Jobs, the iconic tech giant would never have made it without the bold, high-risk investment of Mike Markkula, an angel investor who provided critical seed money and managerial support during Apple's embryonic phase. A sound and efficient financial system that can channel resources to would-be innovators is a crucial component of a viable innovation environment.

In this special chapter, we take a closer look at the link between finance and innovation using cross-economy empirical analysis. We delve into the issue of whether financial intermediaries (e.g., banks) or capital markets (e.g., equity markets) are more conducive to innovation. The details of our empirical analysis are outlined in **Box 6**. There are strong conceptual grounds for why financial architecture matters for innovation. Intuitively, capital markets are better at dealing with risk and uncertainty than banks, which tend to be more conservative. But innovative activity is inherently full of risk and uncertainty. This is why capital markets are likely to matter more for innovation than banks.

Given the widely varying levels of economic development across developing Asia, we also examine whether an economy's income level affects our analytical comparison of intermediaries versus markets.[11] Although the region's financial system has historically been bank-centered, capital markets have expanded rapidly in recent decades and now play a large and growing role in financing. There is also a wide variation in financial development and maturity among the region's economies, ranging from global financial centers such as Hong Kong, China and Singapore to less developed economies with rudimentary capital markets.

The baseline results show that financial structure matters disproportionately to the innovation of an industry in an economy for the full sample of 47 economies from 1997 to 2016. In particular, we find that market-based financial systems, as represented by both the equity market and debt market, have a positive and significant effect on the quantity of innovation, as measured by the number of patents granted. The results of additional analysis indicate that the equity and debt markets also have a positive and significant effect on the quality of innovation, as measured by citation-based quality metrics and claim-based quality metrics. However, intermediary-based financial systems (i.e., banks) fail to encourage innovation and even lower the quality of innovation.

Additional analysis explores whether financial architecture matters differently for small versus large firms. To the extent that some small firms eventually grow into large firms, we can interpret size as a proxy for a firm's development stage. We find that even though the positive effect of a market-based financial system holds for both types of firms, only an equity-based financial system can improve the innovation of small firms. In contrast, a more developed debt market impedes the innovation of small firms but contributes to the innovation of large firms.

The final analysis examines whether financial system architecture matters differently for economies with different levels of national income. High-income and low-income economies are significantly different in their financial architecture, economic growth, and innovation. These differences raise the question of whether it is appropriate to apply a one-size-fit-all approach in analyzing the finance–innovation link. We find that compared to innovation in low-income economies, innovation in high-income economies is more likely to benefit from a market-based financial system and to be impeded by an intermediary-based financial system. In addition, we find that while the development of the equity market benefits the innovation of small firms in both types of economies, it impedes the innovation of large firms in low-income economies. In contrast, large

---

[10] This theme chapter is a revised version of Z. Huang and X. Tian. 2020. Does One Size Fit All? Financial Architecture and Innovation in the 21st Century. Background paper prepared for the *Asian Development Outlook 2020*. https://www.adb.org/documents/asian-development-outlook-2020-background-papers.
[11] Developing Asia comprises the 46 developing member economies of the Asian Development Bank.

Box 6: Econometric Analysis of the Relationship between Financial Architecture and Innovation

We collected innovation and financial architecture information for 47 economies with mixed financial structures and at least one patent granted by the United States Patent and Trademark Office (USPTO).[a] We also collected annual financial market development data and other economy-level information from the World Bank's World Development Indicators and Global Financial Development databases. Since our goal was to compare the degree of innovation in different types of financial system architecture, we restrict their sample to the period 1997–2016 for economies with mixed financial architecture and at least one patent granted by the USPTO as of March 2019. The result is a sample of 47 economies that includes both developed economies such as Canada, Japan, and the United Kingdom, as well as emerging economies such as Brazil and the People's Republic of China.

The quantity of innovation is measured by the number of patents in a two-digit US standard industrial classification industry j that are applied in year t and eventually granted and assigned to individuals or nongovernmental institutions from economy i. We follow the classification of the USPTO and construct Patent_Small as the number of patents filed by small entities and define Patent_Large to capture the rest. We also measure the quality of innovation based on the innovativeness and exclusiveness of patents, proxied by the numbers of citations and independent claims. Financial architecture is captured by the proxies for the level of development of the equity market, private debt market, and financial intermediaries such as deposit money banks and other financial institutions. All the proxies are divided by an economy's gross domestic product.

We further control for several other variables for each economy-year. These characteristics may capture some time-varying features of the economy and are likely to affect both innovation and the development of the financial system. The summary statistics suggest that both the equity market and the intermediary-based financial system are important for the economies in our sample since both occupy a larger portion of gross domestic product than that of the debt market on average.

The main obstacle that hinders any empirical attempt to study the causal effects of financial development on technological innovation is the potential for endogeneity resulting from reverse causality. In this context, the reverse causality concern is really about whether innovation, an important factor for economic growth, renders disproportional changes to the structure of the financial system. We attempt to deal with this endogeneity problem by using a panel-based, fixed-effects approach that has been widely adopted. In particular, we add the fixed effects to each economy–industry pair as well as to each year to capture the unobserved heterogeneity within the groups.

We thus examine the effects of financial architecture on innovation using a fixed-effects approach. In the economy–industry–year level data, the basic regression we estimate is the following:

$$y_{i,j,t+1} = \beta_0 + \beta_1 Equity_{it} + \beta_2 Debt_{it} + \beta_3 Bank_{it} + \rho Controls_{it} \\ + \delta_{i,j} + \mu_t + \delta_{i,j,t+1} \tag{1}$$

where $y_{i,j,t+1}$ is one of the relative innovation measures for each industry j of economy i at time t. We add a 1-year lag in all our explanatory variables to alleviate the concern of reverse causality. By adding the economy–industry fixed effect $\delta_{i,j}$, our coefficient estimates are identified by the variation within each industry of an economy. Thus, the fixed effect absorbs any time-invariant difference across different economies and across different industries in an economy. In addition, we add year fixed effect μ_t to further mitigate the variation of common trends in the economy over time. Following practice in the literature, standard errors are clustered by economy and industry, and adjusted for heteroscedasticity. Our tests center on both the sign and the significance of the estimated β_1, β_2, and β_3.

Table B6 reports the baseline results for a test of the relationship between financial architecture and the quantity of innovation, measured by the number of patents granted. The table only reports the results for the three variables of interest: equity, debt, and bank.

Table B6: Financial Architecture and Innovation

	Relative Number of Patents			
Equity	0.017***			0.030***
	(2.74)			(5.20)
Debt		0.041***		0.047***
		(4.10)		(3.36)
Bank			0.008	−0.020
			(0.40)	(−0.81)
N	28,841	20,445	28,761	20,445
adj. R^2	0.912	0.912	0.912	0.912

Notes: *** indicate statistical significance at the 1% level. The numbers in parentheses represent t-statistics.
Sources: Authors' calculations.

---

[a]   This box is a revised version of Z. Huang and X. Tian. 2020. Does One Size Fit All? Financial Architecture and Innovation in the 21st Century. Background paper prepared for the *Asian Development Outlook 2020*. https://www.adb.org/documents/asian-development-outlook-2020-background-papers.

firms in low-income economies are more likely to benefit from an intermediary-based financial system than a market-based one.

The primary focus of this special chapter was empirical analysis of the effect of financial architecture (i.e., banks and other financial intermediaries, debt markets, and equity markets) on innovation quantity and quality. However, as much as finance can affect innovation, innovation can also affect finance. Financial technology, or the integration of new technology and financial services, is currently reshaping the global financial landscape. Financial technology can potentially become a powerful agent for financial inclusion, which can contribute to inclusive growth. The financing modalities analyzed in this section are by no means complete or comprehensive. Precisely because innovation is an inherently risky and uncertain process, financing innovation has given rise to more specialized forms of financing modalities that are capable of mobilizing and allocating seed money. Silicon Valley is replete with sophisticated mechanisms for channeling risk capital, with venture capital being one well-known example.

Market Summaries

People's Republic of China

Yield Movements

The People's Republic of China's (PRC) yield curve for local currency (LCY) bonds steepened between 28 February and 15 May, driven by a much larger decrease in yields at the shorter-end of the curve (**Figure 1**). Yields fell by an average of 70 basis points (bps) for tenors of 3 years or less. For tenors between 5 years and 10 years, yields fell an average of 29 bps. The yield for the 30-year tenor rose 9 bps. As a result, the 2-year versus 10-year yield spread rose from 50 bps to 117 bps during the review period.

Yields in the PRC fell largely over the ongoing economic impact of the coronavirus disease (COVID-19), which has curtailed both consumer demand and manufacturing supply. In addition, the global impact of COVID-19 has negatively affected PRC exports. This led to the PRC's gross domestic product declining 6.8% year-on-year (y-o-y) in the first quarter (Q1) of 2020 after 6.0% y-o-y growth in the previous quarter. Exports in March also declined, falling 6.6% y-o-y. April exports staged a rebound, rising 3.5% y-o-y. However, the rise in exports was largely the result of production backlogs from previous orders that were not completed when quarantine measures were implemented. Inflation also softened, with the inflation rate coming in at 3.3% y-o-y in April versus 4.3% y-o-y in March.

As a result of the economic contraction, the PRC was forced to implement further monetary easing. On 29 March, the People's Bank of China (PBOC) reduced the 7-day repurchase rate by 20 bps to 2.20%. The PBOC also reduced the rate it charges on its medium-term lending facility by 20 bps to 2.95% on 15 April. On 19 April, it also reduced the rate on the 1-year loan prime rate by 20 bps to 3.85%.

Size and Composition

The PRC's outstanding LCY bonds climbed 4.9% quarter-on-quarter (q-o-q) in Q1 2020, after gaining 2.8% q-o-q in the fourth quarter (Q4) of 2019, to reach CNY88.3 trillion

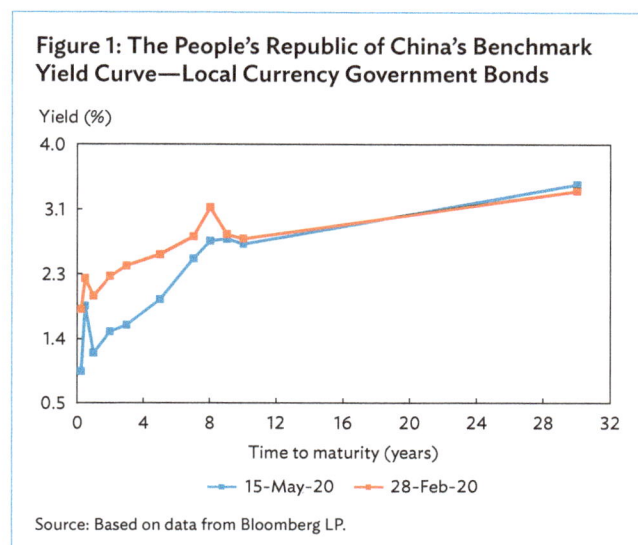

Figure 1: The People's Republic of China's Benchmark Yield Curve—Local Currency Government Bonds

Source: Based on data from Bloomberg LP.

(USD12.4 trillion). LCY bonds grew 16.1% y-o-y in Q1 2020 (**Table 1**).

Government bonds. The growth of government bonds outstanding in the PRC accelerated to 3.5% q-o-q in Q1 2020 after growth of 2.0% in the previous quarter. Growth was driven by an increase in local government bond issuance, which surged more than eightfold on a q-o-q basis to CNY1.6 trillion in Q1 2020, leading to a 6.6% q-o-q increase in local government bonds outstanding. The increase in issuance was driven both by a low base effect, as local governments had completed their bond issuance quotas before Q4 2019, and by the granting of the 2020 bond issuance quota totaling CNY1.8 trillion. Specifically, the State Council issued a directive on 17 March to accelerate bond issuance and the use of proceeds. Treasury bonds and other government bonds fell 0.9% q-o-q in Q1 2020, while policy bank bonds grew 1.8% q-o-q in the same period.

Corporate bonds. Growth in the PRC's corporate bond market accelerated in Q1 2020 to 7.3% q-o-q from 4.1% q-o-q in Q4 2019. The rise in corporate bonds was helped in part by regulations issued in March simplifying

Table 1: Size and Composition of the Local Currency Bond Market in the People's Republic of China

| | Outstanding Amount (billion) | | | | | | Growth Rates (%) | | | |
| | Q1 2019 | | Q4 2019 | | Q1 2020 | | Q1 2019 | | Q1 2020 | |
	CNY	USD	CNY	USD	CNY	USD	q-o-q	y-o-y	q-o-q	y-o-y
Total	76,012	11,325	84,185	12,090	88,270	12,464	3.0	16.7	4.9	16.1
Government	49,061	7,309	53,986	7,753	55,852	7,886	2.5	16.1	3.5	13.8
Treasury Bonds and Other Government Bonds	14,882	2,217	16,698	2,398	16,850	2,379	(0.3)	10.6	0.9	13.2
Central Bank Bonds	2	0	22	3	19	3	–	–	(15.9)	1,133.3
Policy Bank Bonds	14,776	2,201	15,695	2,254	15,985	2,257	1.8	8.6	1.8	8.2
Local Government Bonds	19,401	2,890	21,571	3,098	22,999	3,247	5.2	27.6	6.6	18.5
Corporate	26,951	4,015	30,199	4,337	32,418	4,577	4.1	17.8	7.3	20.3
Policy Bank Bonds										
China Development Bank	8,328	1,241	8,704	1,250	8,875	1,253	2.2	10.0	2.0	6.6
Export–Import Bank of China	2,444	364	2,735	393	2,858	404	1.9	4.9	4.5	17.0
Agricultural Devt. Bank of China	4,005	597	4,256	611	4,252	600	0.8	8.2	(0.1)	6.2

( ) = negative, – = not applicable, CNY = Chinese yuan, q-o-q = quarter-on-quarter, Q1 = first quarter, Q4 = fourth quarter, USD = United States dollar, y-o-y = year-on-year.
Notes:
1. Calculated using data from national sources.
2. Treasury bonds include savings bonds and local government bonds.
3. Bloomberg LP end-of-period local currency–USD rates are used.
4. Growth rates are calculated from local currency base and do not include currency effects.
Sources: CEIC and Bloomberg LP.

Table 2: Corporate Bonds Outstanding in Key Categories

| | Amount (CNY billion) | | | Growth Rate (%) | | | |
| | Q1 2019 | Q4 2019 | Q1 2020 | Q1 2019 | | Q1 2020 | |
				q-o-q	y-o-y	q-o-q	y-o-y
Financial Bonds	4,744	5,832	6,364	1.0	28.7	9.1	34.2
Enterprise Bonds	3,872	3,793	3,707	1.0	(11.7)	(2.3)	(4.3)
Listed Corporate Bonds	6,608	7,724	8,328	1.0	21.5	7.8	26.0
Commercial Paper	2,240	1,994	2,671	1.1	26.9	34.0	19.2
Medium-Term Notes	5,813	6,333	6,829	1.1	19.4	7.8	17.5
Asset-Backed Securities	1,728	2,416	2,388	1.0	72.4	(1.2)	38.2

( ) = negative, CNY = Chinese yuan, q-o-q = quarter-on-quarter, Q1 = first quarter, Q4 = fourth quarter, y-o-y = year-on-year.
Source: CEIC.

the issuance process for listed corporate bonds and enterprise bonds.

The new regulations led to strong growth in listed corporate bonds, which grew 7.8% q-o-q in Q1 2020 (**Table 2**). Increased financial uncertainty and expectations of further declines in interest rates led to commercial paper outstanding rising 34.0% q-o-q on a surge in issuance of 46.9% q-o-q (**Figure 2**). Issuance of financial bonds also rose 50.6% q-o-q in Q1 2020 as financial institutions sought to bolster their capital base and liquidity.

The PRC's LCY corporate bond market continued to be dominated by a few big issuers in Q1 2020 (**Table 3**).

At the end of March, the top 30 corporate bond issuers accounted for a combined CNY8.9 trillion worth of corporate bonds outstanding, representing 27.5% of the total corporate bond stock. Of the top 30, the 10 largest issuers accounted for an aggregate CNY5.7 trillion. China Railway, the top issuer, had four times the outstanding amount of bonds as Industrial and Commercial Bank of China, the second-largest issuer. The top 30 issuers included 15 banks, which continued to generate funding to strengthen their capital bases, improve liquidity, and lengthen their maturity profiles amid ongoing uncertainty.

Table 4 lists the largest corporate bond issuances in the PRC in Q1 2020. The top issuers consisted largely of

Figure 2: Corporate Bond Issuance in Key Sectors

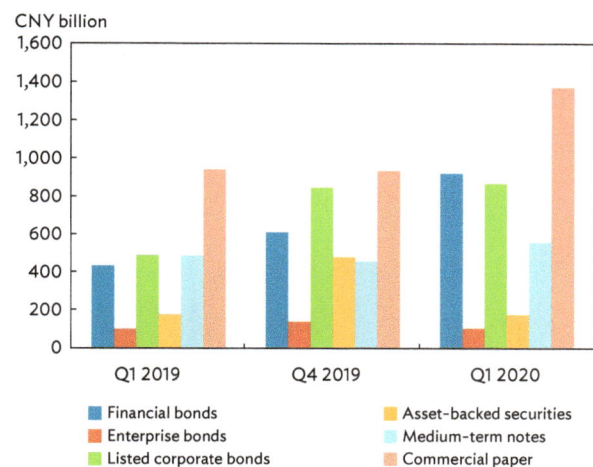

CNY = Chinese yuan, Q1 = first quarter, Q4 = fourth quarter.
Source: *ChinaBond.*

financial institutions that sought to improve their capital bases and liquidity in light of the ongoing economic impact of COVID-19.

Investor Profile

Among the major government bond categories (local government, Treasury, and policy bank bonds), banks were the single-largest holder at the end of March, with a 73.0% share of all outstanding government bonds (**Figure 3**). The concentration of banks' ownership of bonds was highest for local government bonds (87.9%), as banks were asked by the government to help support the funding efforts of local governments. Policy banks were the next largest holder of local government bonds. Unincorporated products were the second-largest holder of policy bank bonds after banks.[12]

Liquidity

The volume of interest rate swaps fell 10.2% q-o-q in Q1 2020. The 7-day repurchase agreement remained the most used interest rate swap, comprising a 79.2% share of the total interest rate swap volume during the quarter (**Table 5**).

Policy, Institutional, and Regulatory Developments

National Development and Reform Commission Eases Bond Issuance Regulations

In March, the National Development and Reform Commission launched a registration-based system for the public issuance of enterprise and corporate bonds to replace the previous approval-based corporate and enterprise bond issuance system. Starting 1 March, the National Development and Reform Commission began registering the issuance of enterprise bonds if a firm's average distributable profits over the last 3 years were enough to cover 1 year of interest. The new system was expected to reduce the issuance period of enterprise bonds to 2 weeks from 2–6 months.

People's Bank of China Reduces Reserve Requirement Ratios for Small Banks

In April, PBOC announced a reduction in the reserve requirement ratio for small banks by a total of 100 bps, a 50-bps cut each on 15 April and 15 May. The reductions released a total of around CNY400 billion into the domestic economy, which has been negatively impacted by the outbreak of COVID-19. The PBOC has stepped up its policy easing measures since February, cutting the benchmark leading rate and encouraging banks to offer cheap loans to firms hit hardest by the pandemic.

---

[12] Unincorporated products include banks' wealth management products, securities investment funds, trust funds, and insurance products.

Table 3: Top 30 Issuers of Local Currency Corporate Bonds in the People's Republic of China

	Issuers	Outstanding Amount		State-Owned	Listed Company	Type of Industry
		LCY Bonds (CNY billion)	LCY Bonds (USD billion)			
1.	China Railway	2,098.5	296.3	Yes	No	Transportation
2.	Industrial and Commercial Bank of China	517.6	73.1	Yes	Yes	Banking
3.	Agricultural Bank of China	500.1	70.6	Yes	Yes	Banking
4.	Bank of China	491.2	69.4	Yes	Yes	Banking
5.	Central Huijin Investment	443.0	62.6	Yes	No	Asset Management
6.	State Grid Corporation of China	358.0	50.5	Yes	No	Public Utilities
7.	Bank of Communications	351.5	49.6	No	Yes	Banking
8.	Shanghai Pudong Development Bank	325.5	46.0	No	Yes	Banking
9.	China Construction Bank	307.1	43.4	Yes	Yes	Banking
10.	China CITIC Bank	291.8	41.2	No	Yes	Banking
11.	China National Petroleum	274.9	38.8	Yes	No	Energy
12.	China Minsheng Banking	234.0	33.0	No	Yes	Banking
13.	Industrial Bank	216.2	30.5	No	Yes	Banking
14.	State Power Investment	202.3	28.6	Yes	No	Energy
15.	PetroChina	195.0	27.5	Yes	Yes	Energy
16.	Tianjin Infrastructure Construction and Investment Group	171.0	24.1	Yes	No	Industrial
17.	China Merchants Bank	169.4	23.9	Yes	Yes	Banking
18.	China Southern Power Grid	167.0	23.6	Yes	No	Energy
19.	China Everbright Bank	164.2	23.2	Yes	Yes	Banking
20.	Ping An Bank	163.7	23.1	No	Yes	Banking
21.	Postal Savings Bank of China	155.0	21.9	Yes	Yes	Banking
22.	Huaxia Bank	155.0	21.9	Yes	No	Banking
23.	CITIC Securities	142.8	20.2	Yes	Yes	Brokerage
24.	Datong Coal Mine Group	135.3	19.1	Yes	No	Coal
25.	Bank of Beijing	132.9	18.8	No	Yes	Banking
26.	Shaanxi Coal and Chemical Industry Group	125.5	17.7	Yes	No	Energy
27.	China Cinda Asset Management	115.0	16.2	Yes	Yes	Asset Management
28.	Shougang Group	108.5	15.3	Yes	No	Steel
29.	China Datang	107.7	15.2	Yes	Yes	Energy
30.	China Three Gorges Corporation	105.0	14.8	Yes	No	Power
	Total Top 30 LCY Corporate Issuers	**8,924.6**	**1,260.1**			
	Total LCY Corporate Bonds	**32,417.6**	**4,577.3**			
	Top 30 as % of Total LCY Corporate Bonds	**27.5%**	**27.5%**			

CNY = Chinese yuan, LCY = local currency, USD = United States dollar.
Notes:
1. Data as of 31 March 2020.
2. State-owned firms are defined as those in which the government has more than a 50% ownership stake.
Source: *AsianBondsOnline* calculations based on Bloomberg LP data.

Table 4: Notable Local Currency Corporate Bond Issuance in the First Quarter of 2020

Corporate Issuers	Coupon Rate (%)	Issued Amount (CNY billion)
Central Huijin Investment		
3-year bond	3.15	15
3-year bond	2.75	15
5-year bond	3.55	6
5-year bond	3.02	6
Bank of Beijing		
3-year bond	2.85	30
5-year bond	3.10	10
China CITIC Bank		
3-year bond	2.75	30

Corporate Issuers	Coupon Rate (%)	Issued Amount (CNY billion)
China Southern Power Grid		
3-year bond	3.30	5
3-year bond	3.30	5
3-year bond	2.94	4
3-year bond	2.90	4
5-year bond	3.19	4
CITIC Securities		
3-year bond	2.95	2
3-year bond	3.02	2
5-year bond	3.20	2
5-year bond	3.31	2

CNY = Chinese yuan.
Source: Based on data from Bloomberg LP.

Figure 3: Government Bonds Investor Profile

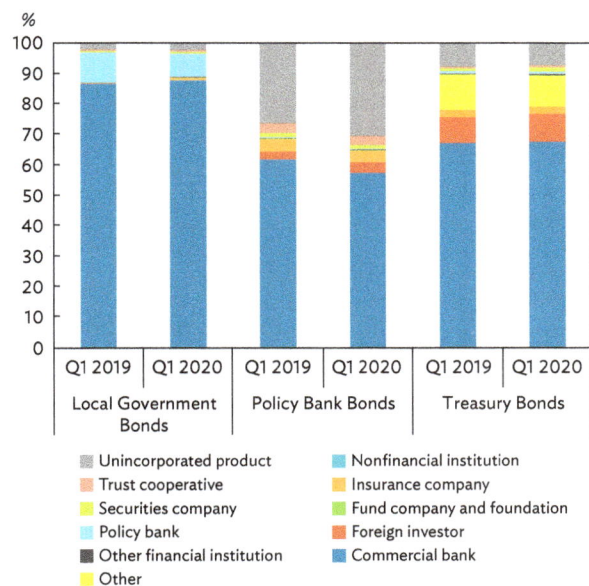

Q1 = first quarter.
Source: Bloomberg LP.

Table 5: Notional Values of the People's Republic of China's Interest Rate Swap Market in the First Quarter of 2020

Interest Rate Swap Benchmarks	Notional Amount (CNY billion)	Share of Total Notional Amount (%)	Growth Rate (%)
	Q1 2020		q-o-q
7-Day Repo Rate	2.0	0.00	(100.0)
7-Day Repo Rate (Deposit Institutions)	33,950.5	79.21	3.7
Overnight SHIBOR	234.0	0.55	170.5
3-Month SHIBOR	7,799.3	18.20	(45.2)
1-Year Lending Rate	728.5	1.70	77.8
5-Year Lending Rate	25.6	0.06	39.7
10-Year Treasury Yield	62.0	0.14	(61.1)
10-Year China Development Bank Bond/10-Year Government Bond Yield	61.0	0.14	(34.1)
Total	**42,862.9**	**100.00**	**(10.2)**

( ) = negative, CNY = Chinese yuan, q-o-q = quarter-on-quarter, Q1 = first quarter,
Repo = repurchase, SHIBOR = Shanghai Interbank Offered Rate.
Note: Growth rate computed based on notional amounts.
Sources: *AsianBondsOnline* and *ChinaMoney*.

Hong Kong, China

Yield Movements

Between 28 February and 15 May, local currency (LCY) government bond yields in Hong Kong, China fell across all tenors, shifting the yield curve downward (**Figure 1**). The drop was more pronounced at the shorter-end of the curve as tenors with maturities of 1 year or below shed an average of 94 basis points (bps). For longer-dated bonds with maturities of 10 years or more, yields fell an average of 50 bps. The 15-year tenor posted the smallest drop at 49 bps.

Hong Kong, China's yield curve was inverted at the beginning of the review period with the spread between the 2-year and 10-year yields at –4 bps. The yield curve had normalized by the end of the review period, with the spread between 2-year and 10-year bonds back in positive territory at 24 bps.

Hong Kong, China's government bond yields tracked United States (US) Treasury yields during the review period. The US yield curve shifted downward, with yields of tenors with maturities of 1 year or below falling an average of 110 bps, and tenors with maturities of 10 years or longer dropping 43 bps on average. The decline in US yields stemmed from a sharp interest rate drop as the Federal Reserve cut the federal funds rate twice in March in response to the coronavirus disease (COVID-19) pandemic. The two rate cuts—a 50-bps cut on 3 March and a 100-bps cut on 15 March—lowered the federal funds target to a range of between 0.0% and 0.25%. To further mitigate risks and address volatility in financial markets, the Federal Reserve also expanded its repo operations and resumed purchasing Treasury and mortgage-backed securities.

To maintain the Hong Kong dollar's peg to the US dollar, the Hong Kong Monetary Authority (HKMA) lowered its base rate by 50 bps to 1.50% on 4 March. In response to the subsequent 100-bps cut by the US Federal Reserve, the HKMA again lowered the base rate to 0.86% on 16 March based on a pre-set formula.[16] Demand for the Hong Kong dollar surged in April, fueled by carry trade activities brought about by the gap between the

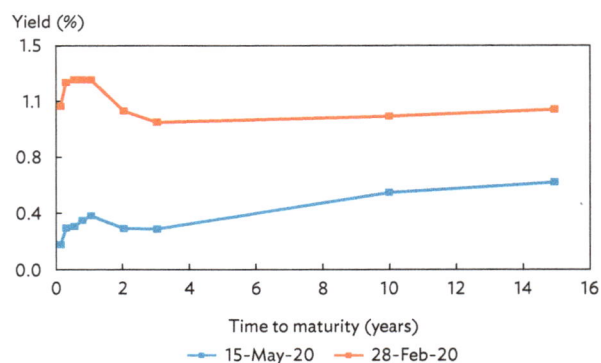

Figure 1: Hong Kong, China's Benchmark Yield Curve— Exchange Fund Bills and Notes

Source: Based on data from Bloomberg LP.

Hong Kong Interbank Offered Rates (HIBORs) over US interest rates, which combined with seasonal and equity-related demand as high-profile initial public offerings resumed in Hong Kong, China's stock market.

The heightened demand for the Hong Kong dollar pushed the strong-side of its trading band against the US dollar, prompting the HKMA to spend a total of HKD20.7 billion to rein in the local currency in April. A series of HKMA interventions brought the aggregate balance—an indicator of liquidity in the financial system—to HKD84.7 billion, up 55.7% year-to-date by the end of April. To inject further liquidity into the market, the HKMA also reduced it issuance of Exchange Fund Bills (EFBs) by HKD20.0 billion between April and May. By 15 May, the aggregate balance reached HKD94.7 billion, up 74.1% since the start of the year. Consequently, domestic interest rates dropped, with the overnight HIBOR at 0.07% and the 1-month HIBOR at 0.64%.

Falling yields also reflected the contraction of Hong Kong, China's economy. The economic recession deepened in Q1 2020 as the onset of COVID-19 disrupted the economy already battered by the combined impacts of trade tensions between the US and the People's Republic of China (PRC), as well as prolonged political unrest. Gross domestic product (GDP) dropped sharply by 8.9%

---

[13]   The base rate is set at either 50 bps above the lower end of the prevailing target range of the US federal funds rate or the average 5-day moving average of the overnight and 1-month Hong Kong Interbank Offered Rates (HIBORs), whichever is higher. As of 15 March, the 5-day moving average of the overnight and 1-month HIBORs was 0.86%.

year-on-year (y-o-y) in the first quarter (Q1) of 2020, following a 3.0% y-o-y decline in the fourth quarter (Q4) of 2019.

The contraction in Q1 2020 was the steepest on record for a single quarter and worse than what the economy experienced following the 1997/98 Asian financial crisis. Private consumption dropped 10.1% y-o-y in Q1 2020 due to disruptions in consumer-related activities, while investment expenditure fell 14.3% y-o-y amid sagging investor confidence.

Exports of goods fell 9.9% y-o-y in Q1 2020, weighed down by disruptions to regional supply chains and the sharp drop in global demand as several governments implemented travel bans and social distancing measures to contain the spread of COVID-19. Exports of services plunged 37.8% y-o-y in Q1 2020 as the pandemic halted tourism and hampered cross-border transport and commercial services in February and March.

Consumer price inflation moderated to 1.9% y-o-y in April from 2.3% y-o-y in March as the recession in the domestic economy and the slowdown in global demand eased pressure on prices.

Size and Composition

Hong Kong, China's LCY bonds outstanding amounted to HKD2,255.4 billion (USD291.0 billion) at the end of March after a 0.5% quarter-on-quarter (q-o-q) contraction in Q1 2020 (**Table 1**). The drop in LCY bonds

outstanding stemmed from a 1.1% q-o-q contraction in the government bond segment combined with tepid 0.2% q-o-q growth in the corporate bond segment. On a year-on-year basis, growth slowed to 0.3% in Q1 2020 from 1.8% in Q4 2019. Government bonds accounted for a 51.9% share of total LCY bonds outstanding at the end of March.

Government bonds. LCY government bonds outstanding stood at HKD1,169.5 billion at the end of March. The stock of government bonds contracted 1.1% q-o-q in Q1 2020, mainly due to the 16.9% q-o-q contraction of Hong Kong Special Administrative Region (HKSAR) bonds. EFBs posted weak 0.4% q-o-q growth, while Exchange Fund Notes (EFNs) posted no growth in Q1 2020. Annual growth of LCY government bonds outstanding decelerated to 0.7% y-o-y in Q1 2020 from 1.2% y-o-y in the previous quarter. Government bond issuance declined 1.8% q-o-q in Q1 2020 as issuance of EFBs, EFNs, and HKSAR bonds contracted during the quarter.

Exchange Fund Bills. EFBs outstanding reached HKD1,059.7 at the end of March on growth of 0.4% q-o-q and 2.4% y-o-y. Issuance of EFBs amounted to HKD833.8 billion in Q1 2020, contracting 1.4% q-o-q.

Exchange Fund Notes. Since 2015, the HKMA has limited its issuance of EFNs to 2-year tenors. In February, the HKMA issued a 2-year EFN worth HKD1.2 billion. Due to maturities, outstanding EFNs remained steady at HKD26.6 billion in Q1 2020.

Table 1: Size and Composition of the Local Currency Bond Market in Hong Kong, China

| | Outstanding Amount (billion) | | | | | | Growth Rate (%) | | | |
| | Q1 2019 | | Q4 2019 | | Q1 2020 | | Q1 2019 | | Q1 2020 | |
	HKD	USD	HKD	USD	HKD	USD	q-o-q	y-o-y	q-o-q	y-o-y
Total	2,249	287	2,266	291	2,255	291	1.1	8.5	(0.5)	0.3
Government	1,161	148	1,182	152	1,170	151	(0.6)	1.1	(1.1)	0.7
Exchange Fund Bills	1,035	132	1,055	135	1,060	137	0.5	2.1	0.4	2.4
Exchange Fund Notes	31	4	27	3	27	3	(3.1)	(15.2)	–	(14.7)
HKSAR Bonds	95	12	100	13	83	11	(10.5)	(3.5)	(16.9)	(12.2)
Corporate	1,088	139	1,084	139	1,086	140	3.0	17.8	0.2	(0.2)

( ) = negative, – = not applicable, HKD = Hong Kong dollar, HKSAR = Hong Kong Special Administrative Region, q-o-q = quarter-on-quarter, Q1 = first quarter, Q4 = fourth quarter, USD = United States dollar, y-o-y = year-on-year.
Notes:
1. Calculated using data from national sources.
2. Bloomberg LP end-of-period local currency–USD rates are used.
3. Growth rates are calculated from local currency base and do not include currency effects.
Source: Hong Kong Monetary Authority.

HKSAR bonds. HKSAR bonds outstanding amounted to HKD83.2 billion at the end of March, down 16.9% q-o-q and 12.2% y-o-y in Q1 2020. The government issued a 10-year HKSAR bond worth HKD1.7 billion in February and a 15-year HKSAR bond worth HKD800.0 million in March under the Institutional Bond Issuance Programme.

Corporate bonds. Corporate bonds outstanding reached HKD1.1 billion at the end of March. The corporate bond segment recovered slightly in Q1 2020 with 0.2% q-o-q growth, reversing the 0.9% q-o-q contraction in the previous quarter. On a y-o-y basis, corporate bonds outstanding dropped 0.2% in Q1 2020, reversing the 2.6% gain posted in the previous quarter.

Hong Kong, China's top 30 nonbank issuers had a combined HKD223.8 billion of bonds outstanding at the end of March, accounting for 20.6% of the total corporate bond market (**Table 2**). Government-owned financial firm Hong Kong Mortgage Corporation remained the top issuer with HKD30.0 billion of bonds outstanding at the end of Q1 2020. Sun Hung Kai & Co. maintained its position as second-largest issuer at HKD17.0 billion. The third-largest issuer was MTR corporation, a government-owned transportation company, with HKD13.7 billion. The top 30 issuers were predominantly finance and real estate companies. A majority of the top 30 issuers were listed in the Hong Kong Stock Exchange; only two were government-owned corporations.

Corporate bond issuance reached HKD213.6 billion at the end of March, as issuance growth rebounded to 44.3% q-o-q in Q1 2020 from an 18.9% q-o-q decline in the previous quarter. Among the top nonbank issuers in Q1 2020, government-owned Hong Kong Mortgage Corporation was the largest issuer with an aggregate HKD4.5 billion from 13 issuances, the largest of which was a 2-year bond with a 1.74% coupon worth HKD1.0 billion (**Table 3**). The next top issuers were Wharf Real Estate Investment and Han Lung Properties, each with aggregate issuance worth HKD2.8 billion. Wharf Real Estate Investment issued two 10-year bonds worth HKD800.0 million each, as well as a 7-year bond with a 2.10% coupon worth HKD1.0 billion. Han Lung Properties' issuances included a 5-year bond with a 2.35% coupon worth HKD950.0 million and a 7-year bond with a 3.01% coupon worth HKD700.0 million. There were two issuances of 15-year bonds in Q1 2020, the longest-dated tenor issued during the quarter. Henderson Land Development issued a 15-

year HKD100.0 million bond with a 2.66% coupon, while Hong Kong Land issued a 15-year HKD400.0 million bond with a 2.72% coupon.

Ratings Update

On 20 April, Fitch Ratings downgraded Hong Kong, China's long-term currency issuer default rating to AA– from AA with a stable outlook, stating that the economy was facing a second major shock from the onset of the COVID-19 pandemic after prolonged political unrest. Fitch Ratings noted that the downgrade reflected Hong Kong, China's increasing integration into the PRC's national governance system and the related rise of economic, financial, and sociopolitical links to the PRC merit a closer alignment of their respective sovereign ratings. The PRC is currently rated one notch below Hong Kong, China at A+. The downgrade puts Hong Kong, China at its lowest rating level since 2007.

Policy, Institutional, and Regulatory Developments

Hong Kong Monetary Authority Reduces Countercyclical Capital Buffer to 1.0%

On 16 March, the HKMA reduced its countercyclical buffer to 1.0% from 2.0% amid worsening economic conditions brought about by the COVID-19 outbreak. The move was intended to release additional funds that would allow banks to extend credit to support financing needs in the domestic economy, particularly for sectors and individuals affected by the downturn. The countercyclical buffer is an integral part of the Basel III regulatory capital framework designed to increase the resilience of the banking sector during periods of excess credit growth.

Hong Kong Monetary Authority Reduces Issuance of Exchange Fund Bills by HKD20.0 billion in April–May

On 9 April, the HKMA announced a reduction in the issuance of EFBs, which was aimed at raising Hong Kong dollar liquidity in the interbank market. The HKMA reduced the issue size of 91-day EFBs by HKD5.0 billion in each of the tenders held on 21 April, 28 April, 5 May, and 12 May. The combined reduction lowered the issuance of EFBs by a total of HKD20.0 billion.

Table 2: Top 30 Nonbank Corporate Issuers of Local Currency Corporate Bonds in Hong Kong, China

	Issuers	Outstanding Amount		State-Owned	Listed Company	Type of Industry
		LCY Bonds (HKD billion)	LCY Bonds (USD billion)			
1.	Hong Kong Mortgage Corporation	30.0	3.9	Yes	No	Finance
2.	Sun Hung Kai & Co.	17.0	2.2	No	Yes	Finance
3.	MTR Corporation	13.7	1.8	Yes	Yes	Transportation
4.	The Hong Kong and China Gas Company	13.3	1.7	No	Yes	Utilities
5.	Link Holdings	11.9	1.5	No	No	Finance
6.	New World Development	11.8	1.5	No	Yes	Diversified
7.	Hong Kong Land	10.9	1.4	No	No	Real Estate
8.	Henderson Land Development	10.9	1.4	No	No	Real Estate
9.	Swire Pacific	10.0	1.3	No	Yes	Diversified
10.	CLP Power Hong Kong Financing	7.7	1.0	No	No	Finance
11.	Hang Lung Properties	7.1	0.9	No	Yes	Real Estate
12.	Smart Edge	6.8	0.9	No	No	Finance
13.	The Wharf (Holdings)	6.7	0.9	No	Yes	Finance
14.	Hongkong Electric	6.3	0.8	No	No	Utilities
15.	AIA Group	6.3	0.8	No	Yes	Insurance
16.	CK Asset Holdings	6.2	0.8	No	Yes	Real Estate
17.	Wharf Real Estate Investment	5.9	0.8	No	Yes	Real Estate
18.	Hysan Development Company	5.9	0.8	No	Yes	Real Estate
19.	Swire Properties	5.6	0.7	No	Yes	Diversified
20.	Future Days	5.5	0.7	No	No	Transportation
21.	Guotai Junan Holdings	3.1	0.4	No	Yes	Finance
22.	Lerthai Group	3.0	0.4	No	Yes	Real Estate
23.	Haitong International Securities Group	2.7	0.3	No	Yes	Finance
24.	Champion REIT	2.5	0.3	No	Yes	Real Estate
25.	China Dynamics Holdings	2.4	0.3	No	Yes	Automotive
26.	South Shore Holdings	2.2	0.3	No	Yes	Industrial
27.	Emperor Capital Group	2.2	0.3	No	Yes	Finance
28.	Emperor International Holdings	2.2	0.3	No	Yes	Real Estate
29.	Cathay Pacific Airways	2.1	0.3	No	Yes	Transportation
30.	Nan Fung Treasury	1.8	0.2	No	No	Finance
	Total Top 30 Nonbank LCY Corporate Issuers	**223.8**	**28.9**			
	Total LCY Corporate Bonds	**1,085.9**	**140.1**			
	Top 30 as % of Total LCY Corporate Bonds	**20.6%**	**20.6%**			

HKD = Hong Kong dollar, LCY = local currency, REIT = real estate investment trust, USD = United States dollar.
Notes:
1. Data as of 31 March 2020.
2. State-owned firms are defined as those in which the government has more than a 50% ownership stake.
Source: *AsianBondsOnline* calculations based on Bloomberg LP data.

Table 3: Notable Local Currency Corporate Bond Issuance in the First Quarter of 2020

Corporate Issuers	Coupon Rate (%)	Issued Amount (HKD million)
Wharf Real Estate Investment		
7-year bond	2.10	1.00
10-year bond	2.69	0.80
10-year bond	2.80	0.80
Hong Kong Mortgage Corporation		
1-year bond	1.90	0.50
2-year bond	1.74	1.00
4-year bond	1.19	0.25
Hang Lung Properties		
5-year bond	2.35	0.95
7-year bond	3.01	0.70
Hong Kong Land		
15-year bond	2.72	0.40
Henderson Land Development		
15-year bond	2.66	0.10

HKD = Hong Kong dollar.
Source: Bloomberg LP.

Hong Kong Monetary Authority Introduces a Temporary US Dollar Liquidity Facility

On 22 April, the HKMA announced the introduction of a temporary US dollar liquidity facility that will provide US dollar liquidity assistance to licensed banks through competitive tenders of 7-day repurchase transactions. Starting 6 May, the HKMA began conducting a tender once per week. Eligible banks can submit a bid of at least USD100.0 million or multiples thereof. The HKMA intends to maintain the facility, which currently has USD10.0 billion of available funds, until 30 September. It will also consider market conditions and revise arrangements as necessary.

Indonesia

Yield Movements

Local currency (LCY) government bond yields in Indonesia climbed across all tenors, leading the yield curve to shift upward between 28 February and 15 May (**Figure 1**). Bond yields rose an average of 95 basis points (bps) for the 1-year maturity through the 13-year maturity. Yields climbed the most for the 3-year, 4-year, 5-year, and 12-year tenors, with upticks of over 100 bps for each during the review period. For maturities of 15 years and longer, bond yields climbed an average of 57 bps. The spread between the 2-year and 10-year maturities narrowed to 154 bps on 15 May from 167 bps on 28 February.

The overall rise in yields was largely driven by a market sell-off as investor sentiments soured amid heightened global market uncertainty. As the coronavirus disease (COVID-19) pandemic spread globally, rising risk aversion led investors to shift toward safe-haven assets. This resulted in the steep decline in Indonesia's foreign holdings share from 38.6% at the end of December to 32.7% at the end of March, and further to 30.3% on 15 May. Record-level foreign capital outflows from Indonesia's bond market were also recorded in March.

Further contributing to the risk-off sentiment was S&P Global's downward revision of the sovereign rating outlook of Indonesia from stable to negative in April. The rise in yields was also reflective of the government's need for a wider budget deficit to fund COVID-19-related stimulus measures and recovery efforts, as well as of Bank Indonesia's less aggressive monetary policy stance compared with regional peers.

While there is room for monetary easing amid tame inflation and given the need to bolster economic growth, Bank Indonesia had only lowered policy rates by a cumulative 50 bps year-to-date through the end of May. The central bank opted to support the Indonesian rupiah, whose value once again weakened to its 1997/98 Asian financial crisis level of IDR16,000 per USD1, which was last seen in 2018 when the United States (US) Federal Reserve tightened monetary policy. To maintain financial market stability, Bank Indonesia has opted to inject liquidity in the money market and banking system through interventions and bond buy-backs, repurchase

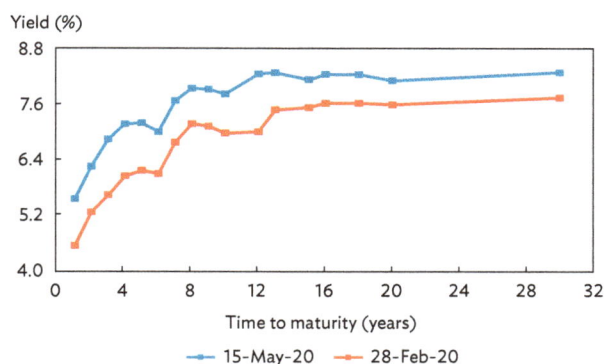

Figure 1: Indonesia's Benchmark Yield Curve—Local Currency Government Bonds

Source: Based on data from Bloomberg LP.

transactions, foreign currency swaps, and a reduction in the rupiah reserve requirement ratio.

The Indonesian rupiah fell to its lowest level year-to-date on 23 March at IDR16,575 per USD1, before recovering after Bank Indonesia signed a deal with the Federal Reserve for a repo facility worth USD60 billion. Between 28 February and 15 May, the Indonesian rupiah depreciated the most among all emerging East Asian currencies, weakening 3.6% versus the US dollar.

Indonesia was among three markets in the region that posted positive economic growth in the first quarter (Q1) of 2020. Real gross domestic product growth moderated to 3.0% year-on-year (y-o-y) in Q1 2020 from 5.0% y-o-y in the fourth quarter (Q4) of 2019. Gross domestic product growth slowed as all expenditure components posted weaker growth. Domestic consumption rose 2.8% y-o-y in Q1 2020 versus 5.0% y-o-y in Q4 2019, while investment growth slowed to 1.7% y-o-y from 5.0% y-o-y during the same period. Bank Indonesia expects economic growth to slow further during the rest of 2020 due to the COVID-19 pandemic.

Size and Composition

The LCY bond market in Indonesia reached a size of IDR3,324.7 trillion (USD203.8 billion) at the end of March on marginal growth of 0.4% quarter-on-quarter (q-o-q) in Q1 2020, down from 2.5% q-o-q in Q4 2019 (**Table 1**). Growth came largely from an expansion in the stock of central government bonds, comprising Treasury bills and Treasury bonds. The stocks of both central bank bills and corporate bonds contracted during the quarter in review. On a y-o-y basis, overall growth of the bond market moderated to 7.8% in Q1 2020 from 16.6% in Q4 2019.

The LCY bond market in Indonesia largely comprises government bonds, with a share of 86.7% of the aggregate bond total at the end of March. The remaining 13.3% share was accounted for by corporate bonds. Similarly, conventional bonds accounted for a larger share of the aggregate bond total, representing an 83.6% share during the period. At the end of March, *sukuk* (Islamic bonds) had a share of 16.4%.

Government bonds. The outstanding size of government bonds reached IDR2,881.8 trillion at the end of March, up 0.6% q-o-q and 8.4% y-o-y. Growth was solely contributed by central government bonds, particularly conventional bonds. The stock of central government *sukuk* declined during the review period. The stock of central bank bonds also contracted, but with declines coming from conventional central bank instruments rather than *sukuk*.

Central government bonds. The outstanding stock of central government bonds stood at IDR2,833.4 trillion at the end of March on growth of 2.9% q-o-q and 12.1% y-o-y. While positive, growth in Q1 2020 moderated

from that of Q4 2019. Despite strong issuance volume in Q1 2020 due to the Ministry of Finance's adoption of a frontloading policy as in past years, a high volume of maturities during the quarter capped the outstanding size of central government bonds.

The issuance of Treasury bills and Treasury bonds climbed to IDR199.0 trillion, up 38.2% q-o-q but down 19.8% y-o-y. The government accepted bids higher than its targeted amount in 9 out of 13 Treasury auctions, in line with its frontloading policy. Two Treasury auctions were under-awarded while two were awarded at par with the target. The government also raised funds from the private placement of select Treasury bonds during the quarter. An Islamic retail bond was offered via bookbuilding in March, with the government raising IDR12.1 trillion from the sale. A higher volume of Treasury issuance is expected during the rest of the year as the government aims for a wider budget deficit to fund its stimulus measures and recovery efforts to combat the impact of the COVID-19 pandemic.

Central bank bonds. At the end of March, the outstanding amount of central bank instruments, comprising Sertifikat Bank Indonesia and Sukuk Bank Indonesia, reached IDR48.4 trillion. The stock of central bank bonds was down 57.1% q-o-q and 63.2% y-o-y in Q1 2020 as maturities greatly exceeded issuance during the quarter. Total issuance of central bank instruments in Q1 2020 was broadly at par with the preceding quarter as the central bank opted to boost financial market liquidity.

Table 1: Size and Composition of the Local Currency Bond Market in Indonesia

	Outstanding Amount (billion)						Growth Rate (%)			
	Q1 2019		Q4 2019		Q1 2020		Q1 2019		Q1 2020	
	IDR	USD	IDR	USD	IDR	USD	q-o-q	y-o-y	q-o-q	y-o-y
Total	3,083,746	217	3,310,632	239	3,324,692	204	8.7	18.7	0.4	7.8
Government	2,659,664	187	2,865,531	207	2,881,782	177	9.6	21.0	0.6	8.4
Central Govt. Bonds	2,527,993	177	2,752,741	199	2,833,359	174	6.7	15.7	2.9	12.1
of which: *Sukuk*	427,277	30	485,534	35	478,152	29	8.7	29.8	(1.5)	11.9
Central Bank Bonds	131,671	9	112,790	8	48,423	3	127.5	913.1	(57.1)	(63.2)
of which: *Sukuk*	24,915	2	31,174	2	36,173	2	148.1	91.7	16.0	45.2
Corporate	424,082	30	445,101	32	442,909	27	3.0	5.9	(0.5)	4.4
of which: *Sukuk*	24,606	2	28,673	2	30,200	2	15.5	49.6	5.3	22.7

( ) = negative, IDR = Indonesian rupiah, q-o-q = quarter-on-quarter, Q1 = first quarter, Q4 = fourth quarter, USD = United States dollar, y-o-y = year-on-year.
Notes:
1. Calculated using data from national sources.
2. Bloomberg LP end-of-period local currency–USD rates are used.
3. Growth rates are calculated from local currency base and do not include currency effects.
4. The total stock of nontradable bonds as of 31 March 2020 stood at IDR204.9 trillion.
Sources: Bank Indonesia; Directorate General of Budget Financing and Risk Management, Ministry of Finance; Indonesia Stock Exchange; and Bloomberg LP.

Corporate bonds. Total corporate bonds outstanding stood at IDR442.9 trillion at the end of March, down 0.5% q-o-q but up 4.4% y-o-y. The stock of corporate bonds declined as issuance during the quarter was reduced by nearly half to IDR18.8 trillion from IDR34.2 trillion in the previous quarter. Corporates reconsidered their issuance plans due to the slowdown in the economy and falling consumption demand. Also, some corporates opted to delay issuing bonds in line with current market conditions as borrowing costs remained high following the uptick in government bond yields.

The 30 largest corporate bond issuers in Indonesia had an aggregate outstanding bond stock of IDR330.3 trillion at the end of March, down from IDR332.1 trillion at the end of December (**Table 2**). The top 30 corporate issuers accounted for 74.6% of the aggregate corporate bond stock during the review period. Firms from the banking and financial sectors continued to dominate the list. Other firms on the list were from the energy, telecommunications, construction, and transportation sectors, among others. A total of 17 institutions on the list were state-owned firms, eight of which were also among the top 10 in Q1 2020. A total of 17 of the top issuers were listed on the Indonesia Stock Exchange.

Leading the list of top 30 corporate issuers were six state-owned entities, with the top spot occupied by energy firm Perusahaan Listrik Negara (PLN). Indonesia Eximbank was bumped to the second spot during the quarter, while Bank Rakyat Indonesia rose to the third spot. Sarana Multi Infrastruktur slid to fourth place, and Bank Tabungan kept the fifth spot.

In Q1 2020, new issuance of corporate bonds declined to IDR18.8 trillion from IDR34.2 trillion in the preceding quarter. Issuance volume fell 44.9% q-o-q and 14.3% y-o-y, dragged down by uncertainties in the economy due to the COVID-19 outbreak. A total of 13 firms tapped the bond market for funding during the quarter, compared with 24 firms in Q4 2019. Most of the new bond issues were conventional bonds. Two firms also issued *sukuk ijarah* (Islamic bonds backed by lease agreements) and one bank issued *sukuk mudharabah* (Islamic bonds backed by a profit-sharing scheme from a business venture or partnership).

The largest issuance during the quarter came from PLN, which issued an IDR4.9 trillion multi-tranche bond in February (**Table 3**). PLN issued both conventional

bonds and *sukuk ijarah*. Financing firm Sarana Multigriya Finansial raised IDR4.0 trillion. This was followed by Astra Sedaya Finance with issuance of IDR2.2 trillion. Medco Energi Internasional and Tower Bersama Infrastructure each issued bonds worth IDR1.5 trillion during the quarter.

Investor Profile

Foreign investors continued to comprise the largest investor group in the LCY central government bond market segment. This was despite a decrease in their holdings to a share of 32.7% at the end of March from 38.3% a year earlier (**Figure 2**). A market sell-off in Q1 2020 resulted in investors dumping Indonesian bonds in favor of safe-haven assets amid heightened uncertainties due to the COVID-19 pandemic. Government bonds held by foreign investors dropped to IDR926.9 trillion at the end of March from IDR927.1 trillion a year earlier.

Long-term government bonds remained the favorite among foreign bond holders. Bonds with remaining maturities of at least 10 years and from over 5 years to 10 years accounted for 35.0% and 31.6%, respectively, of total central government bond holdings among nonresident investors (**Figure 3**). Bonds maturing in more than 2 years to 5 years accounted for a 23.1% share, and bonds maturing in more than a year to 2 years had a 7.9% share. The remaining 2.4% of the government bonds held by foreign investors will mature in less than a year.

Banking institutions continued to hold the biggest share of central government bonds among local investors, increasing their share from 25.7% at the end of March 2019 to 26.9% at the end of March 2020. Bank Indonesia nearly doubled its government bond holdings to IDR255.1 trillion at the end of March from IDR132.0 trillion in March 2019, growing its share of government bonds outstanding to 9.0% from 5.2% a year earlier.

Other domestic investors that posted increases in their holdings of central government bonds were pension funds and mutual funds. Pension fund holdings of central government bonds rose to 9.6% in March from 8.9% a year earlier, and mutual fund holdings inched up to 4.6% from 4.5% in the same period. In contrast, the holdings of insurance providers declined to a share of 8.0% from 8.2% at the end of March 2019.

Table 2: Top 30 Issuers of Local Currency Corporate Bonds in Indonesia

	Issuers	Outstanding Amount		State-Owned	Listed Company	Type of Industry
		LCY Bonds (IDR billion)	LCY Bonds (USD billion)			
1.	Perusahaan Listrik Negara	32,675	2.00	Yes	No	Energy
2.	Indonesia Eximbank	32,487	1.99	Yes	No	Banking
3.	Bank Rakyat Indonesia	25,026	1.53	Yes	Yes	Banking
4.	Sarana Multi Infrastruktur	21,866	1.34	Yes	No	Finance
5.	Bank Tabungan Negara	19,847	1.22	Yes	Yes	Banking
6.	Sarana Multigriya Finansial	16,422	1.01	Yes	No	Finance
7.	Indosat	15,716	0.96	No	Yes	Telecommunications
8.	Bank Mandiri	14,000	0.86	Yes	Yes	Banking
9.	Bank Pan Indonesia	13,427	0.82	No	Yes	Banking
10.	Waskita Karya	12,960	0.79	Yes	Yes	Building Construction
11.	Bank CIMB Niaga	10,350	0.63	No	Yes	Banking
12.	Adira Dinamika Multifinance	9,647	0.59	No	Yes	Finance
13.	Telekomunikasi Indonesia	8,995	0.55	Yes	Yes	Telecommunications
14.	Permodalan Nasional Madani	8,189	0.50	Yes	No	Finance
15.	Federal International Finance	7,986	0.49	No	No	Finance
16.	Pupuk Indonesia	7,945	0.49	Yes	No	Chemical Manufacturing
17.	Semen Indonesia	7,078	0.43	Yes	Yes	Cement Manufacturing
18.	Astra Sedaya Finance	6,958	0.43	No	No	Finance
19.	Perum Pegadaian	6,851	0.42	Yes	No	Finance
20.	Hutama Karya	6,825	0.42	Yes	No	Nonbuilding Construction
21.	Medco Energi Internasional	6,452	0.40	No	Yes	Petroleum and Natural Gas
22.	Bank Maybank Indonesia	5,831	0.36	No	Yes	Banking
23.	Bank Pembangunan Daerah Jawa Barat Dan Banten	5,000	0.31	Yes	Yes	Banking
24.	Mandiri Tunas Finance	4,730	0.29	No	No	Finance
25.	Tower Bersama Infrastructure	4,488	0.28	No	Yes	Telecommunications Infrastructure Provider
26.	Adhi Karya	4,027	0.25	Yes	Yes	Building Construction
27.	Kereta Api	4,000	0.25	Yes	No	Transportation
28.	XL Axiata	3,815	0.23	No	Yes	Telecommunications
29.	Maybank Indonesia Finance	3,550	0.22	No	No	Finance
30.	Chandra Asri Petrochemicals	3,139	0.19	No	Yes	Petrochemicals
Total Top 30 LCY Corporate Issuers		**330,279**	**20.25**			
Total LCY Corporate Bonds		**442,909**	**27.16**			
Top 30 as % of Total LCY Corporate Bonds		**74.6%**	**74.6%**			

IDR = Indonesian rupiah, LCY = local currency, USD = United States dollar.
Notes:
1. Data as of 31 March 2020.
2. State-owned firms are defined as those in which the government has more than a 50% ownership stake.
Source: *AsianBondsOnline* calculations based on Indonesia Stock Exchange data.

Table 3: Notable Local Currency Corporate Bond Issuance in the First Quarter of 2020

Corporate Issuers	Coupon Rate (%)	Issued Amount (IDR billion)
Perusahaan Listrik Negara		
5-year bond	7.70	540.63
7-year bond	7.40	672.50
7-year sukuk ijarah	7.40	40.50
10-year bond	8.00	544.25
10-year sukuk ijarah	8.00	3.50
15-year bond	8.70	1,459.00
15-year sukuk ijarah	8.70	9.00
20-year bond	9.05	1,596.05
20-year sukuk ijarah	9.05	62.50

Corporate Issuers	Coupon Rate (%)	Issued Amount (IDR billion)
Sarana Multigriya Finansial		
370-day bond	6.00	1,460.00
5-year bond	7.00	2,541.00
Astra Sedaya Finance		
370-day bond	5.80	882.00
5-year bond	7.00	1,301.05
Medco Energi Internasional		
3-year bond	8.90	1,023.70
5-year bond	9.30	476.30
Tower Bersama Infrastructure		
370-day bond	6.25	633.00
3-year bond	7.75	867.00

IDR = Indonesian rupiah.
Note: Sukuk ijarah are Islamic bonds backed by lease agreements.
Source: Indonesia Stock Exchange.

Figure 2: Local Currency Central Government Bonds Investor Profile

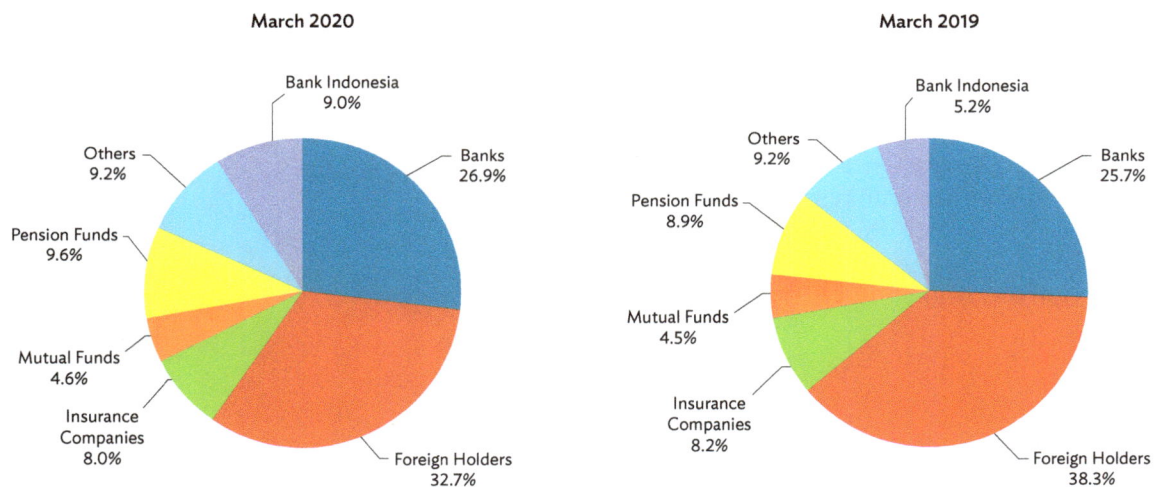

Source: Directorate General of Budget Financing and Risk Management, Ministry of Finance.

Figure 3: Foreign Holdings of Local Currency Central Government Bonds by Maturity

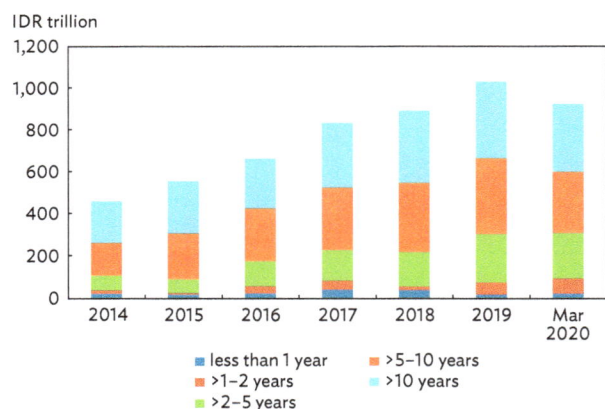

IDR = Indonesian rupiah.
Source: Directorate General of Budget Financing and Risk Management, Ministry of Finance.

Ratings Update

On 17 April, S&P Global affirmed the sovereign credit rating of Indonesia at BBB. The outlook on the rating was revised downward to negative from stable. S&P Global cited Indonesia's stable institutional settings, strong growth prospects, and historically prudent fiscal policy as the factors for the rating affirmation. On the other hand, the negative outlook was based on S&P Global's expectation of increased fiscal and external risks underpinned by higher government borrowing amid the COVID-19 pandemic.

Policy, Institutional, and Regulatory Developments

Otoritas Jasa Keuangan Issues Regulations for the Issuance of Debt Securities Through Private Placements

In March, Otoritas Jasa Keuangan (OJK) issued regulations for the issuance of debt instruments, including *sukuk,* through private placements. The regulations, which are set to became effective in June, placed the legality of instruments issued through private placements similar to that of bonds and provide investor protections. Under the regulations, firms that undertake issuance of debt securities—in particular, medium-term notes or

sukuk—through a private placement will be required to (i) file for registration with OJK, (ii) obtain an investment grade from an OJK-certified credit rating agency for persons outside the scope of public companies, (iii) avail the services of an arranger and monitoring agent, and (iv) limit the buying of medium-term notes to professional investors.

Bank Indonesia Lowers Reserve Requirement Ratios

In April, Bank Indonesia announced a 200-bps reduction in the rupiah reserve requirement ratio for conventional commercial banks and a 50-bps cut for Islamic banks and Islamic business units. The adjustment in reserve requirement ratios took effect in May and formed part of Bank Indonesia's accommodative macroprudential policy stance to stimulate bank intermediation and mitigate the economic impact of COVID-19.

Bank Indonesia and the Federal Reserve Agree to a USD60 Billion Repo Facility

In April, Bank Indonesia reached a deal with the Federal Reserve for a USD60 billion repurchase agreement (repo) facility. According to Bank Indonesia, the repo facility is intended as a second line of defense aside from the bilateral swap agreements it has signed with other markets to boost US dollar liquidity. Bank Indonesia has been engaging in interventions to help stabilize the Indonesian rupiah since February.

Bank Indonesia to Purchase Government Bonds in the Primary Market

In April, Bank Indonesia commenced its participation in the weekly auctions of the government to purchase Treasury instruments. Previously, Bank Indonesia was only allowed to purchase bonds from the secondary market. The regulation in lieu of Law 1/2020 that was passed in March, allows the central bank to participate in the weekly auctions as a noncompetitive bidder. Bank Indonesia and the Ministry of Finance set a limit on the central bank's bond purchases at 30% for Shari'ah Treasury auctions and 25% for conventional Treasury auctions. Bank Indonesia's purchase of government bonds in the primary market is only allowed when the market is unable to absorb the offers.

Republic of Korea

Yield Movements

Between 28 February and 15 May, the Republic of Korea's local currency (LCY) government bond yield curve steepened as yields at the short-end fell, while yields at the long-end rose (**Figure 1**). The yields for 3-month and 6-month paper fell 47 basis points (bps) and 46 bps, respectively. The yield for 1-year paper fell 40 bps. Yields for medium-term tenors of 2 years and 3 years fell 27 bps on average; the 5-year tenor fell the least, dipping 6 bps. The yields for tenors ranging from 10 years to 50 years rose 9 bps on average. The spread between the 2-year and 10-year yields rose to 59 bps from 22 bps during the review period.

Yields at the short-end of the curve fell following the rate cut by the Bank of Korea in its emergency Monetary Policy Board meeting on 16 March, a day after the United States (US) Federal Reserve lowered its target range for the federal fund rate by 100 basis points to 0%–0.25%. The Bank of Korea decided to lower its base rate by 50 basis points to 0.75% to stabilize the financial market and in response to the impending economic impact of the coronavirus disease (COVID-19) pandemic. In its Monetary Policy Board meeting on 9 April, the central bank decided to leave its base rate unchanged.

The Bank of Korea has also announced and implemented several measures since March to provide additional liquidity in the market, which contributed to the fall in yields at the short-end of the curve. These included, among others, a (i) weekly reverse repurchase auction for a period of 3 months, available for financial institutions; (ii) broadening of the securities eligible for its open market operations; and (iii) new lending facility for companies with a ceiling of KRW10 trillion and a term of 3 months.

Despite various stabilization measures and strong foreign demand, yields continued to rise at the long-end of the curve, fueled by bond supply concerns as the government passed two supplementary budgets to support various sectors affected by the pandemic. As of 15 May, the National Assembly had approved a total of KRW23.9 trillion in supplementary budget funds to be partly financed via issuance of government bonds. A third supplementary budget is expected to be

Figure 1: The Republic of Korea's Benchmark Yield Curve—Local Currency Government Bonds

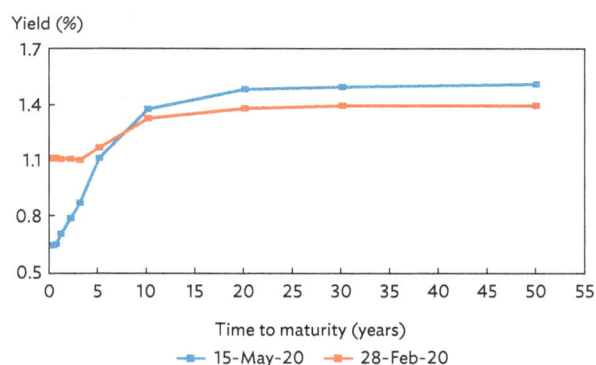

Source: Based on data from Bloomberg LP.

submitted in June. However, market expectations that the Bank of Korea will purchase government bonds to address oversupply concerns have tempered the rise in yields, particularly in early May.

The Republic of Korea's real gross domestic product contracted 1.3% quarter-on-quarter (q-o-q) in the first quarter (Q1) of 2020, a reversal from the 1.3% q-o-q growth in the fourth quarter (Q4) of 2019, based on preliminary estimates by the Bank of Korea. This reflected the economic impact of COVID-19 as the country went on lockdown. Private consumer spending declined 6.5% q-o-q in Q1 2020 after an increase of 0.7% q-o-q in the previous quarter. Exports also fell 1.4% q-o-q from marginal growth of 0.6% q-o-q in Q4 2019. The q-o-q growth in government spending and fixed capital formation also slowed in Q1 2020. On an annual basis, the Republic of Korea's economic growth slowed to 1.4% year-on-year (y-o-y) from 2.3% y-o-y in the previous quarter. Consumer price inflation also decelerated in April to 0.1% y-o-y from an average of 1.2% y-o-y in Q1 2020, amid a slowdown in spending and production, and a drop in oil prices.

The Republic of Korea registered massive net foreign inflows in the months of March and April, providing downward support to bond yields. Foreign demand increased on the economy being considered a safe haven relative to its peers; a high interest rate differential with other bond markets in the region, as well as US Treasuries; the implementation of policies to stabilize financial market volatility and address the economic impact of the pandemic; and a relatively stable Korean won.

The Korean won depreciated versus the US dollar during the review period, particularly in March, due to financial market volatility and foreign selling, with the foreign exchange rate peaking at KRW1,285.7 to USD1 on 19 March. The currency subsequently stabilized toward the end of the month after the Bank of Korea announced a temporary currency swap agreement with the Federal Reserve for a period of at least 6 months. The currency remained in the KRW1,204–KRW1,236 to USD1 range during the rest of the review period.

Size and Composition

The Republic of Korea's LCY bond market grew 2.8% q-o-q to reach a size of KRW2,476.2 trillion (USD2,032.1 billion) at the end of March (**Table 1**). This was higher than the 1.6% q-o-q growth posted in Q4 2019. Growth in Q1 2020 was largely driven by the 4.2% q-o-q increase in the stock of government bonds. Meanwhile, the Republic of Korea's corporate bond segment grew at a slower pace of 1.9% q-o-q.

Government bonds. The size of the Republic of Korea's LCY government bond market rose 4.2% q-o-q to KRW992.3 trillion at the end of March. Growth was boosted by a 5.6% q-o-q expansion in the stock of central

government bonds to KRW645.9 trillion due to the surge in issuance in Q1 2020. The outstanding amount of Monetary Stabilization Bonds issued by the Bank of Korea inched up 1.0% q-o-q to KRW165.7 trillion. Outstanding bonds issued by government-related entities rose 2.5% q-o-q.

Issuance of central government bonds more than doubled in Q1 2020 to KRW42.5 trillion from KRW20.0 trillion in Q4 2019 as the government had a larger annual fiscal budget and a frontloading policy. High issuance volume were seen in the first 2 months of the year and surged even more in March as the government funded policy programs to address the economic impact of the COVID-19 pandemic. Issuance volume is expected to rise further the rest of the year as the government finances its supplementary budgets.

Corporate bonds. The Republic of Korea's LCY corporate bond market marginally grew 1.9% q-o-q to KRW1,483.8 trillion at the end of March on tepid issuance for the quarter. **Table 2** lists the top 30 LCY corporate bond issuers in the Republic of Korea, who together had an aggregate KRW922.1 trillion of bonds outstanding at the end of March, which accounted for 62.1% of the total LCY corporate bond market. Financial companies such as banks and securities and investment firms continued to comprise a majority of the 30 largest corporate bond issuers. Korea Housing Finance Corporation remained the largest issuer with outstanding bonds valued at KRW133.3 trillion.

Table 1: Size and Composition of the Local Currency Bond Market in the Republic of Korea

| | Outstanding Amount (billion) | | | | | | Growth Rate (%) | | | |
| | Q1 2019 | | Q4 2019 | | Q1 2020 | | Q1 2019 | | Q1 2020 | |
	KRW	USD	KRW	USD	KRW	USD	q-o-q	y-o-y	q-o-q	y-o-y
Total	2,277,392	2,006	2,407,623	2,083	2,476,170	2,032	1.7	4.2	2.8	8.7
Government	930,886	820	951,912	824	992,346	814	1.9	1.7	4.2	6.6
Central Government Bonds	584,006	514	611,533	529	645,928	530	3.0	2.7	5.6	10.6
Central Bank Bonds	171,150	151	164,060	142	165,710	136	(0.3)	(2.1)	1.0	(3.2)
Others	175,730	155	176,319	153	180,708	148	0.3	2.5	2.5	2.8
Corporate	1,346,506	1,186	1,455,711	1,259	1,483,824	1,218	1.7	5.9	1.9	10.2

( ) = negative, KRW = Korean won, q-o-q = quarter-on-quarter, Q1 = first quarter, Q4 = fourth quarter, USD = United States dollar, y-o-y = year-on-year.
Notes:
1. Calculated using data from national sources.
2. Bloomberg LP end-of-period local currency–USD rates are used.
3. Growth rates are calculated from local currency base and do not include currency effects.
4. "Others" comprise Korea Development Bank Bonds, National Housing Bonds, and Seoul Metro Bonds.
5. Corporate bonds include equity-linked securities and derivatives-linked securities.
Sources: The Bank of Korea and *EDAILY BondWeb*.

Table 2: Top 30 Issuers of Local Currency Corporate Bonds in the Republic of Korea

	Issuers	Outstanding Amount		State-Owned	Listed on		Type of Industry
		LCY Bonds (KRW billion)	LCY Bonds (USD billion)		KOSPI	KOSDAQ	
1.	Korea Housing Finance Corporation	133,287	109.4	Yes	No	No	Housing Finance
2.	Mirae Asset Daewoo Co.	75,016	61.6	No	Yes	No	Securities
3.	Korea Investment and Securities	68,135	55.9	No	No	No	Securities
4.	Industrial Bank of Korea	57,340	47.1	Yes	Yes	No	Banking
5.	KB Securities	55,090	45.2	No	No	No	Securities
6.	NH Investment & Securities	49,822	40.9	Yes	Yes	No	Securities
7.	Hana Financial Investment	46,860	38.5	No	No	No	Securities
8.	Samsung Securities	35,950	29.5	No	Yes	No	Securities
9.	Shinhan Bank	31,342	25.7	No	No	No	Banking
10.	Korea Land & Housing Corporation	29,700	24.4	Yes	No	No	Real Estate
11.	Korea Electric Power Corporation	28,456	23.4	Yes	Yes	No	Electricity, Energy, and Power
12.	Korea Expressway	23,100	19.0	Yes	No	No	Transport Infrastructure
13.	Woori Bank	21,290	17.5	Yes	Yes	No	Banking
14.	KEB Hana Bank	21,170	17.4	No	No	No	Banking
15.	Shinyoung Securities	19,625	16.1	No	Yes	No	Securities
16.	Korea Rail Network Authority	19,204	15.8	Yes	No	No	Transport Infrastructure
17.	Kookmin Bank	18,950	15.6	No	No	No	Banking
18.	The Export-Import Bank of Korea	18,444	15.1	Yes	No	No	Banking
19.	Hyundai Capital Services	17,440	14.3	No	No	No	Consumer Finance
20.	Shinhan Card	16,727	13.7	No	No	No	Credit Card
21.	Korea Deposit Insurance Corporation	15,280	12.5	Yes	No	No	Insurance
22.	Nonghyup Bank	15,145	12.4	Yes	No	No	Banking
23.	Korea SMEs and Startups Agency	15,038	12.3	Yes	No	No	SME Development
24.	Hanwha Investment and Securities	14,836	12.2	No	No	No	Securities
25.	KB Kookmin Bank Card	13,534	11.1	No	No	No	Consumer Finance
26.	Standard Chartered Bank Korea	13,290	10.9	No	No	No	Banking
27.	Korea Gas Corporation	13,090	10.7	Yes	Yes	No	Gas Utility
28.	Nonghyup	12,100	9.9	Yes	No	No	Banking
29.	Meritz Securities Co.	12,009	9.9	No	Yes	No	Securities
30.	Korea Student Aid Foundation	10,870	8.9	Yes	No	No	Student Loan
	Total Top 30 LCY Corporate Issuers	**922,140**	**756.8**				
	Total LCY Corporate Bonds	**1,483,824**	**1,217.7**				
	Top 30 as % of Total LCY Corporate Bonds	**62.1%**	**62.1%**				

KOSDAQ = Korean Securities Dealers Automated Quotations, KOSPI = Korea Composite Stock Price Index, KRW = Korean won, LCY = local currency, SME = small and medium-sized enterprise, USD = United States dollar.
Notes:
1. Data as of 31 March 2020.
2. State-owned firms are defined as those in which the government has more than a 50% ownership stake.
3. Corporate bonds include equity-linked securities and derivatives-linked securities.
Sources: *AsianBondsOnline* calculations based on Bloomberg LP and *EDAILY BondWeb* data.

The Republic of Korea's corporate bond market saw tepid issuance during Q1 2020, particularly in March, due to market volatility as a result of the COVID-19 pandemic. In addition, the continued pessimistic outlook in economic growth resulted in less borrowing by corporates during the quarter. **Table 3** lists the notable corporate bond issuances in Q1 2020. The market continues to be dominated by issuances from banks and financial institutions such as Woori Bank, Nonghyup Bank, and Mirae Asset Daewoo.

Investor Profile

Insurance companies and pension funds remained the largest holders of the Republic of Korea's LCY government bonds at the end of December 2019 with a share of 35.7%, which was slightly lower than their share of 36.0% in the same period in 2018 (**Figure 2**). General government and banks were next with shares of 17.6% and 17.4%, respectively. The share of the general government declined from 19.2% in December 2018, while that of

Table 3: Notable Local Currency Corporate Bond Issuance in the First Quarter of 2020

Corporate Issuers	Coupon Rate (%)	Issued Amount (KRW billion)	Corporate Issuers	Coupon Rate (%)	Issued Amount (KRW billion)
Woori Bank			National Agricultural Cooperative Federation		
2-year bond	1.42	400	3-year bond	1.51	300
3-year bond	1.25	400	5-year bond	1.62	400
3-year bond	1.46	350	Samsung Securities		
10-year bond	1.94	300	3-year bond	1.48	450
Nonghyup Bank			S-Oil Corp		
2-year bond	1.50	380	5-year bond	1.49	440
5-year bond	1.62	300	Kookmin Bank		
10-year bond	2.38	300	10-year bond	2.02	400
Mirae Asset Daewoo			KB Financial Group		
3-year bond	1.80	350	10-year bond	2.21	370
6-year bond	3.00	500	LG Chem		
SK Hynix			10-year bond	1.57	350
3-year bond	1.61	340	KEB Hana Bank		
5-year bond	1.72	360	10-year bond	2.32	350

KRW = Korean won.
Source: Based on data from Bloomberg LP.

Figure 2: Local Currency Government Bonds Investor Profile

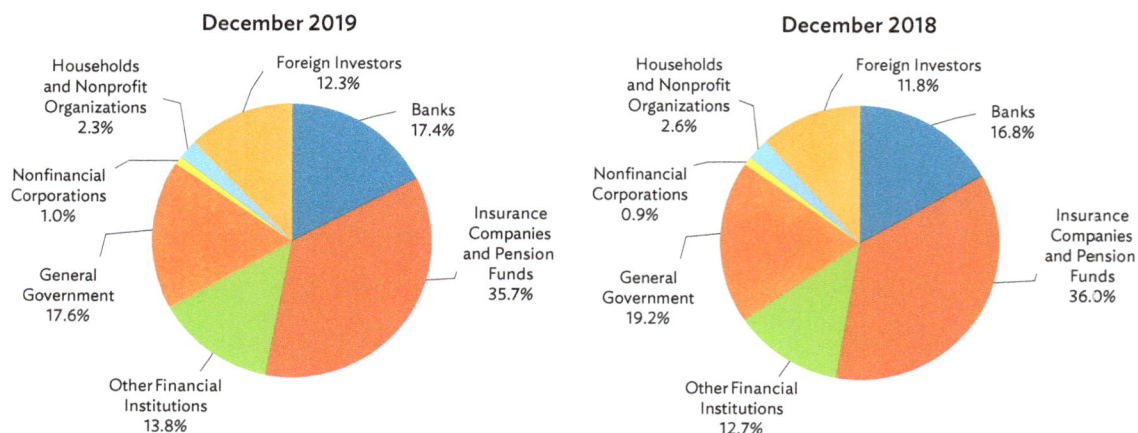

December 2019

Households and Nonprofit Organizations 2.3%
Foreign Investors 12.3%
Banks 17.4%
Insurance Companies and Pension Funds 35.7%
Other Financial Institutions 13.8%
General Government 17.6%
Nonfinancial Corporations 1.0%

December 2018

Households and Nonprofit Organizations 2.6%
Foreign Investors 11.8%
Banks 16.8%
Insurance Companies and Pension Funds 36.0%
Other Financial Institutions 12.7%
General Government 19.2%
Nonfinancial Corporations 0.9%

Sources: *AsianBondsOnline* and the Bank of Korea.

banks marginally increased from 16.8%. The share of other financial institutions rose to 13.8% from 12.7% during the review period. Foreign holdings of LCY government bonds was up marginally to 12.3% from 11.8%.

Insurance companies and pension funds continued to be the largest investor group in the Republic of Korea's LCY corporate bond market with a share of 37.0% at the end of December 2019, a decline from its share of 39.2% in the same period in 2018 (**Figure 3**). Meanwhile, the share of other financial institutions rose to 35.8% from 33.3% during the same period. The share of the general government was barely changed at 13.6% at the end of December 2019, while the share of banks rose to 8.5% from 7.1%. The share of foreign investors remained negligible at 0.1%.

Foreign investor demand for the Republic of Korea's LCY bond market remained strong in the first 4 months of 2020 amid financial market volatility caused by the COVID-19 pandemic (**Figure 4**). The Republic of Korea remained a safe haven relative to its peers in the region as its LCY bond market registered net inflows of KRW4,623 billion in January. A decline to KRW570 billion in net inflows was registered in February, primarily due to risk aversion as domestic COVID-19 cases temporarily surged. However, foreign investors returned in March with net inflows of KRW3,581 billion, followed by a surge in net inflows of KRW7,383 billion in April.

The strong demand for the Republic of Korea's LCY bonds can be attributed to the high interest rate differential with the bond yields of similarly rated peers and with US Treasury yields after the Federal Reserve cut its rate to between 0% and 0.25%. The Republic of Korea also remained a safe haven given its high credit rating, robust external balances, the government's efforts to provide liquidity in the market, and its various programs to cushion the economic impact of the pandemic.

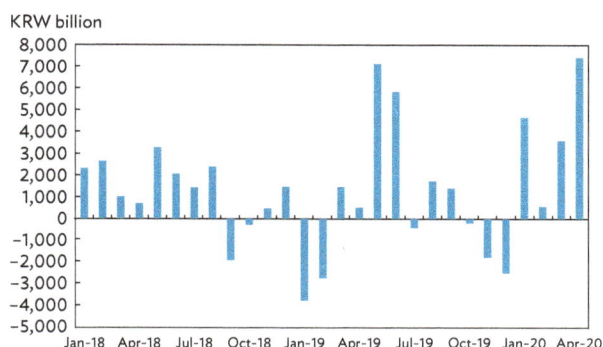

Figure 4: Net Foreign Investment in Local Currency Bonds in the Republic of Korea

KRW = Korean won.
Source: Financial Supervisory Service.

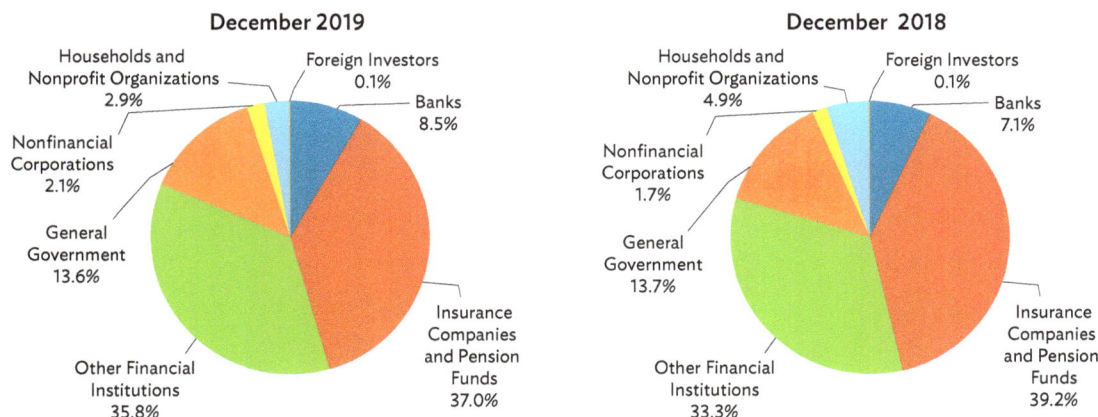

Figure 3: Local Currency Corporate Bonds Investor Profile

December 2019

Households and Nonprofit Organizations 2.9%
Foreign Investors 0.1%
Banks 8.5%
Nonfinancial Corporations 2.1%
General Government 13.6%
Insurance Companies and Pension Funds 37.0%
Other Financial Institutions 35.8%

December 2018

Households and Nonprofit Organizations 4.9%
Foreign Investors 0.1%
Banks 7.1%
Nonfinancial Corporations 1.7%
General Government 13.7%
Insurance Companies and Pension Funds 39.2%
Other Financial Institutions 33.3%

Sources: *AsianBondsOnline* and the Bank of Korea.

Ratings Update

On 11 February, Fitch Ratings affirmed the Republic of Korea's sovereign credit rating at AA– with a stable outlook. The rating affirmation was supported by the economy's steady macroeconomic prospects, which were to be further boosted by the government's fiscal stimulus, sound fiscal management, and robust external finances. Risks to the outlook remain and largely stem from rising cases of COVID-19 and geopolitical risks.

On 21 April, S&P Global affirmed the Republic of Korea's sovereign credit rating at AA and maintained its stable outlook. The rating agency stated that the economy may contract 1.5% in 2020, and it expects the fiscal deficit to widen this year due to fiscal measures being undertaken by the government to address the impact of the COVID-19 pandemic. The rating agency cited the Republic of Korea's strong economic prospects, with growth expected to rebound in 2021; the government's sound fiscal position amid years of surpluses; a favorable policy environment; and strong external metrics as reasons behind the affirmation.

Policy, Institutional, and Regulatory Developments

The Republic of Korea Announces Launch of Financial Support Package in Excess of KRW50 Trillion

On 19 March, the Government of the Republic of Korea announced the launch of a more than KRW50 trillion financial support package to aid businesses and households affected by the COVID-19 pandemic. The package includes nine programs focused on (i) providing liquidity to small businesses, special guarantees for small and medium-sized enterprise loans, guarantees for small merchants; (ii) deferment and or suspension of loan and interest payments by small and medium-sized enterprises and small businesses; and the (iii) creation of a bond market stabilization fund and equity market stabilization fund.

The Bank of Korea Announces Measures to Boost Market Liquidity

On 26 March, the Bank of Korea announced measures to support market liquidity and stabilize financial markets. This included the conduct of weekly repo auctions for a period of 3 months. It also expanded the range of institutions eligible for the auctions from five to 16 nonbanks, eligible securities will now include eight bonds issued by public organizations, and eligible collateral has been extended to eight bonds issued by public organizations and bank debentures.

The Bank of Korea Launches Corporate Bond-Backed Lending Facility

On 16 April, the Bank of Korea launched the Corporate Bond-Backed Lending Facility to allow banks and non-bank financial institutions that can provide high-rated corporate bonds as collateral to access credit from the central bank. The facility will have a ceiling of KRW10 trillion and a term of 3 months; this can be adjusted after an assessment of financial market conditions.

National Assembly Passes KRW12.2 Trillion Supplementary Budget

On 30 April, the National Assembly passed the government's second supplementary budget, which was revised upward to KRW12.2 trillion from KRW7.6 trillion. As part of the government's financial support package, funds will be used to aid sectors affected by the COVID-19 pandemic, particularly financing of the household emergency relief program. KRW8.8 trillion will be sourced from spending restructuring, and the remaining KRW3.4 trillion will be raised via debt issuance.

Malaysia

Yield Movements

Between 28 February and 15 May, movements in Malaysia's local currency (LCY) government bond yields were mixed (**Figure 1**). Yield of bonds with 1-month to 7-year tenor declined an average of 34 basis points (bps). Yields of longer-term tenors (from 8 years to 30 years) increased an average of 11 bps. The yield spread between 2-year and 10-year government bonds expanded from 22 bps to 67 bps during the review period.

The movement at the shorter-end of the yield curve in Malaysia was driven by Bank Negara Malaysia's (BNM) decision to cut its overnight policy rate by a total of 75 bps during its monetary policy committee meetings held on 3 March and 5 May. To enhance liquidity amid the economic fallout from the coronavirus disease (COVID-19) pandemic, BNM also announced in March that banks may use Malaysian Government Securities and Government Investment Issues to fulfill their statutory reserve requirements. The decline in demand for longer-term tenors reflects investors' flight to safety amid an uncertain economic outlook. In March, Malaysia's 10-year yield spiked as a substantial decline in global oil prices hampered sentiments in global financial markets, with investors demanding a higher risk premium. Investors turned wary of the possible effects of oil-related revenues on Malaysia's fiscal balance. The 10-year yield has since fallen as global oil prices rebounded.

On 5 May, the monetary policy committee of BNM decided to lower the overnight policy rate by 50 bps to 2.00%, the third time in 2020 that it has reduced the policy rate. The committee decreased the overnight policy rate by 25 bps during its 22 January and 3 March meetings. The series of reductions were meant to ensure price stability and a stable growth trajectory for Malaysia's economy. But with the COVID-19 pandemic disrupting economic activities worldwide, the decision was viewed as enabling conditions for a sustainable economic recovery.

Prices of basic goods and services in Malaysia declined 0.2% year-on-year (y-o-y) in March, dragged down by the transport industry. This came after consumer price inflation of 1.6% y-o-y and 1.3% y-o-y in January and February, respectively. In May, BNM announced that it

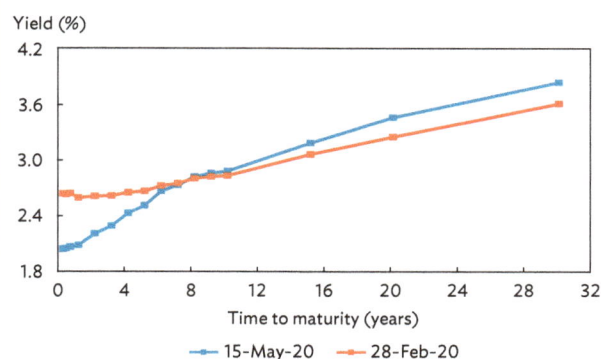

Figure 1: Malaysia's Benchmark Yield Curve—Local Currency Government Bonds

Source: Based on data from Bloomberg LP.

expects inflation for full-year 2020 to be negative due to falling global oil and other commodity prices.

Malaysia's economic growth slowed to 0.7% y-o-y in the first quarter (Q1) of 2020 from 4.4% y-o-y and 3.6% y-o-y in the third quarter and fourth quarter (Q4) of 2019, respectively. In April, BNM's economic growth forecast for full-year 2020 was between −2.0% and −0.5% due to weak global demand that has led to declining oil prices and commodity supply disruptions. During the second half of March, the Government of Malaysia implemented a Movement Control Order to contain the spread of COVID-19. This is expected to lead to limited domestic demand. BNM expects the Malaysian economy to contract in the second quarter of 2020.

Size and Composition

Malaysia's LCY bond market expanded 2.9% quarter-on-quarter (q-o-q) in Q1 2020 to reach a size of MYR1,527.8 billion (USD353.7 billion), up from MYR1,485.4 billion at the end of Q4 2019 (**Table 1**). The growth corresponds to a 6.0% y-o-y jump from MYR1,440.8 billion at the end of Q1 2019. The growth in the LCY bond market in Q1 2020 was supported by expansions in both LCY government and corporate bonds, which accounted for 52.6% and 47.4%, respectively, of total LCY bonds outstanding at the end of March. Total outstanding *sukuk* (Islamic bonds) at the

Table 1: Size and Composition of the Local Currency Bond Market in Malaysia

| | Outstanding Amount (billion) | | | | | | Growth Rate (%) | | | |
| | Q1 2019 | | Q4 2019 | | Q1 2020 | | Q1 2019 | | Q1 2020 | |
	MYR	USD	MYR	USD	MYR	USD	q-o-q	y-o-y	q-o-q	y-o-y
Total	1,441	353	1,485	363	1,528	354	2.9	7.6	2.9	6.0
Government	766	188	773	189	804	186	3.6	8.7	3.9	4.9
Central Government Bonds	720	176	737	180	767	177	4.2	9.8	4.0	6.4
of which: Sukuk	327	80	341	83	362	84	6.7	14.1	5.9	10.6
Central Bank Bills	17	4	9	2	10	2	(9.9)	(13.9)	11.1	(42.2)
of which: Sukuk	5	1.3	1	0.2	2	0.3	40.5	420.0	50.0	(71.2)
Sukuk Perumahan Kerajaan	28	7	27	7	27	6	(1.8)	(1.8)	0.0	(3.9)
Corporate	675	165	712	174	724	168	2.0	6.4	1.7	7.3
of which: Sukuk	520	127	569	139	577	134	3.0	8.3	1.5	11.0

( ) = negative, MYR = Malaysian ringgit, q-o-q = quarter-on-quarter, Q1 = first quarter, Q4 = fourth quarter, USD = United States dollar, y-o-y = year-on-year.
Notes:
1. Calculated using data from national sources.
2. Bloomberg LP end-of-period local currency–USD rates are used.
3. Growth rates are calculated from local currency base and do not include currency effects.
4. Sukuk Perumahan Kerajaan are Islamic bonds issued by the Government of Malaysia to refinance funding for housing loans to government employees and to extend new housing loans.
Sources: Bank Negara Malaysia Fully Automated System for Issuing/Tendering and Bloomberg LP.

end of the review period stood at MYR966.7 billion on growth of 3.1% q-o-q from MYR937.7 billion at the end of the previous quarter, spurred by increased stocks of government and corporate *sukuk*.

Issuance of LCY bonds in Q1 2020 increased 10.7% q-o-q to MYR92.6 billion from MYR83.7 billion in Q4 2019, driven by increased government bond issuance.

Government bonds. The LCY government bond market grew 3.9% q-o-q to MYR803.5 billion in Q1 2020, up from MYR773.2 billion in the previous quarter. The growth was due to the 4.0% q-o-q increase in outstanding central government bonds, which comprised 95.4% of total outstanding LCY government bonds, and the 11.1% q-o-q expansion of outstanding central bank bills, which comprised a 1.2% share of total LCY government bonds outstanding. The outstanding stock of Sukuk Perumahan Kerajaan (3.3% of total outstanding LCY government bonds) remained unchanged from the previous quarter.

LCY government bonds issued in Q1 2020 surged 42.9%, spurred by robust issuance of government bonds and Treasury bills. These were more than enough to offset the decline in BNM bills. Issuance of Malaysian Government Securities and Government Investment Issues jumped compared to the previous quarter.

Corporate bonds. LCY corporate bonds outstanding expanded 1.7% q-o-q to MYR724.3 billion in Q1 2020

from MYR712.2 billion in Q4 2019. Outstanding corporate *sukuk* rose 1.5% q-o-q to MYR576.8 billion at the end of March from MYR568.6 billion in the prior quarter.

The top 30 corporate bond issuers in Malaysia accounted for an aggregate MYR432.9 billion of corporate bonds outstanding at the end of Q1 2020, or 59.8% of the total corporate bond market (**Table 2**). Government institutions Danainfra Nasional, Prasarana, and Cagamas continued to dominate all issuers with outstanding LCY corporate bonds amounting to MYR63.8 billion (8.8% of total LCY corporate bonds outstanding), MYR34.5 billion (4.8%), and MYR32.9 billion (4.5%), respectively. By industry, finance comprised the largest share (53.4%) of the top 30 issuers with MYR231.1 billion in outstanding LCY corporate bonds at the end of March. This was followed by the transport, storage, and communications industry with MYR69.2 billion, which represented 16.0% of total LCY corporate bonds outstanding at the end Q1 2020.

Issuance of LCY corporate bonds declined 14.1% q-o-q in Q1 2020 due to the slow pace of issuance in January.

Government-owned public transport company Prasarana issued the most tranches of Islamic medium-term notes (MTN), issuing five tranches with tenors ranging from 7 years to 30 years, proceeds from which will be used for various Shari'ah-compliant activities of the company (**Table 3**). Prasarana also issued a MYR0.7 billion 20-year

Table 2: Top 30 Issuers of Local Currency Corporate Bonds in Malaysia

	Issuers	Outstanding Amount		State-Owned	Listed Company	Type of Industry
		LCY Bonds (MYR billion)	LCY Bonds (USD billion)			
1.	Danainfra Nasional	63.8	14.8	Yes	No	Finance
2.	Prasarana	34.5	8.0	Yes	No	Transport, Storage, and Communications
3.	Cagamas	32.9	7.6	Yes	No	Finance
4.	Project Lebuhraya Usahasama	29.4	6.8	No	No	Transport, Storage, and Communications
5.	Urusharta Jamaah	27.6	6.4	Yes	No	Finance
6.	Lembaga Pembiayaan Perumahan Sektor Awam	24.7	5.7	Yes	No	Property and Real Estate
7.	Perbadanan Tabung Pendidikan Tinggi Nasional	21.6	5.0	Yes	No	Finance
8.	Pengurusan Air	18.0	4.2	Yes	No	Energy, Gas, and Water
9.	Khazanah	14.2	3.3	Yes	No	Finance
10.	CIMB Bank	14.1	3.3	Yes	No	Finance
11.	Maybank Islamic	13.0	3.0	No	Yes	Banking
12.	Maybank	11.4	2.6	No	Yes	Banking
13.	CIMB Group Holdings	11.2	2.6	Yes	No	Finance
14.	Sarawak Energy	11.1	2.6	Yes	No	Energy, Gas, and Water
15.	Danga Capital	10.0	2.3	Yes	No	Finance
16.	Jimah East Power	9.0	2.1	Yes	No	Energy, Gas, and Water
17.	Public Bank	7.9	1.8	No	No	Banking
18.	GENM Capital	7.6	1.8	No	No	Finance
19.	Bank Pembangunan Malaysia	7.2	1.7	Yes	No	Banking
20.	GOVCO Holdings	7.2	1.7	Yes	No	Finance
21.	Tenaga Nasional	7.0	1.6	No	Yes	Energy, Gas, and Water
22.	Bakun Hydro Power Generation	6.3	1.5	No	No	Energy, Gas, and Water
23.	YTL Power International	6.1	1.4	No	Yes	Energy, Gas, and Water
24.	Telekom Malaysia	5.8	1.3	No	Yes	Telecommunications
25.	Rantau Abang Capital	5.5	1.3	Yes	No	Finance
26.	Danum Capital	5.5	1.3	No	No	Finance
27.	Turus Pesawat	5.3	1.2	Yes	No	Transport, Storage, and Communications
28.	EDRA Energy	5.1	1.2	No	Yes	Energy, Gas, and Water
29.	1Malaysia Development	5.0	1.2	Yes	No	Finance
30.	Sunway Treasury Sukuk	4.9	1.1	No	No	Finance
	Total Top 30 LCY Corporate Issuers	432.9	100.2			
	Total LCY Corporate Bonds	724.3	167.7			
	Top 30 as % of Total LCY Corporate Bonds	59.8%	59.8%			

LCY = local currency, MYR = Malaysian ringgit, USD = United States dollar.
Notes:
1. Data as of 31 March 2020.
2. State-owned firms are defined as those in which the government has more than a 50% ownership stake.
Source: AsianBondsOnline calculations based on Bank Negara Malaysia Fully Automated System for Issuing/Tendering data.

Table 3: Notable Local Currency Corporate Bond Issuance in the First Quarter of 2020

Corporate Issuers	Coupon Rate (%)	Issued Amount (MYR billion)
Prasarana		
7-year Islamic MTN	3.02	0.4
10-year Islamic MTN	3.09	0.6
15-year Islamic MTN	3.28	0.5
20-year Islamic MTN	3.44	1.0
20-year *sukuk murabahah*	3.75	0.7
25-year Islamic MTN	3.90	0.7
30-year Islamic MTN	3.80	1.0
Khazanah		
20-year MTN	4.14	2.9
Aeon Credit Service		
7-year *sukuk wakalah*	3.80	0.3
8-year *sukuk wakalah*	3.85	0.2
10-year *sukuk wakalah*	3.95	0.2

MTN = medium-term note, MYR = Malaysian ringgit.
Notes:
1. *Sukuk murabahah* are Islamic bonds in which bondholders are entitled to a share of the revenues generated by the assets.
2. *Sukuk wakalah* are Islamic bonds backed by an agreement between an investor and an agent. The bondholders are entitled to profits as agreed upon by the two parties.
Source: Bank Negara Malaysia Bond Info Hub.

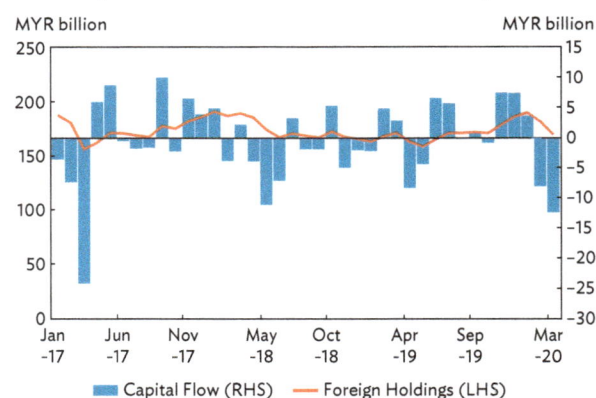

Figure 2: Foreign Holdings and Capital Flows of Local Currency Central Government Bonds in Malaysia

LHS = left-hand side, MYR = Malaysian ringgit, RHS = right-hand side.
Notes:
1. Figures exclude foreign holdings of Bank Negara Malaysia bills.
2. Month-on-month changes in foreign holdings of local currency government bonds were used as a proxy for bond flows.
Source: Bank Negara Malaysia Monthly Statistical Bulletin.

sukuk murabahah (an Islamic bond in which bondholders are entitled to a share of the revenues generated by the assets) with a coupon rate of 3.75%. The *sukuk* was issued under the company's Sukuk Murabahah Programme, and its proceeds will be used to finance Shari'ah-compliant activities related to the LRT3 project. Prasarana issued a 25-year Islamic MTN worth MYR0.7 billion and with a coupon rate 3.90%. Proceeds from the issuance will be used for Shari'ah-compliant capital expenditure and general working capital requirements. Khazanah had the single-largest issuance, which also carried the largest coupon, during the quarter with a MYR2.9 billion 20-year MTN and a 4.14% coupon rate. The sovereign wealth fund of the Government of Malaysia will utilize the proceeds to fund general investments and refinance borrowing. Aeon Credit Service issued two tranches of *sukuk* with tenors of 7 years and 8 years. It also sold a MYR0.2 billion 10-year *sukuk* with a 3.95% coupon rate. The financial institution will use the proceeds from the issuances to finance disbursements to its customers and refinance existing obligations.

Investor Profile

Foreign holdings of LCY government bonds in Q1 2020 jumped to MYR542.2 billion from MYR536.9 billion in Q4 2019, although monthly holdings showed a declining trend (**Figure 2**). A total of MYR16.7 billion in net capital outflows were recorded in Q1 2020, with the largest outflows recorded in March amid recession concerns as global investors became increasingly wary of the economic impact of the COVID-19 pandemic. This reversed the capital inflows of MYR14.4 billion recorded in the previous quarter. As a share of LCY government bonds, foreign holdings of LCY government bonds decreased to 22.2% at the end of Q1 2020 from 25.3% at the end of Q4 2019.

At the end of Q4 2019, social security institutions and financial institutions led all investors in LCY government bond holdings with 33.0% and 31.5% of the total, respectively, both of which were down from a year earlier (**Figure 3**). Foreign holders increased their share of total holdings to 24.9% from 23.5% in Q4 2018. The shares of insurance companies and BNM fell to 4.7% and 0.6%, respectively, from 5.1% and 1.5% during the review period.

Figure 3: Local Currency Government Bonds Investor Profile

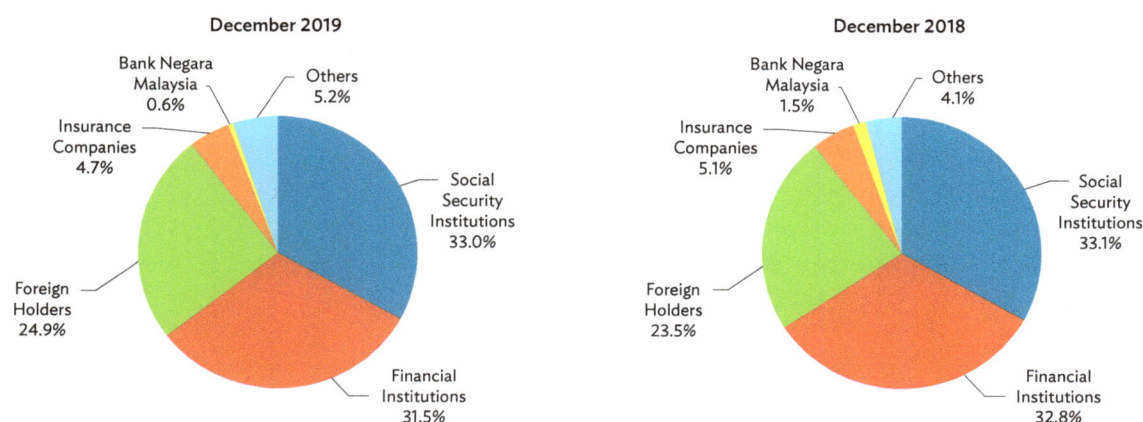

December 2019

- Bank Negara Malaysia 0.6%
- Others 5.2%
- Insurance Companies 4.7%
- Social Security Institutions 33.0%
- Foreign Holders 24.9%
- Financial Institutions 31.5%

December 2018

- Bank Negara Malaysia 1.5%
- Others 4.1%
- Insurance Companies 5.1%
- Social Security Institutions 33.1%
- Foreign Holders 23.5%
- Financial Institutions 32.8%

Note: "Others" include statutory bodies, nominees and trustee companies, and cooperatives and unclassified items.
Source: Bank Negara Malaysia.

Ratings Update

On 27 March, S&P Global affirmed Malaysia's A-/A-2 foreign currency and A/A-1 local currency ratings with a stable outlook for both. Despite falling oil prices and the sudden change in government, the rating agency hailed the economy's strong position in the international market, monetary stance flexibility, and well-established institutions. It also expects the new government to continue the reforms started by the previous administration. On the other hand, increasing net general government debt and rising political risk are placing downward pressure on the economy's ratings.

On 9 April, Fitch Ratings affirmed Malaysia's long-term foreign currency issuer default rating at A− but revised its outlook to negative from stable. Declining economic activities due to the lockdown imposed to fight the COVID-19 pandemic have weakened growth prospects for Malaysia. The uncertainty of the duration of the pandemic contributed to the weak projections for the economy. Fitch Ratings is also wary of political risks hampering improvements in governance for the past 2 years as the new government's plans have yet to be laid out.

Policy, Institutional, and Regulatory Developments

Bank Negara Malaysia Decreases Statutory Reserve Requirement

On 19 March, BNM decreased the statutory reserve requirement ratio from 3.0% to 2.0%. Principal dealers can now include up to a total of MYR1.0 billion worth of Malaysian Government Securities and Government Investment Issues in the computation of their reserves. On 5 May, the central bank allowed all banking institutions to do the same, although no cap on the total amount was mentioned. The measures are expected to release MYR46.0 billion worth of liquidity into Malaysia's banking system to support financial activities in the market.

FTSE Russell Keeps Malaysia on Its Watchlist

On 2 April, FTSE Russell decided to keep Malaysia on its watchlist during its interim March review, saying it would continue to monitor Malaysia for a possible downgrade. To avoid being removed from the FTSE Russell World Government Bond Index, Malaysia has been given 6 months to improve its market conditions. Since its placement on the watchlist last year, Malaysia has implemented regulations to improve bond and foreign exchange liquidity conditions. The decision on whether or not to exclude Malaysia from the benchmark index is expected during FTSE Russell's annual review in September.

Philippines

Yield Movements

The yields of local currency (LCY) government securities in the Philippines fell across the board between 28 February and 15 May (**Figure 1**). Yields of bonds with maturities from 1 year to 10 years declined the most, averaging 106 basis points (bps). Smaller yield declines were observed at the shorter-end and longer-end of the curve. Securities with 6-month tenors or less shed an average of 77 bps from their yield, while longer-term debt paper (20- and 25-year tenors) dropped 52 bps on average. The change in the yield spread between the 2-year and 10-year tenors was minimal, widening only 1 bp during the review period from 45 bps to 46 bps.

Several developments influenced the downward movement of the yield curve. The first was the series of interest rate cuts from Bangko Sentral ng Pilipinas (BSP). The central bank cut the policy rate by 50 bps on 17 April during an off-cycle meeting, bringing the overnight reverse repurchase rate to 2.75%. The move came less than 1 month after the BSP cut the policy rate by 50 bps on 19 March. The unprecedented move sought to encourage lending in various sectors of the economy. The BSP has aggressively cut the key rate by 125 bps thus far in 2020 in an effort to keep the economy afloat during the pandemic. However, the BSP recently hinted at a pause in monetary policy easing to assess the impact of its actions.

The second factor has been investors resorting to safe-haven assets at a time of persistent uncertainty over the economic impact of the COVID-19 pandemic. In an environment clad with risks, investors have become cautious by parking their money in less risky assets such as government bonds. Increased demand from investors, as observed in the auctions, has led to higher bids and lower yields.

Weaker inflationary pressure was also a factor pushing yields downward. Consumer price inflation has moderated since the start of the year. In May, it slowed further to 2.1% year-on-year (y-o-y) from 2.2% y-o-y in April. The Consumer Price Index was weighed down largely by the continued negative price growth in the transport group where prices declined 5.6% y-o-y due to lower

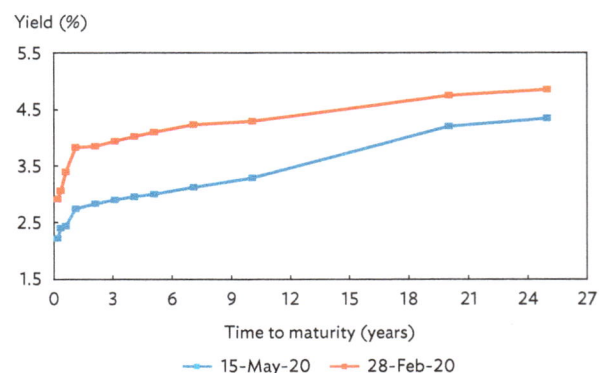

Figure 1: Philippines' Benchmark Yield Curve—Local Currency Government Bonds

Source: Based on data from Bloomberg LP.

domestic petroleum prices. The lower inflation was also underpinned by the slower price adjustments for some food and nonfood commodities.

LCY bond yield declines were also driven by the dovish stance of the United States (US) Federal Reserve and other major central banks. The Federal Reserve cut its policy rate to almost zero in March to shield the domestic economy from the negative impact of the COVID-19 pandemic. This resulted in US Treasury yields tumbling, which Philippine bond yields often track to a degree.

The Philippines' gross domestic product fell 0.2% y-o-y in the first quarter (Q1) of 2020 after expanding 6.7% y-o-y in the fourth quarter (Q4) of 2019, ending the economy's growth streak since Q4 1998. The decline was the result of shocks to the economy, primarily coming from the imposition of enhanced community quarantine, which halted most economic activities, as a measure to control the COVID-19 pandemic. All major sectors showed weaker performance, led by declining output in manufacturing, transportation and storage, and accommodation and food service activities. On the expenditure side, only household and government consumption showed increases, albeit at slower paces than in Q4 2019 at 0.2% y-o-y and 7.1% y-o-y, respectively.

The Philippine peso was relatively stable from the beginning of the year through mid-May, characterized by modest strengthening against the US dollar. Despite the COVID-19 pandemic that has wreaked havoc on both the domestic and global economy, the peso-to-dollar exchange rate has managed to hover around PHP50–PHP51 to USD1. The peso's strength is backed by the economy's sufficient financial buffers that include gross international reserves at a secure level and a sound fiscal position. But the prospect of a weakening peso remains if the impact of the pandemic worsens.

Size and Composition

The Philippine LCY bond market expanded 6.9% quarter-on-quarter (q-o-q) in Q1 2020, registering total bonds outstanding of PHP7,106 billion (USD140.2 billion) at the end of March (**Table 1**). The quarterly growth rate in Q1 2020 rebounded strongly from a decline in the preceding quarter. On an annual basis, the bond market grew 7.9% y-o-y, which was slower compared with Q4 2019. The LCY bond market comprises 77.8% government bonds and 22.2% corporate bonds.

Government bonds. The size of the LCY government bond market grew 7.5% q-o-q in Q1 2020, following a q-o-q decline in Q4 2019 when a large volume of Treasury bonds and bills matured and resulted in a reduced bond stock. The increase in market size was due to Bureau of the Treasury's (BTr) enlarged borrowing plan

from the local market in Q1 2020, which was upped by the issuance of Retail Treasury Bonds (RTBs). Treasury bills and Treasury bonds outstanding grew 14.5% q-o-q and 6.8% q-o-q, respectively, after recording declines in Q4 2019, while the amount of outstanding debt from government-related entities was mostly unchanged.

The government raised a substantial volume of debt in the domestic bond market in Q1 2020. The total issuance of PHP718.2 billion more than doubled issuance volume in Q4 2019 of PHP272.2 billion. The increased borrowing was programmed to take advantage of liquidity in the local market as a result of the reserve requirement ratio cuts in Q4 2019 by the BSP, as well as of lower interest rates. A large portion of government bond sales during the quarter comprised the issuance of 3-year RTBs amounting to PHP310.8 billion, the highest volume recorded for an RTB offering. In Q1 2020, issuance of Treasury bonds amounted to PHP 414.6 billion, and Treasury bill issuance amounted to PHP303.6 billion. Both amounts represented a significant increase from their respective issue volumes in the previous quarter. Proceeds from the government's aggressive Q1 2020 debt sales will be used for general budgetary purposes and for planned increased spending in 2020.

Despite the government's aggressive borrowing stance, it postponed the sale of CNY-denominated Panda bonds in the People's Republic of China that had been scheduled for March 2020. The BTr stated that it needs to evaluate

Table 1: Size and Composition of the Local Currency Bond Market in the Philippines

	Outstanding Amount (billion)						Growth Rate (%)			
	Q1 2019		Q4 2019		Q1 2020		Q1 2019		Q1 2020	
	PHP	USD	PHP	USD	PHP	USD	q-o-q	y-o-y	q-o-q	y-o-y
Total	6,588	125	6,646	131	7,106	140	8.0	17.8	6.9	7.9
Government	5,203	99	5,141	101	5,526	109	8.8	16.2	7.5	6.2
Treasury Bills	608	12	486	10	557	11	22.9	82.8	14.5	(8.4)
Treasury Bonds	4,562	87	4,615	91	4,930	97	7.2	11.1	6.8	8.1
Others	34	1	40	0.8	40	0.8	(0.02)	(16.2)	(0.02)	18.3
Corporate	1,385	26	1,505	30	1,579	31	5.4	24.4	5.0	14.0

( ) = negative, PHP = Philippine peso, q-o-q = quarter-on-quarter, Q1 = first quarter, Q4 = fourth quarter, USD = United States dollar, y-o-y = year-on-year.
Notes:
1. Calculated using data from national sources.
2. Bloomberg end-of-period local currency–USD rates are used.
3. Growth rates are calculated from local currency base and do not include currency effects.
4. "Others" comprise bonds issued by government agencies, entities, and corporations for which repayment is guaranteed by the Government of the Philippines. This includes bonds issued by Power Sector Assets and Liabilities Management and the National Food Authority, among others.
5. Peso Global Bonds (PHP-denominated bonds payable in USD) are not included.
Sources: Bloomberg LP and Bureau of the Treasury.

developments in the market to decide on the timing of the sales amid the COVID-19 pandemic. Meanwhile, the government can take advantage of strong local demand for securities, especially for short-term tenors as liquidity onshore remains high.

The BTr may also adjust its borrowing program upward given the fiscal measures being taken to contain the impact of COVID-19 on the economy. The government must ensure that it has the resources to prop up the economy and support growth in the near-term.

Corporate bonds. The LCY corporate bond market expanded 5.0% q-o-q in Q1 2020, which was slightly faster than the growth recorded in Q4 2019. LCY corporate bonds outstanding registered PHP1,579.3 billion at the end of Q1 2020, an amount that was lifted by a large volume of issuance during the quarter.

Outstanding debt from the banking sector comprised the largest share of the corporate bond market at the end of March at 41.2% (**Figure 2**). This share was up from 33.1% at the end of March 2019 as several local banks raised their funding levels over the past year. Property companies and holding firms remained in the second and third spot, respectively, comprising 22.9% and 14.8% of the market. In both cases, however, the shares were lower compared with Q1 2019.

The combined bonds outstanding of the top 30 issuers in the corporate market amounted to PHP1,388.3 billion, or 87.9% of the total debt stock in the corporate segment (**Table 2**). The top 30 issuers comprised 25 listed firms and 5 unlisted firms. Nearly half of the outstanding bonds were from the banking sector, totaling PHP609.2 million. Metropolitan Bank, BDO Unibank, Ayala Land, and SM Prime Holdings had the largest amount of bonds outstanding with over PHP100 billion each.

Bond issuances from the corporate segment in Q1 2020 sustained the momentum of the previous quarter with double-digit growth of 38.4% q-o-q. Corporate issuance amounted to PHP147.3 billion with the bulk of it coming from the banking sector. The issuance growth came on the back of strong economic prospects prior to the outbreak of COVID-19 as corporates sought to capitalize on investor optimism by tapping the bond market. The reserve requirement ratio cuts in Q4 2019, with expectations of further reductions, also unleashed liquidity that boosted demand in the market. Notable issuances during Q1 2020 included BDO Unibank's PHP40.1 billion 2.5-year bond in February, which was the single-largest bond issuance from the private sector in the Philippines to date. It was met by strong demand and fetched a coupon rate of 4.41%. Arthaland's maiden issuance of a 5-year PHP3.0 billion green bond with a 6.35% coupon rate was also noteworthy (**Table 3**).

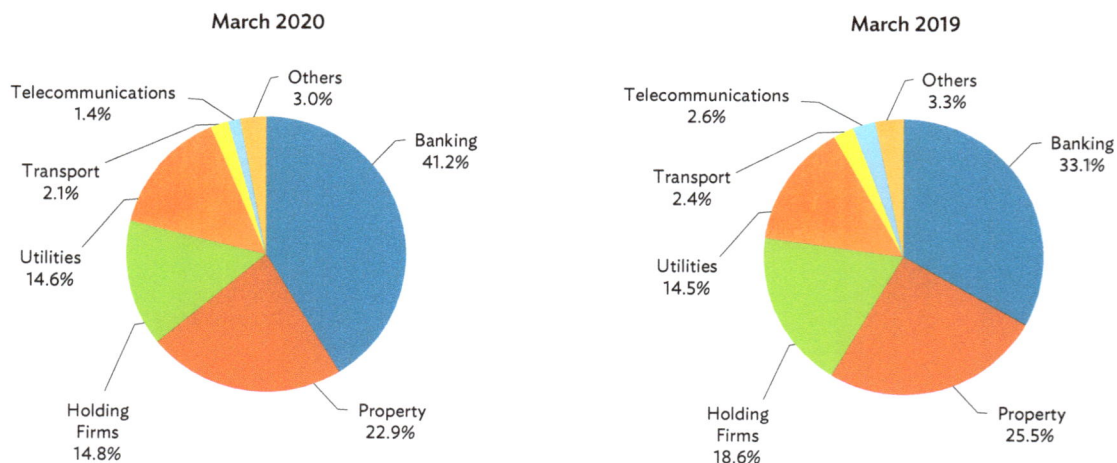

Figure 2: Local Currency Corporate Bonds Outstanding by Sector

March 2020

- Telecommunications 1.4%
- Others 3.0%
- Banking 41.2%
- Transport 2.1%
- Utilities 14.6%
- Holding Firms 14.8%
- Property 22.9%

March 2019

- Telecommunications 2.6%
- Others 3.3%
- Banking 33.1%
- Transport 2.4%
- Utilities 14.5%
- Holding Firms 18.6%
- Property 25.5%

Source: Based on data from Bloomberg LP.

Table 2: Top 30 Issuers of Local Currency Corporate Bonds in the Philippines

	Issuers	Outstanding Amount		State-Owned	Listed Company	Type of Industry
		LCY Bonds (PHP billion)	LCY Bonds (USD billion)			
1.	Metropolitan Bank	128.3	2.5	No	Yes	Banking
2.	BDO Unibank	121.4	2.4	No	Yes	Banking
3.	Ayala Land	105.0	2.1	No	Yes	Property
4.	SM Prime Holdings	103.6	2.0	No	Yes	Property
5.	SMC Global Power	80.0	1.6	No	No	Electricity, Energy, and Power
6.	San Miguel	70.0	1.4	No	Yes	Holding Firms
7.	Bank of the Philippine Islands	64.6	1.3	No	Yes	Banking
8.	Security Bank	59.2	1.2	No	Yes	Banking
9.	Philippine National Bank	56.2	1.1	No	Yes	Banking
10.	SM Investments	52.8	1.0	No	Yes	Holding Firms
11.	Rizal Commercial Banking Corporation	48.7	1.0	No	Yes	Banking
12.	Vista Land	43.6	0.9	No	Yes	Property
13.	Petron	42.9	0.8	No	Yes	Electricity, Energy, and Power
14.	China Bank	42.7	0.8	No	Yes	Banking
15.	Ayala Corporation	40.0	0.8	No	Yes	Holding Firms
16.	Aboitiz Equity Ventures	37.0	0.7	No	Yes	Holding Firms
17.	Maynilad	32.8	0.6	No	No	Water
18.	Aboitiz Power	30.5	0.6	No	Yes	Electricity, Energy, and Power
19.	Union Bank of the Philippines	26.6	0.5	No	Yes	Banking
20.	Philippine Savings Bank	25.4	0.5	No	Yes	Banking
21.	Manila Electric Company	23.0	0.5	No	Yes	Electricity, Energy, and Power
22.	Filinvest Land	22.0	0.4	No	Yes	Property
23.	San Miguel Brewery	22.0	0.4	No	No	Brewery
24.	East West Banking	20.2	0.4	No	Yes	Banking
25.	Robinsons Bank	16.0	0.3	No	No	Banking
26.	GT Capital	15.1	0.3	No	Yes	Holding Firms
27.	Doubledragon	15.0	0.3	No	Yes	Property
28.	PLDT	15.0	0.3	No	Yes	Telecommunications
29.	San Miguel Food and Beverage	15.0	0.3	No	Yes	Food and Beverage
30.	NLEX Corporation	13.9	0.3	No	No	Transport
	Total Top 30 LCY Corporate Issuers	**1,388.3**	**27.4**			
	Total LCY Corporate Bonds	**1,579.3**	**31.2**			
	Top 30 as % of Total LCY Corporate Bonds	**87.9%**	**87.9%**			

LCY = local currency, PHP = Philippine peso, USD = United States dollar.
Notes:
1. Data as of 31 March 2020.
2. State-owned firms are defined as those in which the government has more than a 50% ownership stake.
Source: *AsianBondsOnline* calculations based on Bloomberg LP data.

Table 3: Notable Local Currency Corporate Bond Issuance in the First Quarter of 2020

Corporate Issuers	Coupon Rate (%)	Issued Amount (PHP billion)
Bank of the Philippine Island		
1-year bond	4.05	33.90
2-year bond	4.24	15.33
BDO Unibank		
2.5-year bond	4.41	40.10
SM Prime Holdings		
5-year bond	4.86	11.37
7-year bond	5.06	3.63
San Miguel Food and Beverage		
5-year bond	5.05	8.00
7-year bond	5.25	7.00
Arthaland		
5-year bond	6.35	3.00

PHP = Philippine peso.
Source: Bloomberg LP.

Investor Profile

Banks and investment houses remained the largest investor in LCY government bonds at the end of March, with their combined market share among all investor groups rising to 50.4% from 42.4% from a year earlier (**Figure 3**). On the other hand, contractual savings and tax-exempt institutions; brokers, custodians, and depositories; and BTr-managed funds maintained their respective rankings but all saw declines in their respective market shares. The share of BTr-managed funds declined 5.4 percentage points from March 2019 to March 2020. The shares of the remaining investor groups were mostly unchanged.

Ratings Update

On 7 February, Rating and Investment Information Inc. (R&I) upgraded the Philippines' credit rating to BBB+ from BBB with a stable outlook. The upgrade from R&I was based on the Philippines' continued positive economic performance that is being sustained by the government's aggressive public investment, led by the accelerated infrastructure drive. R&I also noted that the government has maintained a sound fiscal position with the help of tax reforms.

On 7 May, Fitch Ratings revised its outlook for the Philippines downward to stable from positive as near-term macroeconomic and fiscal prospects deteriorated amid the global COVID-19 pandemic and the resulting domestic lockdown to control the spread of the virus. The revision came 3 months after the rating agency had upgraded its outlook to positive from stable on 11 February on the back of expectations of high growth accompanied by moderate inflation and sound fiscal conditions. Fitch Ratings affirmed the economy's BBB rating as fiscal and external buffers remained in place and medium-term growth prospects were still strong.

Figure 3: Local Currency Government Bonds Investor Profile

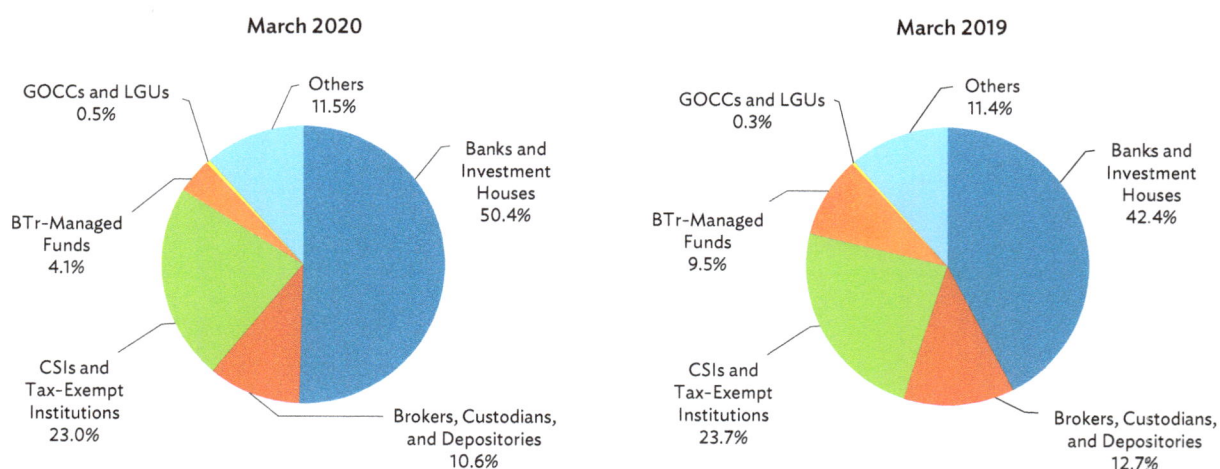

March 2020

- GOCCs and LGUs 0.5%
- Others 11.5%
- Banks and Investment Houses 50.4%
- BTr-Managed Funds 4.1%
- CSIs and Tax-Exempt Institutions 23.0%
- Brokers, Custodians, and Depositories 10.6%

March 2019

- GOCCs and LGUs 0.3%
- Others 11.4%
- Banks and Investment Houses 42.4%
- BTr-Managed Funds 9.5%
- CSIs and Tax-Exempt Institutions 23.7%
- Brokers, Custodians, and Depositories 12.7%

BTr = Bureau of the Treasury, CSIs = contractual savings institutions, GOCCs = government-owned or -controlled corporations, LGUs = local government units.
Source: Bureau of the Treasury.

Policy, Institutional, and Regulatory Developments

Bangko Sentral ng Pilipinas Cuts Reserve Requirement Ratio to Support the Economy amid COVID-19

The BSP announced a cut to the reserve requirement ratio (RRR) of universal and commercial banks by 200 bps on 24 March, effective on 3 April. According to the central bank, the RRR cut was intended to encourage banks to lend to the retail and corporate sectors, and to ensure that there is enough liquidity to support economic activities amid the COVID-19 pandemic. The Monetary Board has authorized the Governor of the BSP to reduce the RRR by as much as 400 bps in 2020. The BSP will assess the pandemic's ongoing impact on the domestic economy to determine the timing and extent of possible further reductions. The possibility of extending the RRR cut to other types of banks and non-bank financial institutions is being explored.

Bangko Sentral ng Pilipinas Announces Measures to Support Domestic Liquidity

On 10 April, the BSP announced measures to support domestic liquidity to ensure stability and the proper functioning of the financial market. Based on BSP's statement, the measures include (i) purchases of government securities in the secondary market, (ii) a reduction of overnight reverse repurchase volumes to encourage counterparties to lend in the interbank market or to rechannel their funds into other assets such as government securities or loans, and (iii) a repurchase agreement with the government where the BSP shall purchase government securities worth up to PHP300 billion from the BTr.

Singapore

Yield Movements

Between 28 February and 15 May, Singapore's local currency (LCY) government bond yields declined for all tenors (**Figure 1**). The shorter-end of the yield curve (from 3 months to 1 year) declined an average of 134 basis points (bps). Yields of longer-term tenors (from 2 years to 30 years) recorded smaller declines, decreasing an average of 68 bps. The yield spread between 2-year and 10-year government bonds expanded from 11 bps to 48 bps during the review period.

The yield curve for Singapore's LCY government bonds shifted downward during the review period amid policy easing by the Monetary Authority of Singapore (MAS) on 30 March, which followed easing measures taken in October 2019. At the end of March, MAS adopted a 0.0% per annum rate of appreciation for the policy band to support the domestic economy amid disruptions caused by the coronavirus disease (COVID-19) pandemic.

In October 2019, MAS reduced slightly the appreciation rate of the Singapore dollar nominal effective exchange rate policy band. In March 2020, this rate was reduced further to 0.0%. Singapore's inflation and economic growth rates have been low since 2019, with recession fears worrying investors. The monetary policy easing supports the economy and ensures price stability over the medium-term. It also complements the Resilience Budget announced in late March.[16]

Singapore's consumer price inflation in March was 0.0% year-on-year (y-o-y) as increases in prices of food and transport were offset by declines in the cost of housing and utilities, and recreation and culture. This came after recording consumer price inflation of 0.8% y-o-y and 0.3% y-o-y in January and February, respectively. In January, MAS inflation projection for full-year 2020 was 0.5%–1.5% y-o-y. In March, the forecast was revised downward to between –1.0% and 0.0%.

Singapore's economy contracted 0.7% y-o-y in the first quarter (Q1) of 2020 after expanding 0.7% y-o-y and

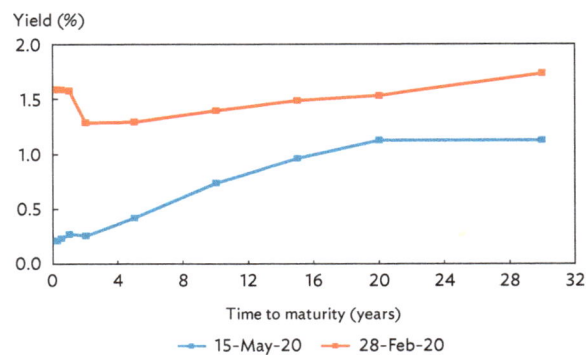

Figure 1: Singapore's Benchmark Yield Curve— Local Currency Government Bonds

Source: Based on data from Bloomberg LP.

1.0% y-o-y in the third quarter and fourth quarter (Q4) of 2019, respectively. In February, Singapore's Ministry of Trade and Industry downgraded its full-year 2020 economic growth to between –1.5% and –0.5% from a November 2019 forecast of between 0.5% and 2.5% as the COVID-19 pandemic was expected to affect the growth prospects of the People's Republic of China and other regional economies, leading to a decline in tourist arrivals and a contraction in domestic consumption. In March, it reduced its growth forecast to between –4.0% and –1.0% amid the escalated COVID-19 outbreak and significantly deteriorating economic activities worldwide. And in May, the forecast was revised downward further to between –7.0% and –4.0%. At the start of April, Singapore started implementing its circuit breaker, limiting movements inside the city-state to prevent the spread of COVID-19.[17]

Size and Composition

Singapore's LCY bond market expanded 2.2% quarter-on-quarter (q-o-q) in Q1 2020 to reach SGD467.2 billion (USD328.5 billion) at the end of March from SGD457.1 billion at the end of December (**Table 1**). On an annual basis, growth was up 12.5% y-o-y. The expansion in the LCY bond market was supported by growth in government and corporate bonds, which

---

[14] The Resilience Budget is a supplementary budget which aims to address the COVID-19 situation and its impact on the economy and society of Singapore.
[15] Circuit breaker is a set of measures implemented by the Singapore government to prevent the spread of COVID-19.

Table 1: Size and Composition of the Local Currency Bond Market in Singapore

| | Outstanding Amount (billion) | | | | | | Growth Rate (%) | | | |
| | Q1 2019 | | Q4 2019 | | Q1 2020 | | Q1 2019 | | Q1 2020 | |
	SGD	USD	SGD	USD	SGD	USD	q-o-q	y-o-y	q-o-q	y-o-y
Total	415	306	457	340	467	329	3.1	8.3	2.2	12.5
Government	256	188	286	212	293	206	4.5	11.1	2.5	14.6
SGS Bills and Bonds	130	96	183	136	188	132	3.8	7.2	2.7	44.8
MAS Bills	126	93	103	77	105	74	5.4	15.4	2.0	(16.5)
Corporate	160	118	171	127	174	123	0.9	4.0	1.7	9.2

( ) = negative, MAS = Monetary Authority of Singapore, q-o-q = quarter-on-quarter, Q1 = first quarter, Q4 = fourth quarter, SGD = Singapore dollar, SGS = Singapore Government Securities, USD = United States dollar, y-o-y = year-on-year.
Notes:
1. Government bonds are calculated using data from national sources. Corporate bonds are based on *AsianBondsOnline* estimates.
2. SGS bills and bonds do not include the special issue of SGS held by the Singapore Central Provident Fund.
3. Bloomberg LP end-of-period local currency–USD rates are used.
4. Growth rates are calculated from local currency base and do not include currency effects.
Sources: Bloomberg LP, Monetary Authority of Singapore, and Singapore Government Securities.

accounted for 62.7% and 37.3%, respectively, of total LCY bonds outstanding at the end of Q1 2020.

Issuance of LCY bonds in Q1 2020 increased 1.3% q-o-q to SGD177.8 billion from SGD175.6 billion in Q4 2019, driven by both rising government and corporate bond issuance.

Government bonds. The LCY government bond market grew 2.5% q-o-q to SGD292.8 billion in Q1 2020 from SGD285.7 billion in the previous quarter. The growth was due to increases in Singapore Government Securities (SGS) bills and bonds, and MAS bills. Outstanding SGS bills and bonds, which comprised 64.1% of total outstanding LCY government bonds, jumped 2.7% q-o-q as 6-month SGS bills gradually replaced 24-week MAS bills starting July 2019. By the end of March, outstanding MAS bills had dropped 16.5% on an annual basis.

LCY government bond issuance in Q1 2020 marginally rose 0.6% q-o-q as lower issuance of SGS bills and bonds was offset by slightly higher MAS bills issuance.

Corporate bonds. LCY corporate bonds outstanding increased 1.7% q-o-q to SGD174.4 billion in Q1 2020 from SGD171.4 billion in Q4 2019, buoyed by the increase in outstanding corporate bonds in the real estate industry.

The top 30 LCY corporate bond issuers in Singapore accounted for combined outstanding bonds of SGD83.1 billion, or 47.7% of total LCY corporate bonds outstanding at the end of Q1 2020 (**Table 2**).

Government institutions such as the Housing & Development Board and the Land Transport Authority remained the largest issuers with outstanding LCY corporate bonds amounting to SGD24.4 billion (14.0% of total LCY corporate bonds outstanding) and SGD10.4 billion (6.0% of total LCY corporate bonds outstanding), respectively. By industry type, real estate companies continued to comprise the largest share (43.9%) among the top 30 issuers of LCY corporate bonds with SGD36.5 billion of LCY corporate bonds outstanding at the end of Q1 2020. Although its share slightly dropped compared with the previous quarter, the transport industry still had the second-largest share of total LCY corporate bonds outstanding at 18.7% (SGD15.6 billion).

Issuance of LCY corporate bonds soared 44.9% q-o-q in Q1 2020 after tepid issuance during the last quarter of 2019.

The Housing & Development Board issued the single-largest LCY corporate bond in Q1 2020, issuing a SGD700.0 million 7-year bond with a coupon rate of 1.76% under its Multicurrency Medium-Term Note Programme (**Table 3**). Proceeds from the issuance will be used to finance the real estate company's development programs and working capital needs, and to refinance existing obligations. PSA Treasury and Singapore Press Holdings both issued SGD500.0 million 10-year bonds, the longest tenor issued during the quarter. PSA Treasury will use the proceeds to support general corporate activities and to refinance existing borrowing, while Singapore Press Holdings plans on utilizing issuance

Table 2: Top 30 Issuers of Local Currency Corporate Bonds in Singapore

	Issuers	Outstanding Amount		State-Owned	Listed Company	Type of Industry
		LCY Bonds (SGD billion)	LCY Bonds (USD billion)			
1.	Housing & Development Board	24.4	17.2	Yes	No	Real Estate
2.	Land Transport Authority	10.4	7.3	Yes	No	Transportation
3.	Singapore Airlines	4.4	3.1	Yes	Yes	Transportation
4.	Frasers Property	4.0	2.8	No	Yes	Real Estate
5.	United Overseas Bank	3.3	2.3	No	Yes	Banking
6.	Mapletree Treasury Services	2.7	1.9	No	No	Finance
7.	Capitaland Treasury	2.7	1.9	No	No	Finance
8.	Temasek Financial	2.6	1.8	Yes	No	Finance
9.	DBS Group Holdings	2.5	1.8	No	Yes	Banking
10.	Keppel Corporation	2.4	1.7	No	Yes	Diversified
11.	Sembcorp Financial Services	2.4	1.7	No	No	Engineering
12.	Capitaland	1.8	1.3	Yes	Yes	Real Estate
13.	City Developments Limited	1.7	1.2	No	Yes	Real Estate
14.	Oversea-Chinese Banking Corporation	1.5	1.1	No	Yes	Banking
15.	CMT MTN	1.4	1.0	No	No	Finance
16.	Shangri-La Hotel	1.4	1.0	No	Yes	Real Estate
17.	GLL IHT	1.3	0.9	No	No	Real Estate
18.	SP Powerassets	1.3	0.9	No	No	Utilities
19.	Public Utilities Board	1.3	0.9	Yes	No	Utilities
20.	Singtel Group Treasury	1.2	0.8	No	No	Finance
21.	Mapletree Commercial Trust	1.1	0.7	No	Yes	Real Estate
22.	Singapore Press Holdings	1.0	0.7	No	Yes	Communications
23.	Hyflux	0.9	0.6	No	Yes	Utilities
24.	Ascendas	0.9	0.6	No	Yes	Finance
25.	Olam International	0.8	0.6	No	Yes	Consumer Goods
26.	Suntec REIT	0.8	0.6	No	Yes	Real Estate
27.	DBS Bank	0.8	0.6	No	Yes	Banking
28.	SMRT Capital	0.8	0.6	No	No	Transportation
29.	Sembcorp Industries	0.8	0.6	No	Yes	Shipbuilding
30.	Singapore Technologies Telemedia	0.8	0.6	Yes	No	Utilities
Total Top 30 LCY Corporate Issuers		**83.1**	**58.4**			
Total LCY Corporate Bonds		**174.4**	**122.6**			
Top 30 as % of Total LCY Corporate Bonds		**47.7%**	**47.7%**			

LCY = local currency, MTN = medium-term note, REIT = real estate investment trust, SGD = Singapore dollar, USD = United States dollar.
Notes:
1. Data as of 31 March 2020.
2. State-owned firms are defined as those in which the government has more than a 50% ownership stake.
Source: *AsianBondsOnline* calculations based on Bloomberg LP data.

Table 3: Notable Local Currency Corporate Bond Issuance in the First Quarter of 2020

Corporate Issuers	Coupon Rate (%)	Issued Amount (SGD million)
Housing & Development Board		
7-year bond	1.76	700.0
PSA Treasury		
10-year bond	1.63	500.0
Singapore Press Holdings		
10-year bond	3.20	500.0
Oxley Holdings		
3-year bond	6.50	75.0
Aspial Corporation		
3-year bond	6.50	50.0

SGD = Singapore dollar.
Source: Bloomberg LP.

proceeds for working capital, capital expenditure, and debt refinancing. The highest coupon rate in Q1 2020 was offered by Oxley Holdings and Aspial Corporation, which both issued 3-year bonds. Oxley Holdings' issuance was drawn from its Euro Medium-Term Note Programme. Aspial Corporation will use the proceeds from the issuance to fund general corporate use and to refinance debt obligations.

Policy, Institutional, and Regulatory Developments

Monetary Authority of Singapore and Federal Reserve Establish Swap Facility

On 19 March, MAS and the United States Federal Reserve established a USD60.0 billion swap facility to address liquidity concerns amid the COVID-19 pandemic. In place for at least 6 months, the swap facility provides stable liquidity conditions in the US dollar funding market in Singapore. It also complements MAS' management of the Singapore dollar market. Together, these measures reinforce the robustness and efficiency of Singapore's financial market.

Monetary Authority of Singapore Adjusts Regulations to Support Financial Institutions

On 7 April, MAS adjusted regulatory and supervisory measures to support financial institutions as they deal with the impacts of the COVID-19 pandemic. To help financial institutions sustain their lending activities, MAS adjusted downward the net stable funding ratio requirement to 25% from 50%. It will also allow financial institutions to factor in the government's fiscal assistance and banks' relief measures in accounting loan loss allowances. As businesses focus on managing the impact of COVID-19, the implementation of Basel III reforms for Singaporean banks has been deferred for 1 year. MAS will coordinate with financial institutions for revised timelines for the submission of regulatory reports. Regular on-site inspections and supervisory visits will be suspended indefinitely; MAS assessments will focus instead on how financial institutions handle the impacts of COVID-19 on their businesses.

Thailand

Yield Movements

Between 28 February and 15 May, the local currency (LCY) government bond yield curve in Thailand shifted downward at the shorter-end and slightly upward at the longer-end (**Figure 1**). Yields fell an average of 28 basis points (bps) for tenors with maturities of up to 6 years, while yields rose an average of 9 bps for tenors with maturities of 7 years or longer. The 1-month bill exhibited the steepest drop at 55 bps, while the 30-year bond showed the largest gain at 31 bps. On average, yields dropped 10 bps across all tenors. The spread between the 2-year and 10-year tenors widened from 25 bps on 28 February to 47 bps on 15 May.

The decline in yields at the shorter-end of the curve stemmed primarily from the easing of the Bank of Thailand's (BOT) monetary policy in response to the economic headwinds brought by the coronavirus disease (COVID-19). The BOT cut its benchmark policy rate by 25 bps three times during the review period, bringing it to a record low of 0.50%. Aside from the policy rate reduction, the BOT also expressed its readiness to use additional monetary measures if necessary.

The uptick in longer-term bond yields was partly due to capital outflows from the Thai bond market. Risk-off sentiment, brought about by softening global growth and exacerbated by uncertainties due to COVID-19, drove investors away from emerging market assets, including Thai sovereign bonds. Between February and April, the Thai bond market recorded net foreign outflows totaling THB131.3 billion. Domestic demand was also depressed, resulting in heightened volatility and tight liquidity in the Thai bond market, particularly for longer-dated tenors. In March, the BOT tapered its bond issuances and cancelled some offerings to improve market liquidity and reduce volatility.

Another factor contributing to the upward pressure on long-term bond yields were the declining growth prospects and heightened risk associated with the economic fallout from COVID-19. Thailand's economy is highly reliant on exports and tourism, which were both battered by travel bans and social distancing measures imposed by governments around the world to contain the pandemic.

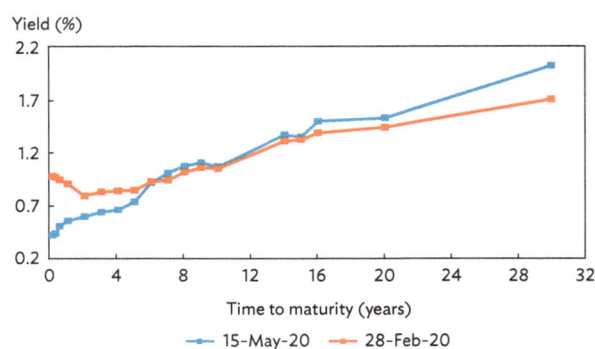

Figure 1: Thailand's Benchmark Yield Curve—Local Currency Government Bonds

Sources: Based on data from Bloomberg LP and Thai Bond Market Association.

Thailand's economy fell into recession in the first quarter (Q1) of 2020, with gross domestic product shrinking 1.8% year-on-year (y-o-y), the deepest contraction since the fourth quarter (Q4) of 2011. Consumption growth slowed to 3.0% y-o-y in Q1 2020 from 4.1% y-o-y in Q4 2019. Government spending and investment dropped 2.7% y-o-y and 6.5% y-o-y, respectively. Exports of goods and services plunged 6.7% y-o-y, while imports of goods and services dipped 2.5% y-o-y. In May, the National Economic and Social Development Council revised its forecast for full-year 2020 gross domestic product growth to a contraction of 5.0%–6.0% from an earlier projection of 1.5%–2.5% growth.

Consumer price inflation fell 3.0% y-o-y in April, following a 0.5% y-o-y drop in March. The deflation resulted from a plunge in energy prices and a reduction in costs of goods and services due to government support measures. The headline inflation rate has been well below the BOT's target range of 1.0%–3.0%. The central bank expects inflation to remain in negative territory for the rest of the year amid subdued energy prices.

The Thai baht depreciated 1.7% against the United States dollar between 28 February and 15 May as weak investor confidence and risk aversion drove foreign capital away from Thai assets, dampening demand for the baht. Prior to the onset of COVID-19, the baht had been outperforming its regional peers. The BOT has expressed concern over the possible strengthening of the baht, which could undermine economic recovery.

Size and Composition

Thailand's LCY bonds outstanding amounted to THB13,168.9 billion (USD402.1 billion) at the end of March after a 0.5% quarter-on-quarter (q-o-q) contraction in Q1 2020 (**Table 1**). The decline reversed the 2.2% q-o-q rise seen in Q4 2019. A contraction in the government bond segment, coupled with tepid growth in the corporate bond segment, drove the quarterly decline in outstanding LCY bonds. On an annual basis, the growth of outstanding LCY bonds decelerated to 4.1% y-o-y in Q1 2020 from 16.0% y-o-y in the previous quarter. The Thai bond market is largely composed of government bonds, which accounted for 71.0% of the total bonds outstanding at the end of March.

Government bonds. The size of the LCY government bond market stood at THB9,353.3 billion at the end of March, with the 1.0% q-o-q contraction in Q1 2020 reversing the 2.5% q-o-q growth posted in Q4 2019. BOT bonds and state-owned enterprise and other bonds posted contractions of 6.1% q-o-q and 1.4% y-o-y, respectively. In contrast, the growth of government bonds and Treasury bills picked up, rising 2.8% q-o-q in Q1 2020 after a 2.3% q-o-q increase in the previous quarter. On an annual basis, the growth of total government bonds outstanding decelerated to 2.7% y-o-y in Q1 2020 from 15.2% y-o-y in the previous quarter.

Total issuance from the government amounted to THB2,032.5 in Q1 2020, with the 3.7% q-o-q growth reversing the 0.9% q-o-q contraction in the previous quarter. The growth stemmed solely from an expansion

in the issuance of BOT bonds, which rose 5.2% q-o-q. There were no new issuances of state-owned enterprise and other bonds, while government bonds and Treasury bills contracted 11.1% q-o-q in Q1 2020. On a y-o-y basis, issuance of government bonds dropped 8.8%, brought down by contractions in the issuance of government bonds and Treasury bills, as well as BOT bonds.

Corporate bonds. Outstanding corporate bonds totaled THB3,815.5 billion at the end of Q1 2020, with q-o-q growth decelerating to 0.8% from 1.6% in the previous quarter. Annual growth was also weaker at 7.9% y-o-y in Q1 2020 compared with 18.0% y-o-y in Q4 2019. The contraction in corporate bonds outstanding was due to a sharp drop in issuance during the review period. Corporate issuance plunged 12.5% q-o-q and 28.6% y-o-y as the onset of the COVID-19 pandemic and the government's containment measures caused wide-scale disruptions in business activities, raising volatility and depressing demand for corporate bonds.

The LCY bonds outstanding of the top 30 corporate issuers amounted to THB2,142.4 billion at the end of March, accounting for 56.1% of the total corporate bond market (**Table 2**). Among the top 30 issuers, food and beverage, commerce, banking, and communication firms together held over half of the outstanding bond stock. Food and beverage firms dominated the list, with total bonds outstanding amounting to THB411.1 billion from five issuers. The majority of the top 30 issuers were listed in the Thai Stock Exchange, while only five were state-owned. Thai Beverage remained the top issuer, with outstanding debt of THB179.5 billion at the end

Table 1: Size and Composition of the Local Currency Bond Market in Thailand

| | Outstanding Amount (billion) | | | | | | Growth Rate (%) | | | |
| | Q1 2019 | | Q4 2019 | | Q1 2020 | | Q1 2019 | | Q1 2020 | |
	THB	USD	THB	USD	THB	USD	q-o-q	y-o-y	q-o-q	y-o-y
Total	12,649	399	13,236	446	13,169	402	1.6	10.9	(0.5)	4.1
Government	9,111	287	9,451	318	9,353	286	1.4	11.1	(1.0)	2.7
Government Bonds and Treasury Bills	4,774	150	4,940	166	5,079	155	0.8	7.9	2.8	6.4
Central Bank Bonds	3,579	113	3,718	125	3,492	107	3.0	20.5	(6.1)	(2.4)
State-Owned Enterprise and Other Bonds	758	24	793	27	782	24	(1.7)	(6.2)	(1.4)	3.1
Corporate	3,538	111	3,786	127	3,816	117	2.3	10.3	0.8	7.9

( ) = negative, q-o-q = quarter-on-quarter, Q1 = first quarter, Q4 = fourth quarter, THB = Thai baht, USD = United States dollar, y-o-y = year-on-year.
Notes:
1. Calculated using data from national sources.
2. Bloomberg LP end-of-period local currency–USD rates are used.
3. Growth rates are calculated from local currency base and do not include currency effects.
Source: Bank of Thailand.

Table 2: Top 30 Issuers of Local Currency Corporate Bonds in Thailand

	Issuers	Outstanding Amount		State-Owned	Listed Company	Type of Industry
		LCY Bonds (THB billion)	LCY Bonds (USD billion)			
1.	Thai Beverage	179.5	5.5	No	No	Food and Beverage
2.	Siam Cement	172.8	5.3	Yes	Yes	Construction Materials
3.	CP All	152.8	4.7	No	Yes	Commerce
4.	Bank of Ayudhya	135.2	4.1	No	Yes	Banking
5.	True Move H Universal Communication	121.2	3.7	No	No	Communications
6.	Berli Jucker	119.2	3.6	No	Yes	Commerce
7.	Charoen Pokphand Foods	100.3	3.1	No	Yes	Food and Beverage
8.	True Corp	91.4	2.8	No	No	Communications
9.	Toyota Leasing Thailand	87.2	2.7	No	No	Finance and Securities
10.	PTT	82.4	2.5	Yes	Yes	Energy and Utilities
11.	Thai Airways International	74.3	2.3	Yes	Yes	Transportation and Logistics
12.	Minor International	66.9	2.0	No	Yes	Hospitality and Leisure
13.	Indorama Ventures	65.3	2.0	No	Yes	Petrochemicals and Chemicals
14.	CPF Thailand	59.5	1.8	No	No	Food and Beverage
15.	Banpu	49.5	1.5	No	Yes	Energy and Utilities
16.	Bangkok Commercial Asset Management	45.8	1.4	No	Yes	Finance and Securities
17.	Krungthai Card	45.8	1.4	Yes	Yes	Banking
18.	Krung Thai Bank	45.5	1.4	Yes	Yes	Banking
19.	Global Power Synergy	42.7	1.3	No	Yes	Energy and Utilities
20.	PTT Global Chemical	41.4	1.3	No	Yes	Petrochemicals and Chemicals
21.	Land & Houses	39.5	1.2	No	Yes	Property and Construction
22.	TPI Polene	39.3	1.2	No	Yes	Property and Construction
23.	Mitr Phol Sugar Corp	38.4	1.2	No	No	Food and Beverage
24.	Bangkok Expressway & Metro	37.5	1.1	No	Yes	Transportation and Logistics
25.	TMB Bank	37.2	1.1	No	Yes	Finance and Securities
26.	Muangthai Capital	36.7	1.1	No	Yes	Finance and Securities
27.	Sansiri	36.0	1.1	No	Yes	Property and Construction
28.	Thai Union Group	33.4	1.0	No	Yes	Food and Beverage
29.	Frasers Property Thailand	33.0	1.0	No	Yes	Property and Construction
30.	CH Karnchang	32.8	1.0	No	Yes	Property and Construction
	Total Top 30 LCY Corporate Issuers	**2,142.4**	**65.4**			
	Total LCY Corporate Bonds	**3,815.5**	**116.5**			
	Top 30 as % of Total LCY Corporate Bonds	**56.1%**	**56.1%**			

LCY = local currency, THB = Thai baht, USD = United States dollar.
Notes:
1. Data as of 31 March 2020.
2. State-owned firms are defined as those in which the government has more than a 50% ownership stake.
Source: *AsianBondsOnline* calculations based on Bloomberg LP data.

of March. Siam Cement remained the second-largest issuer, with total bonds worth THB172.8 billion at the end of March. CP All, Bank of Ayudhya, True Move H Universal Communication, Berli Jucker, and Charoen Pokphand Foods were the next largest issuers, all with bonds outstanding over THB100.0 billion at the end of March.

In Q1 2020, Berli Jucker issued the largest amount of corporate debt totaling THB12.0 billion, comprising bonds with tenors ranging from 3 years to 10 years and carrying coupons ranging from 1.40% to 2.43% (**Table 3**). Toyota Leasing was the second-largest issuer during the quarter, with total issuance amounting to THB8.0 billion from bonds with tenors ranging from 1.5 years to 3 years and coupons ranging from 1.22% to 1.34%. Bank of Ayudhya, True Corp, and Frasers Property were the next largest issuers, with issuances amounting to THB7.0 billion, THB5.5 billion, and THB5.0 billion, respectively.

Investor Profile

Central government bonds. The profile of LCY government bonds investors at the end of March was little changed from last year (**Figure 2**). The combined shares of the four largest holders of LCY government bonds in Thailand remained at 91.5% at the end of March. Financial corporations continued to hold the largest share of government bonds, with their share inching up to 42.5% at the end of March from 41.7% a year earlier. Between March 2019 and March 2020, the central government's share of government bond holdings rose to 18.2% from 13.5%, while that of the BOT dipped to 15.5% from 18.4%. During the same period, the share of nonresidents dropped to 15.3% from 18.0% amid foreign capital outflows from Thailand's government bond market as investors reduced their holdings of emerging market sovereign bonds amid rising uncertainty. The BOT bought government bonds worth THB100.0 billion in the week of 13–20 March to inject liquidity into the bond market given the thin demand for government bonds.

Central bank bonds. Between March 2019 and March 2020, the combined shares of the four largest holders of BOT bonds rose to 96.1% from 92.3% (**Figure 3**). Other depository corporations held the largest share of BOT bonds at 49.5%, up from 37.6% a year earlier. Financial corporations remained the second-largest holder of BOT bonds, although their share of the total holdings fell to

Table 3: Notable Local Currency Corporate Bond Issuance in the First Quarter of 2020

Corporate Issuers	Coupon Rate (%)	Issued Amount (THB billion)
Berli Jucker		
3-year bond	1.40	1.0
5-year bond	1.63	1.0
8-year bond	2.16	7.0
10-year bond	2.43	3.0
Toyota Leasing		
1.5-year bond	1.22	2.0
2.1-year bond	1.27	3.0
3-year bond	1.34	3.0
Bank of Ayudhya		
2-year bond	1.44	2.9
3-year bond	1.57	4.1
True Corp		
1.2-year bond	2.88	0.5
3-year bond	3.43	4.3
5.5-year bond	4.65	0.7
Frasers Property		
3-year bond	2.00	0.5
3.5-year bond	2.10	1.0
5-year bond	2.36	1.8
7-year bond	2.85	0.5
10-year bond	3.20	1.2

THB = Thai baht.
Source: Bloomberg LP.

21.7% at the end of March 2020 from 31.2% the year before. The BOT and the central government remained the next largest holders of BOT bonds. The BOT's holdings of its LCY bonds nearly doubled to 16.0% at the end of March 2020 from 8.8% a year earlier. The central government's share dipped to 8.9% in March 2020 from 14.7% the year before. Nonresidents held a marginal amount of LCY BOT bonds at the end of March 2020 at 1.1%, down from 2.5% a year earlier.

Foreign investors in Thailand's LCY bond market recorded net outflows of THB101.8 billion in Q1 2020, following net outflows of THB5.5 billion in Q4 2019 (**Figure 4**). The capital outflows in Q1 2020 were the largest quarterly totals in the last 3 years. The Thai bond market saw net foreign fund outflows for most of 2019 but experienced a slight reprieve in December and January with net inflows of THB3.9 billion and THB11.4 billion, respectively. However, the spread of COVID-19 in Thailand once again prompted an exodus of foreign funds, with outflows amounting to THB21.3 billion in February and THB91.9 billion in March. In April, smaller outflows of

Figure 2: Local Currency Government Bonds Investor Profile

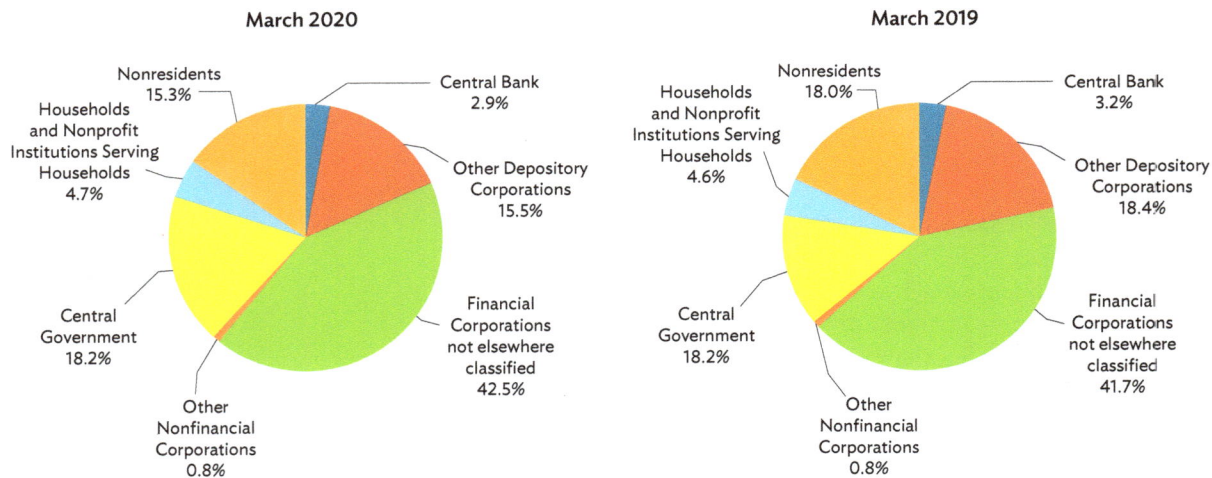

March 2020

- Nonresidents 15.3%
- Households and Nonprofit Institutions Serving Households 4.7%
- Central Bank 2.9%
- Other Depository Corporations 15.5%
- Financial Corporations not elsewhere classified 42.5%
- Central Government 18.2%
- Other Nonfinancial Corporations 0.8%

March 2019

- Nonresidents 18.0%
- Households and Nonprofit Institutions Serving Households 4.6%
- Central Bank 3.2%
- Other Depository Corporations 18.4%
- Financial Corporations not elsewhere classified 41.7%
- Central Government 18.2%
- Other Nonfinancial Corporations 0.8%

Notes:
1. Government bonds include Treasury bills and bonds.
2. Local Government not presented in the chart due to its relatively small shares of 0.005% in March 2019 and 0.00003% in March 2020.
Sources: *AsianBondsOnline* and Bank of Thailand.

Figure 3: Local Currency Central Bank Securities Investor Profile

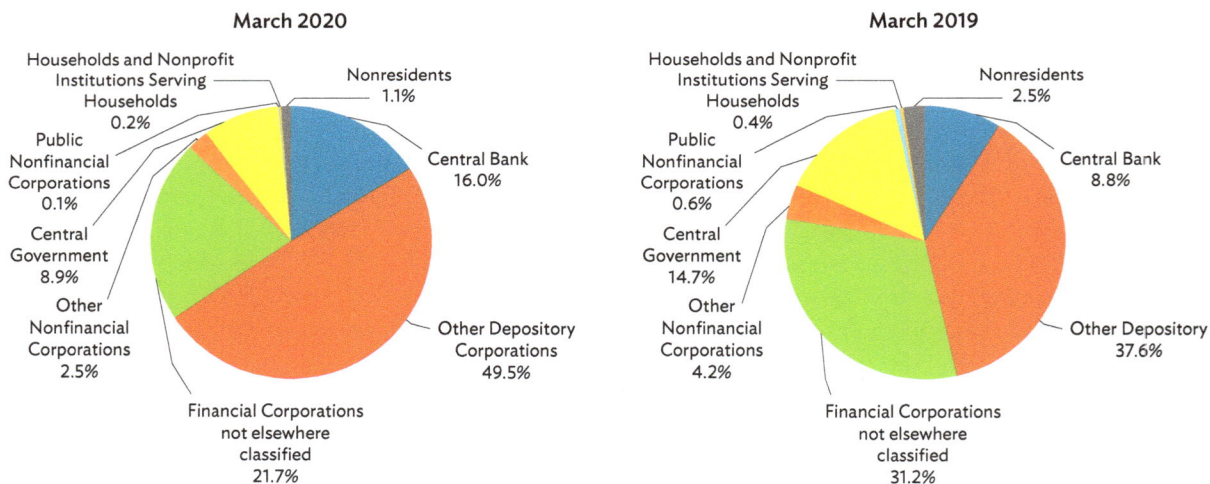

March 2020

- Households and Nonprofit Institutions Serving Households 0.2%
- Nonresidents 1.1%
- Public Nonfinancial Corporations 0.1%
- Central Bank 16.0%
- Central Government 8.9%
- Other Nonfinancial Corporations 2.5%
- Other Depository Corporations 49.5%
- Financial Corporations not elsewhere classified 21.7%

March 2019

- Households and Nonprofit Institutions Serving Households 0.4%
- Nonresidents 2.5%
- Public Nonfinancial Corporations 0.6%
- Central Bank 8.8%
- Central Government 14.7%
- Other Nonfinancial Corporations 4.2%
- Other Depository 37.6%
- Financial Corporations not elsewhere classified 31.2%

Source: Bank of Thailand.

Figure 4: Foreign Investor Net Trading of Local Currency Bonds in Thailand

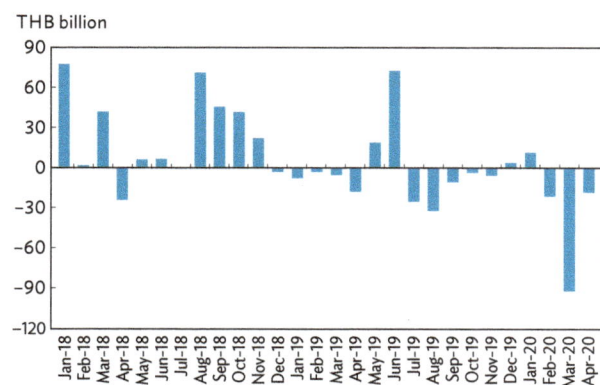

THB = Thai baht.
Source: Thai Bond Market Association.

THB18.1 billion were recorded as the Government of Thailand approved a stimulus package worth at least THB117.0 billion to mitigate the impact of COVID-19 on the economy.

Ratings Update

On 14 April, S&P Global revised downward its outlook on Thailand to stable from positive amid uncertainties over the extent of economic fallout from the COVID-19 pandemic. The revised outlook reflected the rating agency's assessment that the risks being generated by COVID-19 and the ensuing containment efforts could delay the political transition under the civilian government. The rating agency noted that another downgrade is possible if the sluggish economic recovery continues. It affirmed Thailand's BBB+ long-term and A-2 short-term foreign currency sovereign credit ratings.

Policy, Institutional, and Regulatory Developments

Public Debt Management Office to Issue Shorter-Dated Bonds

In March, the Public Debt Management Office (PDMO) announced that it will adjust its bond issuance plan to include shorter-dated bonds amid weak demand for government bonds due to heightened uncertainties caused by the COVID-19 pandemic. The PDMO announcement came after a wave of fixed-income

redemptions as alarm over COVID-19 drove investors to switch from debt instruments to cash.

Bank of Thailand Implements Measures to Stabilize Bond Market

In March, the BOT implemented several measures to alleviate the impact of COVID-19 on the Thai bond market. It established a mutual fund liquidity facility to provide liquidity for mutual funds through commercial banks. The BOT promised to inject about THB1.0 trillion into the bond market through the facility, which will be available until market conditions normalize. Commercial banks that buy investment units of high-quality mutual funds in money market and daily fixed-income funds can apply for liquidity support and use the underlying investment assets as collateral.

Along with the Thai Bankers' Association, the Government Savings Bank, Thai insurance providers, and the Government Pension Fund, the BOT also launched a Corporate Bond Stabilization Fund amounting to THB70 billion–THB100 billion. The fund will be used to inject liquidity into the corporate bond market by buying newly issued investment-grade bonds by corporates that cannot fully rollover maturing debt. The BOT will also continue to purchase government bonds to ensure stability in the government bond market.

Bank of Thailand Revises Bond Issuance Program

On 11 May, the BOT launched a revised bond issuance program for 2020 to accommodate the government's financing needs to fund relief measures and respond to changes in investor sentiment amid the COVID-19 pandemic. The auction days and frequency will remain as announced at the beginning of the year, but the BOT may adjust the issue sizes and will notify market participants of relevant changes at least 2 days before the auction dates. If necessary, the BOT will adjust the auction frequency of 3-month and 6-month BOT bills and of fixed-coupon bonds to accommodate the issuance schedule of Treasury bills and government bonds of comparable tenors. The ranges and minimum issue size per auction were expanded to between TH10.0 billion and THB60.0 billion for all maturities of BOT bills. The BOT will closely coordinate with the PDMO and take into consideration domestic and global market conditions in setting the issue sizes of BOT bills and bonds.

Viet Nam

Yield Movements

Viet Nam's local currency (LCY) bond yield curve shifted downward for short-term tenors and upward for medium- to long-term tenors between 28 February and 15 May (**Figure 1**). Bonds with maturities of 3 years or less saw yield falls between 10 basis points (bps) and 25 bps. The yield for the 1-year bond fell the most, dipping 25 bps. In contrast, yields for 7- to 15-year bonds were up between 13 bps and 31 bps, while the yield for the 5-year bond only rose 7 bps. The opposing movements at the different ends of the yield curve led to a widening of the 2-year versus 10-year yield spread from 103 bps to 131 bps during the review period.

The yield decline at the shorter-end of the curve can be traced to the interest rate cuts of the State Bank of Vietnam (SBV). The central bank cut its key policy rate to 4.5% from 5.0% on 13 May, following a 100-bps cut on 17 March, resulting in a cumulative 150-bps rate reduction for the year through the middle of May. The aggressive stance of the SBV's interest rate reduction sought to spur the domestic economy against the negative impact of the coronavirus disease (COVID-19) pandemic, which is in line with many central banks' unprecedented rate cuts around the world. Amid such an uncertain economic environment, investors are resorting to holding safe assets like government securities in the short-run, taking a wait-and-see approach to developments in the COVID-19 pandemic.

On the other hand, the increase in yields at the medium- to longer-end of the curve reflects investors seeking higher returns at the same time the government needs to secure money to finance its socioeconomic development programs to support the economy. Some upward bias, especially at the longer-end of the curve, can be observed amid rising expectations of expanded and extended fiscal stimulus. The upward pressure therefore reflects investors demanding a higher premium to invest in longer-term bonds.

Viet Nam's economic expansion decelerated in the first quarter (Q1) of 2020 due to the global pandemic, with gross domestic product growth significantly moderating to 3.8% year-on-year (y-o-y) from 7.0% y-o-y in the

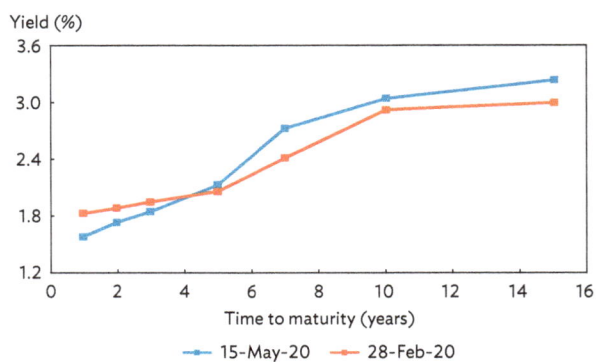

Figure 1: Viet Nam's Benchmark Yield Curve—Local Currency Government Bonds

Source: Based on data from Bloomberg LP.

fourth quarter (Q4) of 2020. The economy's growth hit a 10-year low as the pandemic took a toll on the domestic economy. All key sectors bore the brunt of the pandemic, recording slower y-o-y growth rates in Q1 2020 than in the previous quarter as activities were halted due to strict measures to mitigate the spread of the virus.

Prices of consumer goods in Viet Nam slightly moderated to 2.4% in May from 2.9% y-o-y in April, largely due to lower prices for oil. Falling oil prices caused the transport group's price index to drop sharply by 23.4% y-o-y. Postal services and telecommunication, and culture, entertainment, and tourism also saw negative y-o-y price growth, while the rest of the commodity groups saw price increases. On a month-on-month (m-o-m) basis, consumer prices marginally declined 0.03% in May. In the first 5 months of 2020, the inflation rate reached 4.4% y-o-y.

The Vietnamese dong has been relatively stable against the United States dollar thus far in 2020, trading at VND23,349 per USD1 on 15 May, which reflected a marginal depreciation of 0.8% from the start of the year. A decrease in exports and remittances amid subdued global economic activities affected the supply of foreign exchange in the system. However, with large abundant foreign exchange reserves and the appropriate management of monetary policies by SBV, the exchange rate has been kept stable.

Table 1: Size and Composition of the Local Currency Bond Market in Viet Nam

	Outstanding Amount (billion)						Growth Rate (%)			
	Q1 2019		Q4 2019		Q1 2020		Q1 2019		Q1 2020	
	VND	USD	VND	USD	VND	USD	q-o-q	y-o-y	q-o-q	y-o-y
Total	1,201,959	52	1,243,214	54	1,360,742	58	0.8	0.5	9.5	13.2
Government	1,092,228	47	1,141,009	49	1,260,287	53	0.9	(2.4)	10.5	15.4
Treasury Bonds	919,151	40	978,904	42	970,246	41	2.3	9.0	(0.9)	5.6
Central Bank Bills	4,900	0	0	0	136,986	6	–	(94.6)	–	2,695.6
Government-Guaranteed and Municipal Bonds	168,177	7	162,105	7	153,055	6	(8.5)	(9.0)	(5.6)	(9.0)
Corporate	109,731	5	102,205	4	100,455	4	(0.1)	43.7	(1.7)	(8.5)

– = not applicable, ( ) = negative, q-o-q = quarter-on-quarter, Q1 = first quarter, Q4 = fourth quarter, USD = United States dollar, VND = Vietnamese dong, y-o-y = year-on-year.
Notes:
1. Bloomberg LP end-of-period local currency–USD rates are used.
2. Growth rates are calculated from local currency base and do not include currency effects.
Sources: Bloomberg LP and Vietnam Bond Market Association.

Size and Composition

Viet Nam's LCY bonds outstanding totaled VND1,360.7 trillion at the end of March. The market expanded 9.5% quarter-on-quarter (q-o-q) in Q1 2020 after recording a decline in Q4 2019. The rebound was entirely driven by the government segment as outstanding bonds in the corporate sector remained subdued. On an annual basis, overall market growth accelerated to 13.2%y-o-y in Q1 2020 from 4.3% y-o-y in the previous quarter. Government bonds comprised the bulk of the bond market with a 92.6% share at the end of the quarter versus a 7.4% share for corporate bonds.

Government bonds. Total LCY government bonds outstanding at the end of Q1 2020 amounted to VND1,260.3 trillion on a rebound in growth to 10.5% q-o-q after a decline in the preceding quarter. The increase in market size in Q1 2020 was solely driven by the jump in the stock of central bank bills. On the other hand, outstanding Treasury bonds and outstanding government-guaranteed and municipal bonds decreased in Q1 2020.

Outstanding central bank bills totaled VND137.0 trillion at the end of Q1 2020, up from zero in Q4 2019 on new issuances during the quarter after all previously outstanding central bank bills had matured in Q4 2019.

Treasury bonds outstanding saw a marginal decline of 0.9% q-o-q in Q1 2020 to VND970.2 trillion despite the

government issuing VND33.5 trillion during the quarter. The decline can be attributed to an increase in maturities in Q1 2020. At the same time, Treasury bonds accounted for the largest share of the government bond stock at the end of March, accounting for 77.0% of the total.

The State Treasury had planned to raise VND50 trillion–VND60 trillion via government bond issuance in Q1 2020. However, the bond sales were not well supported by investors as yields are at historic lows. As a result, issuance during the quarter fell short.

Government-guaranteed and municipal bonds outstanding contracted in Q1 2020 after increasing in Q4 2019. Together they amounted to VND153.1 billion, reflecting a decline of 5.6% q-o-q. On a yearly basis, this bond segment declined 9.0% y-o-y.

Corporate bonds. Corporate bonds outstanding leveled off at VND100.5 trillion at the end of Q1 2020, reflecting a decline of 1.7% q-o-q and 8.5% y-o-y. The primary reason for the decline was the absence of new issuance in Q1 2020 as well as the maturation of some outstanding debt during the quarter. Furthermore, a number of corporates in Viet Nam issue bonds through private placements in which information is mostly undisclosed.[16]

The aggregated bond outstanding of the top 30 issuers in Viet Nam's corporate market amounted to VND96.9 trillion (**Table 2**). This nearly comprised the total debt stock of the corporate segment as there are

---

[16] *AsianBondsOnline* data on corporate bonds in Viet Nam is obtained from Bloomberg. As most bonds in Viet Nam are issued via private placement, our data on corporate bonds may be understated.

Table 2: Top 30 Issuers of Local Currency Corporate Bonds in Viet Nam

| | Issuers | Outstanding Amount | | State-Owned | Listed Company | Type of Industry |
		LCY Bonds (VND billion)	LCY Bonds (USD billion)			
1.	Vinhomes	12,500	0.53	No	Yes	Real Estate
2.	Masan Consumer Holdings	11,100	0.47	No	No	Diversified Operations
3.	Asia Commercial Joint Stock Bank	8,300	0.35	No	No	Banking
4.	Vietnam Joint Stock Commercial Bank for Industry and Trade	8,200	0.35	Yes	Yes	Banking
5.	Vinpearl	7,500	0.32	No	No	Hotel Operator
6.	Vingroup	7,000	0.30	No	Yes	Real Estate
7.	Lien Viet Post Joint Stock Commercial Bank	3,100	0.13	No	Yes	Banking
8.	Hoang Anh Gia Lai	3,000	0.13	No	Yes	Real Estate
9.	Vietnam Technological and Commercial Joint Stock Bank	3,000	0.13	No	No	Banking
10.	Bank for Investment and Development of Vietnam	2,700	0.11	Yes	Yes	Banking
11.	Sai Dong Urban Investment and Development	2,600	0.11	No	No	Real Estate
12.	Ho Chi Minh City Infrastructure Investment	2,470	0.10	No	Yes	Infrastructure
13.	Hoan My Medical	2,330	0.10	No	No	Health-care Services
14.	Refrigeration Electrical	2,318	0.10	No	Yes	Manufacturing
15.	Vietnam International Commercial Bank	2,203	0.09	No	Yes	Agriculture
16.	Hong Phong 1 Energy	2,150	0.09	No	No	Utility
17.	Agro Nutrition International	2,000	0.08	No	No	Agriculture
18.	Joint Stock Commercial Bank for Foreign Trade of Vietnam	2,000	0.08	Yes	Yes	Banking
19.	Nui Phao Mining	1,710	0.07	No	No	Mining
20.	Masan Group	1,500	0.06	No	Yes	Finance
21.	Masan Resources	1,500	0.06	No	Yes	Mining
22	SSI Securities	1,150	0.05	No	Yes	Finance
23.	Mobile World Investment	1,135	0.05	No	Yes	Manufacturing
24.	Pan Group	1,135	0.05	No	Yes	Consumer Services
25.	Sai Gon Thuong Tin Real Estate	870	0.04	No	Yes	Real Estate
26.	TTC Education Joint Stock Company	801	0.03	No	No	Education Services
27.	Vietnam Bank for Agriculture and Rural Development	760	0.03	Yes	No	Banking
28.	Nam Long Investment	660	0.03	No	Yes	Real Estate
29.	Saigon-Hanoi Securities	650	0.03	No	Yes	Finance
30.	Khang Dien House	534	0.02	No	Yes	Real Estate
	Total Top 30 LCY Corporate Issuers	96,876	4.10			
	Total LCY Corporate Bonds	100,455	4.25			
	Top 30 as % of Total LCY Corporate Bonds	96.4%	96.4%			

LCY = local currency, USD = United States dollar, VND = Vietnamese dong.
Notes:
1. Data as of 31 March 2020.
2. State-owned firms are defined as those in which the government has more than a 50% ownership stake.
Sources: *AsianBondsOnline* calculations based on Bloomberg LP and Vietnam Bond Market Association data.

only 46 companies currently tapping the bond market. Companies in the banking and real estate sectors are the top fundraisers with VND28.1 trillion and VND27.2 trillion of outstanding bonds, respectively, at the end of March. Together, these two sectors comprise over half of the total corporate bond market. Of the top 30, 19 are listed companies, 11 are unlisted companies, and 4 are state-owned enterprises.

Ratings Update

On 8 April, Fitch Ratings revised its outlook on Viet Nam downward to stable from positive but maintained the economy's credit rating of BB. The outlook revision reflects decelerating economic growth in the near-term due to the impact of the COVID-19, which resulted in muted domestic demand and the abatement of many activities in the export and tourism sectors. Strict measures intended to contain the spread of the virus largely contributed to the weakening. The affirmation of the BB rating was based on medium-term growth prospects, which remained strong, coupled with a sound fiscal position and healthy external finances.

On 21 May, S&P Global maintained Viet Nam's sovereign credit rating at BB with a stable outlook. The rate affirmation reflected the economy's strong macroeconomic performance and improved government institutional settings, which remained intact amid the ongoing global COVID-19 pandemic. The stable outlook was based on the economy's strong growth potential following a deceleration due to the COVID-19 pandemic.

Policy, Institutional, and Regulatory Developments

State Bank of Vietnam Issues Circular on Reserve Requirements

In December, the State Bank of Vietnam issued a circular that grants credit institutions either a lower reserve requirement ratio or a reserve requirement waiver. Circular 30/2019/TT-NHNN identified cases where credit institutions would be granted a reserve requirement waiver: (i) the credit institution is placed under special control; (ii) the credit institution has not yet started its business; and (iii) the credit institution is given an approval for dissolution, issued a decision to institute bankruptcy proceedings, or issued a decision on the revocation of a business license by a competent authority. The circular also granted credit institutions that support the system restructuring a 50% reduction in the reserve requirement rate.[17] The new circular took effect on 1 March.

Ministry of Finance Reduces Securities Fees by Half

On 7 May, the Ministry of Finance issued Circular No. 37, which reduced 20 out of 22 securities fees by 50%. The measure aims to help businesses negatively impacted by the COVID-19 pandemic in line with the government's effort to keep the economy afloat. The reduction will be effective from 7 May to 31 December.

---

[17] Footnote 9.

www.ingramcontent.com/pod-product-compliance
Lightning Source LLC
Chambersburg PA
CBHW042036220326
41599CB00045BA/7476